THE DREAM ARCHITECTS

THE DREAM
ARCHITECTS

Adventures in the
VIDEO GAME INDUSTRY

DAVID
POLFELDT

GRAND CENTRAL
PUBLISHING

NEW YORK   BOSTON

Grand Central Publishing
Hachette Book Group
1290 Avenue of the Americas, New York, NY 10104
grandcentralpublishing.com
twitter.com/grandcentralpub

First Edition: September 2020

Grand Central Publishing is a division of Hachette Book Group, Inc. The Grand Central Publishing name and logo is a trademark of Hachette Book Group, Inc.

The publisher is not responsible for websites (or their content) that are not owned by the publisher.

The Hachette Speakers Bureau provides a wide range of authors for speaking events. To find out more, go to www.hachettespeakersbureau.com or call (866) 376-6591.

Print book interior design by Tom Louie.

Library of Congress Cataloging-in-Publication Data
Names: Polfeldt, David, author.
Title: The dream architects : adventures in the video game industry / David Polfeldt.
Description: First edition. | New York : Grand Central Publishing, [2020]
Identifiers: LCCN 2020000159 | ISBN 9781538702611 (hardcover) | ISBN 9781538702598 (ebook)
Subjects: LCSH: Polfeldt, David. | Video games industry--Sweden--History. | Video game designers--Sweden.
Classification: LCC HD9993.E453 .S876 2020 | DDC 338.7/617948092--dc23
LC record available at https://lccn.loc.gov/2020000159

ISBNs: 978-1-5387-0261-1 (hardcover), 978-1-5387-0259-8 (ebook), 978-1-5387-5418-4 (int'l trade paperback)

Printed in the United States of America

LSC-C

10 9 8 7 6 5 4 3 2 1

To my fellow dreamers, in particular Isa and Harry, with love

There seem to be two moons now,
the one I see in my back yard
and the one I remember from up close.
                    —Michael Collins, *Carrying the Fire*

CONTENTS

THE DREAM ARCHITECTS

INTRODUCTION

WATCHER OF THE SKIES

My friend Jonas and I were having coffee in Stockholm. We sat in a poorly lit corner of the Ritorno café, as we had done many times before. The place hadn't been renovated or touched in ages. It looked like a backdrop to a silent movie, and we enjoyed the sensation of sitting in exactly the same chairs, eating cheap sandwiches from the same plates as several generations of artists must have done before us.

"Do you remember Paul K.?" Jonas asked.

Paul was a mutual friend of ours from art school, a guy I greatly admired. His artwork was astute and elegant, he dressed like an English shoegazer, and he was dating Linda, one of the coolest girls in school. They were two hipsters decades before the term was invented. The couple lived in a run-down apartment they'd transformed into a cozy, tasteful home, decorated with rare collector's items—a Lisa Larson ceramic figurine on a living room shelf, a casually placed original Joost Swarte sketch. Paul K. and Linda had always been the art school "it-couple." They'd set the hipness bar very high.

"Yes, yes, of course. How's he doing?"

"Well," said Jonas, "Paul has become completely obsessed with *World of WarCraft*. He can't stop playing. He's in love with it. Linda is too."

"Paul K. loves *World of WarCraft*?" I looked at him carefully. Was he joking?

When I first joined the video game industry, it was universally seen as a very suspicious business. I often felt as if those of us who worked on games were thought to be part of the porn industry or some ultraviolent, under-the-desk, VHS black market. This wasn't just my imagination; it was what people told me to my face.

At a dinner with friends from art school, confessing that I'd begun to dabble in computer games was akin to burping out loud at a castle dinner with the king. The crowd I hung out with was made up of musicians, filmmakers, writers, artists, and academics. All very respectable, sophisticated bohemians who prided themselves on having very good taste in art and culture. All of us were born in the mid- to late '60s. We were just a few years too old to come of age during the advent of the first gaming consoles, like the Magnavox or the early Ataris. In fact, we didn't grow up with computers at all, which meant that we were at risk of becoming a very outdated generation. But at the very last minute, most of us made the giant leap, landed right at the edge of the digital frontier, and managed to stay in tune with the future. Still, many of my friends never discovered the joys of computer games and remained suspicious of them even as their love for the digital realm grew.

Teachers and parents expressed concerns about my choice of profession too. As an adult, going to a meeting at my children's school and admitting I worked in game development was a bad idea. I'd immediately get bombarded with questions and openly challenged as if I were a satanic worshipper hell-bent on corrupting the youth.

I leaned on a few provocative lines for use whenever people felt like attacking my job. *Yes*, I'd say, *it's correct that games are like jazz: highly damaging to the youth!* This was puzzling to my friends who associated jazz with nice, safe, wholesome values. Wasn't jazz something that our grandparents were into? Something that you'd hear at a retirement home? Yes, and that was my point. Once, even jazz was demonized by concerned parents who believed that the music was corrupting the young and turning them into a lost generation. Older generations always cry wolf as soon as their kids are into something different. It's inevitable. Sometimes it's precisely the reason a younger generation takes up certain hobbies: to alienate the elders. *What on earth is this invention from the evil mind of Beelzebub? It's just jazz, my friend.*

While my career began to take off, and my love for games intensified, so did my outsider status in the art crowd. Although my best friends were themselves outsiders, my unusual new hobby put my belonging at risk. I was hanging out more and more with programmers and computer-based artists (who would draw only in pixels—an unimaginable thing!). But I didn't get involved in making games because I wanted to impress anyone. My choices were based on passion and curiosity as much as luck and chance. It took years and many twists to get anywhere at all, because when my journey began, there wasn't much of a video game industry to explore.

I'd been working with games for more than a decade when the *WoW* phenomenon first happened. I, too, became fully immersed in my new alternate life as the Night Elf Titov, a hunter who strayed from the beaten path, taming legendary spirit beasts. The game that Blizzard created transcended the old boundaries that had kept the industry in a narrow niche for such a long time. With *World of WarCraft*, the developers showed the world what we had all suspected for decades, that the future of games could become much more than a diversion or just a hard-core entertainment product for computer nerds. Games carried the potential to offer entirely new worlds of possibilities—vast landscapes that were more than a playground. This was a world that offered an alternative life, one just as rich and complex as the physical one.

"Paul K. playing *WoW*?" I said. "That is unexpected. What kind of character does he play?"

"I honestly have no idea. But you know, we got to talking about the medium, about games, and Paul said, 'In fact, maybe David has the coolest job of all of us.'"

"The coolest job?"

Fast-forward to the present, and my life has become like an endless, chaotic, beautiful spiral of events that takes me across the globe. I've met world leaders, rigid and hard-nosed lawyers, seen drunkards and addicts try to keep up with the ever-increasing pressure of the entertainment industry, run into a fair share of plain liars wanting to sell some amazing new gizmos, been approached by Freemasons on a recruitment drive, worked with mad geniuses, struggled with a few psychopaths, had dinner with the King and Queen of Sweden, established a creative alliance with the world's most successful movie director, and worked with some of the most brilliant video game developers on the planet.

I've seen projects crash and burn, dreams lost, and witnessed the type of success that turns people into billionaires practically overnight. I've watched as hundreds of millions of dollars evaporated on barely playable projects, and I've seen basement enthusiasts create global hits on shoestring budgets.

As a part of the job, and perhaps as an illustration of the job itself, I once went through real survival training with an old paratrooper in the rainy Swedish forest of Nowhere. There, I spent days trying to stay warm, drinking swamp water filtered through moss, and eating ants. It was brutal, but part of my mind really enjoyed it—not in a masochistic way, but in the same way that I enjoy making games: It's really fucking hard. It really is difficult to make triple-A games. But if it's hard, that means only the best people will figure out a way to survive and succeed. And I want a worthy challenge. Hard is exciting.

These days, as the head of Massive Entertainment, I'm in charge of more than six hundred people spread out over three offices. We are in the middle of rebuilding an entire city block in Malmö where the teams will move once the new office is ready. Massive is home to two of the most exciting brands in the game industry, *The Division* franchise and the forthcoming *Avatar* game.

I started in a basement with nothing, and I matured alongside the video game industry. I was there to see the emergence of a new medium, and I experienced it as it grew. Today, the youngest generation plays more games than ever. By 1998, the global game industry had generated around 35 billion USD, a number that has grown every year for two decades in a row to reach its current status as the entertainment world's new superstar, generating over 150 billion USD yearly. Still, depending on the speed of technological innovations like cloud-gaming, analysts expect the industry to double that number yet again and reach 300 billion USD in 2025.

The average American football fan is just under fifty, and the average baseball fan is fifty-three. Are these dying forms of entertainment? I don't know, but the trend suggests they're losing ground to the digital alternatives. And games deliver, in abundance: A movie is around ninety minutes long, while a great game easily provides entertainment for hundreds of hours. While old media is one-way, offering only passive participation, games are interactive and intensely social, allowing lifelong friendships to develop through the ether. For someone like me, who initially approached video games as nothing more than a basement hobby, this is hard to process, and it's even harder to keep up with. The demands are growing fast. Creative stagnation is a constant obstacle.

Beyond the excitement, still only barely visible, an even bigger future is coming. The games of today will be primitive compared to what we'll see in the decades to follow. We won't be able to predict this development accurately, because our understanding of the virtual world and artificial intelligence (AI) capacity is still quite shallow.

Already, machines are learning to simulate life, and code is able to perfectly emulate nature. Water, weather, light, physics, materials, and dancing particles like smoke and clouds have never been as beautiful as they are in games today. The mathematics is slowly conquering the vast richness of reality. Games are capable of building photo-realistic replicas of everything we can dream of, in higher fidelity than the human eye can perceive.

Elsewhere, experimental submarine data centers are being sunk into the oceans, and Elon Musk is launching his low-orbital horde of eleven thousand microsatellites to finally create a lightning-fast digital web that connects every single human in every remote spot on the planet in one shared virtual experience. If these projects don't succeed, others will. Soon, every person with a screen will have permanent access to the cloud, the digital spirit surrounding everything. All humans will become citizens of the same world, and in that process, every single one will become a potential gamer too.

I suspect future generations will look back upon us as naive and childlike, barely conscious of the world we've started to build.

PART I

1998–2008

I

A PAINTER DIES

Growing up, I spent most of my time drawing.

As soon as I could hold a crayon, I drew cars and portraits of my family and friends. I sketched animals I dreamed of having one day in magical lands of adventure that sprawled out into gigantic imagined maps on other planets. Countless hours of my childhood were spent in my room examining the visual details of album covers and graphic novels, then attempting to create my own. When we went to Italy in the summer, I visited the local museum in every city we traveled to and studied the old masters up close.

My friends were either the guys who played football like me, or the other geeks who liked to draw in class. But my real best friend was always my big brother. Ours was the only reliable relationship I had when I was growing up because we never stayed in one place for long. We lived a vagabond kind of lifestyle, moving every so often. This might sound more exotic than it was. Ours wasn't a hippie life on the road with surfing and psychedelic parents. It was the tidy young academics' version of life.

My mom was a straight-A student from Italy with very old-fashioned parents who'd lived through both World Wars. She fell in love with a quiet Swedish student when they both attended an international summer camp in Romania for highly talented adolescents. My parents married and had three kids—two boys, and my little sister.

We moved to California when I was two, back to Sweden when I was three, to Tanzania when I was five, and then back to Sweden again when I was seven. And somehow, we still managed to spend most of our summers in Sardinia, in a little town on the north coast called Santa Teresa di Gallura.

When I was nine, my parents divorced, and from then on we stayed in Sweden. By that time I'd already decided that the most important part of my life was the dream world I was creating in my drawings. It was a peaceful place, and, opposed to other parts of my life, it was consistent and safe, and I had control of it. I could spend hours just letting the pen travel across the paper, slowly shaping places where epic adventures played out in front of my eyes. I never knew where the stories were heading when I began; I just followed along, and it was as exciting to me as if someone else were reading me a fairy tale. Every time we moved, I left my drawings behind like a trail of fading memories and started a new collection.

As an increasingly quiet kid caught up in my dreamworlds, I became hard to reach. But inside, I understood well the difference between a beautiful fantasy and a real-life challenge. I was never as dreamy as people imagined me to be. Not then, not now.

The things I experienced might have seemed like distant fantasies to others, especially in gray, serene Sweden, but the green mamba in the climbing tree behind our house in Tanzania was real, not a fictional monster in a Dungeons & Dragons adventure. My brother and I almost got killed by the mamba. We carefully climbed down while the venomous snake leered at us. We ran for help, and the village elder summoned an albino man called the Snake Killer. I watched as he defeated the mamba in a chaotic process involving a brick tied to the end of a long stick.

Another time, when I fell asleep on the deck of a fisherman's boat in the waters between Corsica and Sardinia, I was vaguely cognizant that it looked like a scene from a Tintin book, but it wasn't. It was my reality. I remember the warmth of the Mediterranean sun in a summer that never seemed to end, and I can still hear the heavy *tuk-tuk-tuk* from the diesel engine. During the day at the beach, my brother and I built magnificent sand velodromes that rivaled castles.

The stories my grandfather never told me or anyone about the hell he'd lived through in World War I were not part of some abstract homework assignment. I'd watch his eyes from a meter away, shifting as he avoided his memories from the trenches; the fear he never acknowledged, the sorrow he felt for his lost friends, the pride of his accomplishments in the face of death. A fading diploma from the last Italian king hung on a wall in his sunlit apartment in Torino. This was no imaginary king from a Tolkien book. The proof was there, right in front of me, and I could almost touch the paper with the king's elaborate autograph behind the glass frame. After my grandfather's death, my Italian relatives found a diary that confirmed what we'd always guessed; World War I was truly hell. The old man had been there and come back with scars that stayed with him for life.

Neither was it a dream when I visited my dad's university and operated an unforgiving moon-landing simulator on a giant IBM computer that took up an entire room. Nor when I discovered that my Swedish grandparents' cellar was filled to the brim with original paintings and prints from my great-grandfather, who'd been a conservative painter. He'd lived during the most artistically liberating times but was reluctant to participate in them. He kept painting incredibly skillful photo-realistic landscapes, while all of Europe's art scene was on fire with modernism, futurism, Dadaism, and surrealism. He was certainly aware of these revolutions, and I couldn't help but wonder what made him choose to ignore them. Maybe he thought the major art movements were just temporary, overhyped gimmicks, like Nintendo Wiis?

I've lived my life with a mirage of California etched into my brain. A pale image of a place far, far away that quietly calls my name, trying to lure me to *come home*. The dry hills with pine trees, the Case Study Houses, and the skateboarders in Palo Alto. The smell of American asphalt after rainfall. I know them so well. Except...it's not really a mirage, *it's a memory*. It's where I learned to speak. I didn't dream any of this.

In Sweden, it rains a lot, and it's not warm. The streets don't ever dry up, they just remain damp and cold, and the air is filled with an earthy aroma of wet leaves, stone, grass, and mud. In California, though, the rains are short and the streets are wide. The sun will quickly boil the patches of water into steam, and there's a crisp feeling in the air.

I've never stopped knowing that the world is bigger and more exciting than what we see in front of us. I've always felt that dreams are not a product of the unreal, but more like suggestions of alternate realities that can become real if we want them to. In fact, I knew as I was growing up that the world really *is* out there, waiting for us to show up one day. Those faraway mythical lands exist.

Once my parents divorced, I tried to adjust to my new reality, but I was too young to properly digest the collapsing family structure, and the emotions I felt were merely distant clouds moving across the sky on a cold winter day. If I was aching for a stable home before, the longing got worse, and I retreated inward to safe places of fantasy.

The new friends I was drawn to were always the outliers, the odd and the different. One was the heir of a little-known Swedish noble family who had turned communist and smoked a whole lot of dope. To the frustration of our teachers at school, he'd never remove his tam-o'-shanter, a Scottish bonnet, and he'd fiercely lecture people about the name and spelling of it. He was extremely intelligent but more angry than clever, and consequently his youth was wasted picking all the wrong fights. Nonetheless, he had a big impact on me; he was the first one who suggested I become a professional artist. It was a revolutionary thought, but once the words had been spoken out loud, I never forgot them.

Another friend came from Scotland, where he'd grown up in the Outer Hebrides with four siblings and parents who wanted to escape modern society. He came to Sweden alone with his mother when his parents split up. He used to talk to ghosts in my wardrobe, and once he threatened to kill me with an ax and bury me under the ice of a small pond in a frozen field. He was and still is one of the people I trust most in the world. We formed an incredibly strong alliance around our melancholy, our lost connection to remote places, the guilt we felt for our lonely mothers, our mutual interest in drawing, and our longing for our fathers, who lived far away.

In high school, my life was warped again when my childhood friends and I all went to different schools. It was a horrible time. I just wanted school to end and to live my own life. I hated my classmates and I hated my teachers. My few friends were musicians and weirdos, and we wrote very sad, angsty songs, and we always dressed in black. We were serious, pretentious smokers and liked talking about suicide. We never got invited to any parties.

Eventually I befriended many aspiring artists, writers, and musicians, but not a single gamer. The circles I moved in seemed to consist of people from academic families, where culture was more important than technology. There was no one in my sphere who considered games a hobby, let alone a potential profession. However, even though we didn't think of ourselves as gamers, mostly because the term hadn't been properly coined, my brother and I designed board games together. We created several elaborate, complex, and slow-to-play pen-and-paper games. The biggest pleasure, apart from all the illustration tasks that fell upon me, was diving into the algorithmic structure behind the games. There is an almost musical beauty in creating hidden mathematical rules that give way to a long adventure.

My brother grew up and became a cool rock-and-roll guitarist, and I remained the mysterious, quiet, artsy guy in the shadows. Drawing was *my thing* during my entire childhood. As high school came to a close, it seemed only right that I apply to art school and just keep going. After all, what were the alternatives? I couldn't think of any at all.

I got accepted to Konstfack in Stockholm, where I studied graphic design and illustration. Wonderful Konstfack! A school in the Bauhaus tradition. Hidden in a giant concrete building, looking so serious and pretentious, the school was filled with the most fantastic circus of young aspiring artists and craftspeople. The place smelled like paint and melting silver.

I loved it for so many reasons, including that it was the first time I'd felt at home anywhere, and it was the first time I'd fully enjoyed the company of my classmates.

After taking my master's degree, I started up a tiny one-man company and made a living as an illustrator working on comic books, graphic novels, and advertisements.

It seems so incredibly obvious now, but what I didn't understand even remotely back then was that my art was never meant to be *for sale*. Without exception, all my drawing and painting had its origin in the highly private; they had been created as parallel realities through which I could escape. Painting was perhaps the only thing that had unfailingly been my own. I couldn't sell that, and I was beginning to discover that I didn't want to.

For a while I plowed on with my company. I worked for no money making comics, and I worked for good money selling illustrations to weekly and monthly magazines. Occasionally, I'd get a gig for a tech start-up, which was even better money, but at the same time very confusing, since I hadn't initially paid much attention to the digital world.

The longer I kept going, the more I hated myself. It was as if another person had taken the liberty of selling my most personal assets, and not even for a good price. I felt cheap and dirty, and I stopped pitching for new work entirely. I didn't want illustration assignments anymore; business was killing the most precious thing I had. Of course, the heroic act of not going to sales meetings slowly put me in a financial bind, and eventually I had to take other jobs.

Originally, none of those *other* jobs mattered to me. They were my rebound relationships. I was just buying time until I could figure out what to do with my painting. My real mission in life was to repair my relationship with art, but I didn't know how. I still painted in my spare time, but without direction. The magic was gone, and I knew just who had destroyed it. I tried to apologize to my younger self for my incredible clumsiness, but of course the space-time continuum doesn't work that way.

I quit painting entirely. The next time I picked up a brush was on a computer screen.

2

THE MAGIC DOOR

Oskar had been working on something in his spare time.

He was a programmer who, like me, was employed at a small web agency called Out There Communications. He looked like a skinny cousin of Apple's genius Steve Wozniak. Oskar always seemed to be hunching over something, turning his back to the rest of the world. He had thin, long hair like dark curtains that partially hid his pale face. His eyes were intelligent and peered at you from behind expensive glasses (because of course he loved good engineering). Oskar hid his true personality behind a wall of tech-speak, and if you weren't fluent in it, he'd remain distant and unapproachable.

We had a cool industrial-style office in central Stockholm, Sweden, with around thirty-five to forty employees. This was in 1998, the advent of the Swedish so-called "IT Miracle." We were just making web pages, but we were considered part of the "New Economy"—made up of people who kept talking about hocus-pocus internet tricks that would transform everything. It was a crazy time. Every idiot got a job, and a lot of them became millionaires simply because they happened to drink Coke and play flipper in one newly refurbished office and not the identical one across the street. Ours, for instance, looked like a suave steel-and-glass office, with a complete set of large secondhand desks bought from a bankrupt architectural firm. The desks, when paired with the *gigantic* computers we had back then, created an office of minifortresses. Behind the walls of humming machines, we dove down into our own small worlds of pixels and lines of code. Our managers liked expensive furniture, so the place was filled with uncomfortable designer classics such as a Barcelona sofa and an egg chair by Arne Jacobsen.

We sat right in the middle of town, with huge windows that faced the busy street below and had a small balcony toward the backyard where the smokers hung out.

Sweden has always been a country infatuated with *the modern*, no matter what it is. We really, really want to be modern, all the time. Supermodern. We have optimistically embraced everything new: metallurgy, democracy, railroads, telephones, sexual liberation, the Industrial Revolution, gender equality, internationalism, pop music, and so on until the digital revolution came along, and of course we passionately embraced that too. (The only time we don't get involved in the latest fad is when it's war, which we have avoided for many centuries now. But then again, wars aren't really modern.)

Why was I working in a web agency, and why didn't I particularly care? Well, my young identity had been built at art school, a truly great one, and I was snobbish about it. I thought that a real job was one where a single individual could make something with his or her own hands. Like painting. Like lithography. Like sculpture. Proper jobs.

When you paint, you have access to every single color a human eye can perceive, which is several million, and yet there I was, stuck with the insanely frustrating Netscape palette consisting of a ridiculous 256 colors. This was all the web could handle in. And that wasn't the only circumstance I struggled with. As any art student knows, magic can be created in a short and efficient process that starts with your own imagination and ends in something you can complete, happily chugging away at the task in solitude. It's genuinely amazing. Like shaping thin air into meaning and being able to observe the whole process from the front row. But web pages? Producing them was a messy process involving designers, art directors, user interface (UI) experts, and my newest professional acquaintances, programmers. Having a great vision for a website didn't help, because there were so many limiting factors in creating one.

I took the job as an art director only so my girlfriend at the time and I could afford to live somewhere in the city and eat a little better. Landing a job at Out There was easy, because as I said, any idiot with no skill got a job in the IT industry back then if they wanted one. Me included.

"So, you can paint? That's pretty cool," the man in the turtleneck said during the interview.

"Yes, but to be honest, I'm not great with digital tools." I didn't want to be called out later.

"Hmm. Well, okay. But can you code?"

"What, no! Of course not," I replied, feeling the potential job drift away.

"Right. Well. You're hired!" he said with a smile that left me wondering what on earth I'd done.

Ironically, my complete lack of digital skills is the origin of my career in games. In art school I'd learned to recognize quality, perfection, obsession, beauty, and solid craftsmanship. But at Out There I couldn't directly apply any of the things I'd patiently studied for years, which made me look for other challenges in the office. What piqued my interest the most was *teamwork*, especially between artists and programmers. On a more abstract level, I became very interested in figuring out the conditions needed to inspire my new coworkers to embark on professional self-improvement journeys. It was obvious that most people would do better work if they felt that their tasks played into something that mattered to them personally. We all work harder when we follow a (imagined) worthy cause. Peripherally, I picked up a lot of knowledge about the digital world. More than anything, though, I became fascinated by the social dynamics involved in delivering big, complex projects, and I began seeing the office as a sensitive ecosystem in which one could be either poisonous or benevolent.

There was a programmer I knew at the studio named Chris. A tall, bespectacled guy with an intimidating, quiet anger about him. Like many programmers, he was blindingly smart, but his jerky movements made it appear as if he were about to have a nervous breakdown any second. He was clearly a man on the run, maybe from a nasty cybercrime he'd secretly committed or from some inner demon, no one could tell. All we knew was that his constant paranoia made him hard to work with.

Our boss was an unpredictable and pretentious man from Finland with a large square body like a moving refrigerator. He was obsessed with high-polished style and he used to smoke Gauloises and sit with the French magazine *Le Monde* in cafés, though the rumor was he didn't understand any French at all. I remember his pedantic and judgmental opinions about everything design-related, which he'd randomly deliver with a smirk. It was impossible to win his respect because he was always, in his own mind, many steps ahead of everyone else.

"Our cables are a BRANDING STATEMENT!" he'd yell, reminding us to keep the various power cords around our desks in immaculate form.

One day the boss started screaming at our sensitive, shy programmer, Chris. He claimed that Chris wasn't productive enough and that he should spend more time on clients. We all knew this was completely unfair, since the boss himself had a habit of asking Chris to take care of a lot of other things, most of them unrelated to clients, like fixing the boss's internet connection in his own apartment.

It upset me to see Chris being stepped on, so I invented something called the "OT Production Index." It was a simple math formula, an illustration of how much work any single person could realistically do in a workweek, factoring in fixing apartment internets and R & D, and once the index was maxed out, it would illustrate how "Person X has now delivered 100 percent of what is physically possible." At that point, the individual was not available for more work.

The idea was to stop our managers from asking for too much. I ordered a large blackboard with the weekdays printed above a row with each employee's name so that we could use good old chalk to keep track of what everyone was doing. Sometimes we hit the maximum limit: two full weeks on the board! We couldn't imagine the need to plan ahead any further.

A few days later, the boss thundered up the stairs to where I sat with the developers. We were playing Bungie's best game ever, *Marathon*, and getting paid for it. Without looking at me, the boss just shouted from below, "David! You're the new production manager!" And then he left again, his hairless Chinese dog following obediently.

That special morning in 1998, when I got to work, Oskar showed me and a few colleagues the small piece of software he'd been working on. As we huddled around his computer fortress, he loaded up a simple game, a side-scrolling shooter. It was tiny in size and lacked complexity, but it was *astonishing*, a revolution. Some ancient thought process far back in my head clicked into place with an odd feeling of relief.

Like the moment Lucy discovers the wardrobe in the Narnia tales, the experience opened a magic door for me that I didn't even know existed. Even when I knew where it was, the door still took me quite awhile to properly walk through. But once I did, I discovered the place that became the heart of my career.

In Oskar's game, the player controlled a small spaceship that traveled along the horizon from left to right at an ever-increasing speed. With a few keystrokes from the player, the ship would dodge up and down and shoot incoming obstacles. And there were a few pickups along the way: health, weapon upgrades, ammo, shields.

It was brilliant; I couldn't believe it! I had to ask Oskar several times before I could process the unimaginable: *He'd created a game with his own bare hands!* Seriously?

Sure, I'd played computer games in my life. During my first year at Konstfack, there was a single, enormous computer locked up in a room, and it was presented to us as an advanced course for the last year. We swiftly ignored the rules laid down by the professors and found a way to sneakily access the lonely Macintosh named "Mother." But we had no intent to explore the machine as an artistic tool. Instead, just like the legendary original generation of hackers at MIT, we just wanted to play games. Between classes, we lost hours to games like *Prince of Persia*, *4D Boxing*, *Tetris*, and *The 7th Guest*.

Somehow, I'd failed to realize where these games came from and how they were made. I was too busy thinking about things like acrylics, paper qualities, and futurism to understand that each game I'd played in the computer room at art school had an origin in a similar creative process. And Oskar's game made me realize, *Games are made by humans*.

Suddenly, my job at Out There Communications seemed *a lot* more interesting.

Up until that point in 1998, I had entertained a distant love affair with games, thinking of them as more a form of addictive meditation than anything worth serious attention. But Oskar's project made me look at the industry in a new light, and I realized that it was in the midst of an exciting revolution. In 1994 and 1995, after an aborted partnership with Nintendo, Sony had decided to build a gaming machine of their own, with the intention to reach every family's living room. They successfully entered the video game market with the first disc-based console with CD-quality sound, designed around polygon-based graphics, which brought the games to a new, mind-boggling visual level that could be rendered in real time.

Nintendo followed suit a year later with the Nintendo 64, which brought their famous *Mario* series to full 3-D and open-ended level design. This was a revelation to gamers and pushed the art of playable levels (maps) to entirely new heights of complexity and beauty. The flat, static sprite-based images of the late '80s and early '90s had given birth to a rigid linear design, basically taking the adventure from the left side of the screen, through a side-scrolling landscape, to a rewarding conclusion on the right side of the screen. The arrival of the new machinery from Sony and Nintendo made it possible to go beyond these limits and gave way to 3-D characters moving around freely in a virtual space, where the camera could be manipulated to virtually any angle by the player.

Meanwhile, whole new concepts were being created on PCs and Macs seemingly every year, with major advancements in the first-person shooter genre led by id Software and on to Blizzard's ultrapolished and pioneering work in the real-time strategy genre, originally brought to the big audiences by Westwood Studios' *Command & Conquer* in 1995.

The opportunities in the game industry seemed to open up everywhere, as if game developers had suddenly discovered a new continent and everyone was rushing to explore its frontiers, pushing forward, further and further, hoping to realize dreams and maybe find elusive riches.

It seemed to be an opportunity I shouldn't miss.

In the Out There office, Oskar's java game made us pause and think. Especially me and my colleague Jörgen. We were already in love with all sorts of cheap culture: horror movies, comics, toys, pulp novels, and even reality-TV shows—you name it; but we were certainly not in love with our job, building web pages. Thanks to Oskar, we'd quickly caught a new fever for games, and we knew that with the people in the office, we were probably capable of creating something of our own.

Jörgen was a chubby guy born in Örebro who looked like he might have been the chairman of Depeche Mode's fan club. He was half Swedish and half Chinese, with black hair, black clothes, black Bakelite glasses, black Doc Martens, and black everything else, usually with a mouth full of tobacco producing juice that would run down his teeth in a menacing way. Jörgen was, by a broad margin, the best and most creative art director at Out There. He was also hilarious and annoying. When he got bored, he used to get drunk and embark on nightly trips through Stockholm, looking for neo-Nazis to fight. As much as I admired his courage, this was totally suicidal, and I'm surprised that he survived. At work, he wouldn't pick real fights, he'd just find ways to mess around. He'd unplug coworkers' computers, secretly change their customized menu layouts, randomly uninstall software, and make desk chairs disappear. He'd smoke in the office and draw charming and cruel portraits of the rest of us. Some days, I'd hear a little voice saying my name repeatedly: "Davidavidavidavidavidavidavidavidavid...," on and on, like tinnitus, until, after an endless three minutes, it would reach a crescendo in volume and intensity. It would be Jörgen. Not wanting anything, just claiming that he liked to say my name.

The subtlest thing he'd do to annoy the rest of us was to invite us to a multiplayer match (yes, *Marathon*) and rig the controls so that, after a bit of playing, we'd discover that he'd logged in to our computers earlier in the day and changed some basic game setting. It would be something small, something that you didn't perceive at once, like slowed-down mouse speed, or changing "turn left" to "strafe left," or reversing "fire" and "secondary fire." It took a moment to process what was wrong. *What's wrong with my character? There's an input problem? Where?* It felt like trying to play a fast-paced game after too many beers, foggy and disconnected. In the meantime, Jörgen would use the situation to his advantage and take the lead in the match, giggling like a maniac.

Jörgen was my favorite weird guy, but he was still a lone wolf at the core. As much as we chatted about making games or banding up with some folks to start our own project, it gradually occurred to me that such a partnership would be impossible. My feeling was that Jörgen didn't like people much, and by that I mean he didn't like anyone, and for him all kinds of collaboration would ultimately lead to a form of suffering. But he had a friend, he said, someone he'd met a few times named Kim Nordström. Kim had created a wonderful website called c64.com, a tribute to all games created for the Commodore 64. The C64 was a cheap and efficient PC that was home to some of the first original video games. The computer was interesting for aspiring young hackers and game designers due to its accessibility and friendly interface for making homemade demos. Jörgen had made the logotype for the c64.com website, but Kim was the one who could write the code for the games.

In those days, I didn't consider myself to be a legitimate gamer, but Kim was 100 percent the "real deal." He was a Commodore kid, a coder-demon, and already a bit of a legend in the demo scene. He was positive, fun to hang out with, and had an amazing work ethic. As an art school grad, I was a bit judgmental about how people dressed and what music they listened to, but soon enough I laid my prejudice aside and saw Kim for what he was: a genuine, honest, well-intentioned, and entrepreneurial person with a big smile who liked to wear proper clothes—neat jeans with a light-blue ironed shirt. He looked preppy next to me in my patchy, worn jeans and black polo, still steeped in art school fashion. His well-polished shoes were made for the city, while I wore practical boots for walking the dog in the rain over muddy fields on the outskirts of Stockholm. Kim looked professional and reliable, while I just looked like someone who had no money.

We formed an alliance revolving around our unfulfilled ambitions. I'd finally learned how to create art with pixels—the tiny one-size screen squares that all computer art was made of. My job was like building images out of minimalistic LEGO blocks, while Kim's work was much more advanced. He'd weave together long lines of incomprehensible digits that would make computers do stuff, also known as "code." We had a complete team!

Neither of us had thought much about what we wanted to do with this new two-person guild. We were just two guitarists jamming. We didn't care if we were forming a band or not.

Until Poppoo.

3

A FAT BEAR CHANGED MY LIFE

The IT Miracle in Stockholm had gone overboard. I'd moved on from Out There to Icon Medialab, another, much larger, company in the IT industry that focused on expensive consulting and strategic advice for companies eager to understand the digital future. Now and then, the consulting advice the company doled out would result in our actually doing something, like building increasingly sophisticated websites.

I'd been rewarded with a new fashionable title: "Competence Coach, Interface," which in real English meant I was nothing more than a regular head of a department. But in the start-up community, the traditional was detested and every title had to be "New Economy" too. Thousands of people had been employed just to inflate the numbers before the company's IPO, which was supposed to make all of us rich. And the stock market was biting! Every company that got their act together quickly enough was rewarded by new investors and new funding. It seemed that everyone I knew was getting hired by a start-up or starting up a start-up themselves. The word *start-up* became so common, it was like a refrain being shouted everywhere in the Swedish capital.

We knew the digital revolution would fundamentally change almost everything from surgery to slot machines, from travel to telephones, but no one knew how. Investors were simply assuming that the companies with the largest numbers of consultants were the ones capable of taking on the biggest, most lucrative projects. It wasn't crazy to think.

Some months I'd get a Post-it Note with nothing but a number written on it, like "17." It meant that I had to hire seventeen people that month. Did it matter who? *No.* Did it matter what they were good at? *Not really.* Was there any work for them? *No, not at the moment.* I'd normally just hire people I thought were cool and nice. Some of them from art school.

But it was all too fast, too naive. Too many important people visiting, telling us we were the future. Too many spaced-out meetings about man-machine interfaces. At some companies, this madness didn't lead to exploration of new and relevant technologies; instead, it warped into excess and decline. There were madly expensive parties thrown, outlandish trips abroad, bizarre luxury offices built, and many Ferraris purchased. Too many people getting rich doing nothing. In Scandinavian tradition, those who became rich kept a low profile. Everyone dressed the same, in worn jeans and rock band T-shirts, but gradually the watercooler conversations turned from sneakers to sailboats and summerhouses. In the end, the ones who really believed the hype got burned the worst.

It had been a year and some since I'd seen Oskar's spaceship game, and during that time Kim and I had developed a few projects of our own. The first games Kim and I made were pretty good toys, but the problem we had was that we had nothing particular to say. We just wanted to play around with the process of creation itself. We mostly made advertising games for companies to stick on their websites. Some of them we made for Icon's customers, and some of them just for our own creative satisfaction.

The art was crafted, pixel by pixel, by me, and then Kim would apply his enigmatic programming skills through the Mighty God of

Macromedia Director, a software tool that could handle interactivity, movement, movies, audio, and basic code. It was a brilliant piece of software, and it taught us about the DNA of making games, the very essence of the craft. To the outside world it might not have amounted to much, just two dudes huddled behind their big screens, but for the two of us, the projects allowed us to journey deep into the digital unknown.

We made two browser-based games for ICA supermarkets in 1998, and we created a fun 2-D shooter for my fan site about Yury Gagarin, the first man in space. (For no logical reason whatsoever, we both thought that this serious, factual, and biographical web page of mine needed a game about Russians fighting aliens over Mars.)

Far away, in places we had yet to properly discover, the gaming industry kept growing at lightning speed. Sony's challenger, the PlayStation console, had basically knocked pioneering SEGA out of the market entirely. More than twenty million consumers had bought and fallen in love with a PlayStation. With a broad margin, it had become the leading platform for video games in Asia and in the West. But while Sony's first generation of PlayStation had no internet connection, the web that connected PCs all over the world gave birth to another extremely important innovation: the online multiplayer scene. Not only could players engage with each other in intense battles for victory, but they could also create their own maps and share them with their peers. Suddenly, as in no other medium before, the audience became creators, too, and immediately they began tweaking AI and creating experimental game modes, bringing an avalanche of innovation that would leave a significant mark on the future of the industry.

Most people over thirty thought of video games as violent and inherently dangerous. That had changed in 1996, when the Tamagotchi, a virtual pet, became a local hit in Japan, and then almost instantly became a major sensation across the rest of the globe. Tamagotchis were cute, fun, and harmless. But the most important effect the Tamagotchi phenomenon had was in how it broadened people's understanding of what games could be.

At Icon, Kim and I didn't consider ourselves capable of creating something advanced like a PlayStation game or a Tamagotchi machine. Still, it struck us that we'd become quite familiar with the mechanics and the ideas behind such creations. It was possible for us to play, watch, and begin to deconstruct how other games had been developed. And meanwhile, Sweden's IT revolution kept spinning, faster and faster.

An investigative journalist named Peter Kadhammar was particularly skeptical of the IT boom and tried to puncture the balloon of excitement. He was often on the lookout for problems within booming companies, anything negative that would allow him to write an alarmist article about the IT industry being fraudulent. He was the kind of writer who looked forward to saying "I told you so!" when a company fell apart. I'm not a fan of this school of journalism, mostly because it's so easy and destructive to be negative, but in this case, let's face it, the emperor was pretty naked.

Mr. Kadhammar managed to join the founder of Icon Medialab, a serial entrepreneur named Johan Staël von Holstein, on a trip to Asia, where they planned to do a deep, appreciative personal profile, the type Johan was used to.

Johan was normally a clever chap, but he'd been drinking his own Kool-Aid for too long, and genuinely believed that Icon Medialab was changing societies and the global political landscape forever. His plan was to open several sister companies in Asia and initiate the digital revolution all over the East. Johan Staël was overworked, overhyped, lived in the fast lane, and had very recently become very rich. On top of all that, he had a big optimistic ego that would often escalate into hyperbole. When Kadhammar joined the flight, Johan upgraded them both to first class and reportedly drank several bottles of champagne while rambling on about his impact on the human race (*expect the footprint to be super positive!*). The journalist played along. Johan Staël relaxed, let his guard down, and revealed a lot more than he'd intended to.

Of course, this resulted in a big negative article about Johan Staël von Holstein and Icon Medialab, which my colleagues and I found incredibly cruel and damaging. Johan was a man who forced people to choose: Was he a crazed, drunken, bragging scam artist who had lost the plot entirely, or was he a gentle and genuine genius who ignored social norms? The article took a firm stance: Johan Staël was a delusional idiot. I didn't necessarily agree with everything Johan was up to, and, occasionally, some of his word choices made me cringe, but I thought the published piece was a brutal character assassination and a work of sensationalistic journalism masquerading as serious reporting.

I found it to be unsportsmanlike to attack the head of our company so coldly. I decided to express my frustration in a way that made sense to me at the time: through a game.

I made up an innocent, cute character, a polar bear (well, some kind of fat bear anyway) that I called Poppoo, and I made a pixel version of a journalist with glasses. Once this was done, I called Kim (on my *cell phone*, yeah!), who was working in another department at Icon Medialab at the time. He looked at the pixel sketches, we brainstormed for ten minutes, and then we got ready to enter production. The idea for the game was simple; all I wanted to do was to illustrate what I thought Peter Kadhammar had done: use a medium you control 100 percent to screw someone over, and then leave them with no chance to defend themselves. We got to work that evening, and before dawn we'd created a functional piece of software.

The game started deliberately slow, with a pixelated title screen scrolling into place, accompanied by chirpy 6-bit music: *POPPOO MEETS PIITER KADHAMMAR*. The gamer would play as Poppoo the Friendly Bear, who held a gun in his hand. The gun could be aimed in any direction. At the other end of the banner-sized game was a lonely sheep. If the player aimed at it and fired, the poor animal would explode. But if the player aimed elsewhere, the potential victim would escape death. After a few sheep were killed or spared, a man (named "Piiter," not "Peter"), vaguely resembling the real-life journalist Kadhammar, showed up instead of an animal. Once the player fired Poppoo's gun again, the bullet bounced around the edges of the banner until it killed Piiter in a splash of ridiculously exaggerated pixelated blood. Players who tried to avoid shooting the journalist soon realized that no matter what they aimed at, the bullet would always end up taking out the man. Game over. And this was the point I wanted to make: We could have chosen to offer optional endings, interpretations, and perspectives to the audience, but we didn't. The game always ended with a character assassination. And the one who got hurt would not have a single say in the matter.

This was perhaps not the brightest and most earth-shattering review of journalism ever, but we thought it was hilarious. We assumed that no one would ever see the game and that it would remain just an inside joke between friends. We were of the impression that not a single person on earth had played our previous games, perhaps aside from our friends. And anyway, we couldn't fathom anyone taking the game seriously, because it was made in tiny pixel art.

But let me put it this way: If you plan to express something that can be interpreted as a death threat to a journalist, my simple recommendation is *just don't do it.*

A few hours after we'd completed *Poppoo Meets Piiter Kadhammar* it went viral, which at the time meant that it was spread through emails and simple chat programs like ICQ in which you could include links. Soon enough, every joker in Stockholm's IT world had seen (and played) the game, but what was terrifying was that every serious journalist from the printed press had *also* seen (but not played) the game. Kim and I took it down from our obscure website, but it was too late. Copies had been made and blood splatter had been recorded. The distribution of the game was completely out of our hands. Most people took it for what it was, a silly, bad game, and forgot about it. But the newspaper where the real Kadhammar worked made a big fuss about it, trying to make it appear as a threat to freedom of speech. Their front page the following day was covered in heavy war-style typography: "ICON ATTACKS WITH COMPUTER GAME." However, as hard as the press tried, they couldn't manage to make Poppoo the Friendly Bear look threatening. Even those who got mildly upset at first would get a bit of perspective when they saw Poppoo. Like, come on! Do you really feel threatened by *that*?

I was out of town on a business trip when the headline hit the front page. The poor director of corporate communications at Icon was asked to comment on the "death threat" to Kadhammar. She said the game was obviously not an official statement, that it must have been made by a single unruly employee, and that they'd look into it. After hanging up the phone, I was told, she ran around in circles in the elegant office, screaming "Take it down! Take it down!" oblivious to who the culprit was.

I expected this to end badly for me. I walked into my boss's office the following morning and told him I'd created the game. I tried to keep Kim out of it, although they'd already figured out that we must have made it together. My boss told me upper management had been calling frantically the day before, after the story made the headlines, trying to understand what had happened and who was responsible. I waited to get axed. But these were upside-down days when Alice in Wonderland logic was ruling the world, and weirdly enough, my boss seemed pleased with the whole situation, almost proud.

"Will you fire me? Us?" I asked meekly.

"What? No, not at all! We were thinking about asking you to open a department that makes games. They seem to have a huge impact on people, you know?"

Later Johan called me from Asia on a crackling cell phone and thanked Kim and me for standing up for him.

"I won't forget it," he said.

I felt like a nude streaker crossing the football field in a clumsy attempt to make a point, only to unexpectedly discover that the audience and club owners saw my protest as a true highlight.

"I've got your back if something happens," Johan said before hanging up.

That evening when I called Kim to tell him we'd been asked to start a games department because of Poppoo, I could almost hear his jaw drop through the receiver.

4

FROM INSIDE A BUBBLE

As cool as we felt, Kim and I didn't immediately fly toward the stratosphere like triumphant geek gods.

The game industry is a business of false starts. You need to apply an almost naive interpretation to your own reality. And we did just that! We felt like we'd won the lottery. We were getting paid to experiment and learn about things that we'd until only recently done for fun. We hadn't planned and plotted to end up with the opportunity the Icon Gameslab presented, but no matter how we approached it, we were discovering that making great games wasn't as simple as we'd thought. It wasn't because we didn't try hard enough. We were pushing our limits, but we were still in an early phase, planting seeds, gaining experience, and harvesting insights.

Still, it was impossible not to be excited. *We were being paid to make games!*

I was frustrated that my bosses at Icon Medialab didn't allow me to spend all my time with Kim and the new games department. And the Gameslab was quickly developing into an advertising agency. Clients interested in being at the technical forefront wanted minigames for their brands. As with our previous projects, these games were still developed in Macromedia, which Kim had now fully mastered. We'd sign up an artist, an art director, and sometimes an additional coder or two. Kim was involved in the real production of games, while I was busy in some other part of the ecosystem, signing deals, enabling the projects, building relationships, and fighting against our own organization when they questioned the artistic freedom that I'd given Kim. I did everything necessary to keep our little lab protected.

We were sitting among the clouds on the top floor of a sky-scraper in central Stockholm. Kim and I shared the corner office. Our desks were positioned in an L in front of an elegant glass facade that overlooked Stockholm. In the winter, the city below us would become an abstract painting in subtle shades of blue, white, and turquoise. For some inexplicable reason, no one had wanted the room until we made it ours, and once it had become a cozy cave where a childlike sense of wonder was welcome, everyone got jealous. When the compact winter nights turned the skies black and gray, we'd see the lights of the city sparkle far below, like some distant dream world.

Next to my desk, my huge dog Maltsev would lie sleeping. He was a Rhodesian ridgeback named after a Soviet ice-hockey player from the '70s. Even for a ridgeback, he was big, weighing in around fifty kilos (over one hundred pounds). His slow, deep breathing gave the room an atmosphere of calm, no matter how stressed we were. I remember feeling that I was safe only in that room; everything outside, a form of battle. Too often, I'd found myself in situations that were far too complicated for my taste, and much too difficult for my capacity.

From the sanctuary of our glass cave, the Icon Gameslab released nine or ten games during 2000 and 2001. As we progressed, the projects became more and more advanced and demanding, but output remained astonishingly efficient.

As formative as this period was, we weren't exploring the medium to express ourselves at all. We made games for paying clients, and they used them to promote their own brands. We made games for Ericsson, Axe, Compaq, and Telia. Compaq was sponsoring BMW's

Formula One Team and had asked us to build an F1 manager game. When it was released, the Compaq servers went down due to the heavy load of gamers playing it, which was a first, but not the last such occurrence for Kim and me.

One day late in 2001, I was contacted by a guy named Martin Walfisz, who wanted to sell us part of his alleged game studio. Icon Medialab had certainly proven their will to invest over the years and had bought quite a few companies in several countries, so it wasn't a far-fetched proposal. I met Martin in the meeting room where we usually received clients. These rooms were the same in every IT start-up, as if the new industry had spawned interior architects with very expensive tastes: rust-colored rooms, weird-looking lamps made of steel and canvas, a fully functional pinball game to symbolize street savviness and appreciation for underground culture. Management wanted to advertise success, so the entire office was designed to establish a narrative: "Work with us; we create wealth!"

Martin was nice, no doubt about it. Immensely energetic and eager. He was the son of Polish-Jewish immigrants (mentioned in his pitch), and he, too, seemed to have something to prove to the world. He was openly restless and ambitious.

He told us that we'd miss an opportunity of a lifetime if we didn't buy his children's games division. He showed us a chart of his huge organization, consisting of a mother company with many subdivisions: Mobile, Triple-A, Children's Games, IP Management, and more. Here was a guy in a completely different league than me, a proper motormouth. It wasn't conscious exaggeration; this man truly believed the words rolling off his tongue. He was a poet-on-fire. Martin was personally and wholeheartedly convinced about the promises he made, and he was dead certain that the many wonderful things he had in mind would soon come true.

Think about it. Everything amazing starts with someone taking a leap of faith, with someone saying the Big Words: "I want to marry you," or "Let's build a spaceship and fly to the moon." It's those who dare to dream, who dare to take risks, who push the world forward. Don't get me wrong, pragmatism is one of my favorite traits, but pragmatism needs to be aligned with a strong vision. Pragmatism without vision is nothing more than pessimism.

Anyway, Martin Walfisz kept going, a million words coming out of his mouth without any hesitation or time to breathe. The PowerPoint slides looked slick, advanced, and impressive, and I wouldn't have been surprised if my upper management had been ready to buy something from this wordsmith.

In the end Icon passed up on the opportunity, and my only clever contribution to the negotiation was my conscious choice to keep a bridge to Martin intact. Most people tend to dismiss each other too quickly, in my opinion. It requires a bit of energy to remain open-minded. As I see it, relationships are ultimately defined by how you approach them: curiosity or arrogance. One approach will deliver a rich life; the other will cost you many opportunities.

In this case I remained genuinely curious. We had good chemistry, and I found the ambition quite contagious.

After my visitor left, I opened up an AltaVista window on my laptop and looked up "Martin Walfisz." I learned that he was not a fantasizing mega-entrepreneur at all; he was in fact the founder of Massive Entertainment, a hip independent game developer based in the south of Sweden. Massive had created a very beautiful, well-received game called *Ground Control*, and everyone seemed convinced that they were destined for larger triumphs. *Hmm, there you go*, I thought, disappointed in myself for labeling the guy as only a great salesman.

Our Icon Gameslab projects had started winning marketing awards. Perhaps the coolest of the winners was a game called *Nerdolympics*, which was used as a recruitment campaign for Icon Medialab. It was Kim's craftsmanship at its best.

Nerdolympics was set up a little like a wrestling match, or a game of chess. On one side of the screen, there was a champion nerd, hunched over his computer. Facing him there was another nerd, who was controlled by the player, and in the background was a stadium with an enthusiastic nerd audience. The AI nerd would type lines of code that were visible on the game screen. The player's job was to copy the same line of code without a single error as fast as possible. The beauty of this was that since code utilizes so many uncommon symbols, digits, and signs, only a person with a lot of practice from real-life programming would be able to copy the lines fast enough to get to the top of the scoreboard. It was fun, perfectly appropriate for the audience, and it ensured that the people who were on the high-score list were genuinely the best coders, which meant that *Nerdolympics* also was the perfect recruitment tool for the Gameslab.

Amazing! If only it weren't for the fact that we weren't recruiting anymore. In fact, the opposite was about to happen. We were too innocent to understand, too excluded from the boardrooms to know, and too focused on ourselves to see that the IT bubble was about to burst like an infected wound. Sure, we noticed that there seemed to be a fast turnover of directors and managers; and certainly, it seemed a bit like a witch hunt when the newspapers regularly challenged the inflated share prices; and yes, there had been a few collapses among our competitors. If we'd paid more attention to the stock market early in 2001, the signs were blindingly obvious, too, but it all seemed distant somehow. Kim and I had a narrow perspective of the situation, and, as far as we could tell, our games department was thriving.

Eventually, though, my instincts caught up. I'd quickly risen through the ranks of the company, and I was invited to a meeting with the board and other top brass in Brussels. In the meeting, I picked up a bad vibe. I wasn't used to this kind of environment, where big companies meet to make big decisions. The meeting was in an ostentatious hotel conference room with polarized windows, thick carpets, and a solid-oak table that looked like someone had ripped it off the side of a sail boat.

There was a sense of desperation among those in management

who knew more than I did, and I was struck with a strong feeling that it was all over. The finance team took the lead in the meeting and asked strange questions about concepts that hadn't been mentioned before. "What's the expected return on this investment?" "Can you do it with a smaller team?" "Will this pitch lead to a new contract, and if so, how soon?"

What was going on? Was our relentlessly optimistic gazing at the wonderful future becoming a crass question of cash?

I wasn't an idiot.

Things were clearly going to go to hell, not just for Icon Medialab but for an entire line of promising start-ups. The approaching disaster was now palpable, and there was no way our tiny games team could survive the certain collapse of our parent company. The only thing I could think about on my flight home was an escape hatch. How could Kim and I leave this imploding mother ship and move on to a better future?

When I came back to Sweden, I told Kim we needed to split with Icon. "No problem," he said. I knew we didn't even need a handshake (though I realized later that he thought we were headed for New York).

The next day I called Bert Wihlborg, whom I'd met when I was renting an office as a freelance illustrator (another bridge preserved). It was the right call to make; he knew some special people. Bert was at least twenty years older than me and worked for a company called Modern Times Group, or MTG. He was a short, stocky man who wore tailored suits, and he moved with the slickness of a lawyer who'd abandoned his ethics. He had an opaque, professional personality, but I had apparently made enough of an impression as a young illustrator for him to take my call and hear me out.

Bert was also a close friend to one of Sweden's richest men, Jan Stenbeck. Stenbeck's story dates all the way back to the early 1900s. Here's the short version: Jan's father, Hugo Stenbeck, was a lawyer, deeply involved in the businesses of Ivar Kreuger, a genius and a swindler who built up an empire that crashed during the

Great Depression. Ivar subsequently took his own life. After his suicide, his financial empire was either "split up in an organized and civilized manner" or "plundered by scoundrels with only their own interests in mind." I wasn't there, but I know which version I believe is more likely. In any case, Hugo Stenbeck came out of the depression with riches he cleverly invested in the coming decades.

Second-generation superrich kid Jan Stenbeck started to transform Daddy's empire by investing the profits from "old money" (wood, steel, paper, construction) in "new money" (IT, cell phones, commercial TV, entertainment). He had corporations everywhere, and he'd collected many of the new media companies under the umbrella of MTG.

I thought it was obvious that MTG needed to have a proper game studio. And why not? During this time, in other parts of the world, the gaming industry was growing up quickly, and the money was getting bigger. Core Design, a British game developer, had made *Tomb Raider*, which became one of the first games to attract real attention from nongamers, ultimately putting the hero, Lara Croft, on the cover of the influential pop magazine *THE FACE* in 1997. *The Sims*, released before the turn of the century, enriched the interactive entertainment world and inspired the industry to think beyond early formulas. The game appealed to the casual audience by offering access to a huge, living dollhouse world and almost infinite possibilities to grow and play with a virtual family.

In offices around the world, one could see hard-core gamers secretly using their office internet connection at night (and of course during work hours too) to play an online game called *EverQuest*, the first proper massive multiplayer online game (MMO), which would later inspire Blizzard to create the phenomenon *World of WarCraft*.

With the game industry growing and expanding at such incredible speed, and starting to break into the mainstream, all that remained was to convince the right person at MTG that they needed to join the race.

* * *

I closed the heavy glass door to my corner office in the top floor of the Icon tower, watching unknown citizens of Stockholm cross Sergels Torg far below. The perspective made them look tiny, as if they were nothing but small animated units in a real-time strategy game.

Outside my room, self-proclaimed IT gurus in their early twenties moved confidently across the vast floor, seemingly on their way to another million-dollar deal. I knew it was a bubble. Our professional reality was built on distorted predictions and hopeful lies. It was all going to disappear soon, in what I assumed would be a devastating and embarrassing disaster.

I dialed the number.

"Hey Bert, how's life?"

"Ah, David! LONG TIME NO SPEAK. I'm at a team-building thing with the top brass of MTG," he shouted. I could hear go-karts roaring amid tumultuous cries for more beer.

"MTG's management? Perfect. That's what I wanted to talk to you about. Can you hear me?"

"YES," he shouted and laughed at some joke someone made in the background.

"Does MTG have a game development team?" I asked.

"No, not that I know of; why?"

"I think you should hire me and my buddy Kim. We can set it up for you."

And that was my entire pitch. No budget, no business plan, nothing. Just an idea that there were pieces of the puzzle that would match, and the knowledge that I could make it happen.

"Interesting," said Bert. "I'll call you back in a few days."

5

THE CULT OF THE CHEAP

The shiny blond hair of the well-dressed receptionist looked like plastic firmly glued to his head. I tried not to stare at it as I asked him for directions to the restroom.

He opened a drawer in a gigantic wooden cabinet with a red velvet top and from it produced a large rusty key that looked like it would fit a cemetery gate.

Once I had locked the door behind me, I noticed something: On the wall next to the toilet was a small, elegant plate of brass, bolted on top of the expensive tapestry. You could see it only if you were standing up when you were taking a leak. I leaned in closer to read the message etched in the henna-colored metal. "If you're not paranoid, it's because you don't know enough," it read. Something to think about when standing up with your pants down.

I was at MTG's head office on Skeppsbron in Stockholm, a building that had been erected in the early 1700s only a few blocks away from the Royal Palace. The interior sent a self-confident message from someone who had enough money to keep this citadel in top form. The office was covered in dark precious woods and somber wallpaper with swirling patterns. Light from the pale Swedish winter sun bounced off the waters outside and in through the tall windows. A few lonely dust particles caught the light and glittered in the deep windowsills. Teak desks the size of hangar ships sat in front of steampunk chairs with green leather seats. The interior decorator from 1920 was apparently still in charge.

I was meeting Holger Albrecht, the CEO of Modern Times Group. I'd heard he was a shrewd guy who was interested in only the bottom line. I was nervous.

"Why are you here?" he asked less than a minute into our meeting, with a distinct German accent that added a fierceness to his expressionless face.

"Bert set up the meeting," I replied, not sure where he was going.

"Ja, well. Okay. Pitch!" he said and leaned back with his arms behind his head in the classic *impress-me!* pose.

I did my best, but it was like performing in front of an audience just waiting for the main act. I was the warm-up no one had paid to see.

While Albrecht kept staring at me like a failing stand-up comedian, it struck me that he seemed indifferent to me and to the entire entertainment industry in general, which made me wonder why he was in such a prominent position. After a few generic questions, he sent me off with the vague words "Kinna will take care of everything." Apparently, decisions had already been made (or perhaps I wasn't paranoid enough, and being "taken care of" meant that "Kinna" would take me out).

One of the many young, impeccable-looking trainees escorted me to the exit, which also functioned as a portal leading back to the present century. He explained that Kinna was a nickname for Christina Bellander, the managing director of one of the many smaller companies owned by MTG.

A twenty-minute tube ride later, I was in her office in the southern part of the city. I was planning to focus the meeting on the games studio I was dreaming about building for MTG, but coming directly from the MTG headquarters, something else caught my attention: Kinna's MTG office reflected a completely different view on spending. There were way too many people packed into the cramped space, working in an uncoordinated mix of cheap office furniture that looked like it could fall apart any second. Someone should have cleaned the place some time ago, but there was a dusty air of resignation hanging in the room.

They were producing TV, the new kind: reality shows, celebrity stuff, and cheap competitive programs where participants were duped into embarrassing situations, looking like fools in exchange for their fifteen minutes of fame.

"Do you want a coffee?" Kinna asked me. She was a woman in her fifties and dressed smart and simple like my art school professors. But unlike my soft-spoken teachers, she was all business. Professional and hard.

"Coffee, yes, please." I said, trying to gauge the situation.

The pitch-black drink I got tasted like it was made from tree bark and was served in one of the assorted and not-paid-for mugs with unclear origins (private? promotional?).

My "job interview" began. Here, too, it was clear that the almighty had already given a thumbs-up behind the scenes, so it wasn't much of a conversation. Kinna was predominantly interested in displaying further features of her low-cost universe. Behold: a reused cardboard box filled with a mix of pens and pencils "borrowed" from banks and business meetings, every single one for free! And admire: the employees own cleaning schedule in the toilet—no need to pay for professional cleaning here! And voilà, a tip of the year: Don't pay for heating. A cold office stops people from sitting around doing nothing!

I'd been looking forward to a discussion about building a games department. I was prepared to start with my grand vision, move on to strategy, and then translate the whole package into tactics. But here we were, discussing the potential of saving money on pencils. *Really?* Are you telling me *this is MTG?* Kinna shared some additional advice:

- Never buy furniture. We'll send you something old we have stored somewhere.
- Never buy bookshelves or any other storage space; people just use them to collect junk anyway.
- Don't ever hire anyone; just put them on short temporary contracts so you don't get stuck with people and cost.

Okay, okay, I understood. The legend at MTG was that the surreal stinginess originated from Jan Stenbeck himself. The word on the floor was that he derived an almost perverse pleasure from asking managers to be as cheap as possible, while allegedly indulging in the most exorbitant lifestyle imaginable himself. Those who had met him came back with stories of wild parties in castles, improvised races in expensive sports cars, spontaneous weekend trips to the Bahamas in private jets, and exotic big-game hunting trips.

But to win Stenbeck's heart, you needed to be more than his party buddy, you needed to be cheap. Those looking for promotion in his corporate empire competed by aggressively slashing expenses wherever possible to impress the godfather.

There was a story about when Stenbeck visited one of his own start-ups abroad. The new company was supposed to grow to over a hundred employees, so they had a spacious office in the early days. This apparently annoyed Stenbeck so much that he had a wall built right through the middle of the office so the staff would have to squeeze into half the space. The other half of the office remained empty. Everything at MTG was taken as an opportunity to out-cheap the competition. Once I understood this, I stopped paying attention.

After the lecture on the virtues of being financially prudent, Kinna threw a contract on the table and told me to sign, which I did, with an especially cost-effective pen. Deal done. I didn't need MTG to help me understand games, media, or pop culture; all I needed was funding. As long as they were willing to pay the salaries, I felt confident that I could handle the rest together with Kim.

I had married earlier that year, in a small anonymous office in the otherwise impressive city hall of Stockholm, with my year-old daughter in a cute dress and diapers on my arm as my best man. Our son was born soon thereafter, on a night when heavy thunderstorms shook the earth as if Thor himself were celebrating the birth of the baby boy.

Meanwhile, Kim's girlfriend dreamed about horses and a house in the country. Righty-o. We decided to leave the capital. Kim and I happily took our imaginary bag of cash and moved down south to set up the new company, MTG Modern Games. We were going to become ridiculously successful game developers and our respective families embraced the chance to experience something new. Horses would be bought, kids would grow up, dogs and humans would enjoy leaving the city. It was perfect.

Farewell, Stockholm, you high-strung diva!

And boom, we were in Malmö, a five-hour train ride from the capital. Founded sometime in the 1200s, Malmö is located right where the Baltic Sea squeezes through a narrow strait to join the North Sea. Here was a place for a great natural harbor, and a city painted in shades of brown and gray popped up around it. For a time, Malmö was an important Hansa city, where trade flourished. In the years after World War II, the town became an industrial hub with the biggest shipping wharf in the world. But in the '80s, the bright future collapsed, the factories closed one by one, and the town dipped into a deep financial crisis that lasted more than two decades.

Still, Malmö had many advantages: affordable apartments, cheaper offices in the town center, a family-friendly lifestyle, a great football team, friendlier-looking people than in Stockholm, and a pronounced humble-and-hungry comeback attitude that had a positive influence on the whole population. "Yeah, this could be good," we said to each other, smiling, and as a sign of our newfound, superhero courage, we went and defiantly bought brand-new pens and bookshelves to keep all our junk in.

6

SPUTNIKS IN THE BALLROOM

The man had the shortest neck I'd ever seen in my life. It was like a giant pear had been stuck on top of his shoulders. Kim and I tried not to stare, because this odd fellow might become our landlord if we just made a good impression. We were being led through a tour of carefully selected rooms that could potentially become offices. Not a word about cost. Clearly, this was going to be a case of personal chemistry and not money.

Kim and I were expected to find the dumpiest office in Malmö and fill it with the worst secondhand furniture we could get our hands on. But then, why should we? This was our chance to fulfill our dreams, an opportunity we felt we had created ourselves, almost out of nothing, and we had no interest in proving to Kinna Bellander and her faithful acolytes that we could be cheap.

Even before we'd moved down to Malmö, we started checking out various places to rent, all of them in perfect MTG-style (i.e., low-cost and depressing). But then, by accident, we stumbled upon a surreal and unexpected opportunity: The local Odd Fellows Order needed a tenant. Apparently, the secret cult/organization/UFO-spotters/fraternity/devil-worshippers/Christians were not very successful in attracting new recruits, and the Malmö lodge was shrinking quickly. The building in the center of the city was a magnificent relic of better times. The entire house was constructed by the Odd brothers in 1904, and later, after having personally spent quite a lot of time there, I became convinced that it contained several secret rooms and passageways.

In 2001, the Odd Fellows Brothers Lodge, No. 34, had concluded that they didn't use their vast ballroom often enough and they decided to put it up for rent. It was half the size of a football field, and at least five meters high to the ceiling, maybe more. You'd arrive through a modest wooden door that set your expectations low, then walk through the dark hallway to find an incredibly well-crafted wooden staircase with Art Deco handrails of steel. After turning right, you were hit with a huge open room bathed in sun-yellow light reflecting from old oak floors. The whole place was immaculately kept, a celebration in honor of the Fellows, of course. This was exactly the kind of place that MTG would hate, and naturally we fell instantly in love. In our defense, though, it was also the least expensive place we'd found, even though it was at a minimum five times bigger than the alternatives. It seemed ludicrous considering that we were expecting to have four employees, but, nevertheless, it became our office. It was like working in the dining hall at Hogwarts; we could have biked to visit each other's desks if we'd wanted to.

Once the original tour was over and we'd been accepted as tenants, I called MTG and told them we'd found a *really cheap office*, which delighted them, until a month later when Kinna came to visit and stepped into our space. Her eyes widened in horror. But the price was right, so she couldn't fight us on it.

The idea Kim and I had for our new little game studio was simple: MTG owned a lot of content, especially movies and TV shows. They also owned several commercial TV channels. And they owned us. We wanted to create games based on the most appropriate MTG brands.

Others saw this opportunity just as clearly as we did, especially a Swedish game publisher called PAN Vision. They were already investing in original games made for the Scandinavian market, but their projects were mostly new intellectual properties with no fan base or exposure. TV advertising was unimaginable for games at the time; no one had that kind of money. Paying us to make a game based on an MTG property and then sharing the profit would be a lot better for MTG/PAN, we all agreed. The only question was, which brand?

As we started pulling some strings and developing our network from the base of our newfound home, we spent a tremendous amount of time playing games together from the sofa that stood in a distant corner, surrounded by a churchlike echo. Through the screen, we discovered a world far away, where budgets were excessive, technology unlimited, and artists supreme. It was frightening, in the same way that the signal from the Soviet Sputnik satellite had once shocked the rest of the world with its apparently futuristic and unattainable abilities. In awe, we enjoyed the experiences at the expense of our self-confidence.

There were games where the narrative had grown deep and rich, touching profound human emotions and eternal questions about life, relationships, and philosophy. We visited wonderful digital worlds, crafted with insane attention to detail. Sometimes, we were the gods of vast empires that would last for centuries, struggling through complex scenarios of trade, exploration, politics, war, the birth of the Age of Discovery, and the effects of religion. In the racing game *Gran Turismo*, the wonderfully accurate reflections of light on the rain-covered city streets led us to pause the game and take photographs of the television screen, which we studied to figure out how they'd achieved such an effect. We played a lot of different games, and when we found something we liked, we'd analyze it properly to understand how it was made. The big difference was that we no longer put ourselves in the seat of the passenger; we'd switched to the cockpit. If we could play it, that meant we could create it. Every game was now a learning experience.

But playing those games, and truly beginning to understand them, wasn't making me happy. It was making me furious about our own inabilities and frustrated about our ridiculously slow progress.

The experience reminded me of a course in art school, one that almost broke my spirit. The course was (innocently) called Study of Old Masters, and the professor who was responsible had set it up as a trap.

"Welcome to my little course," he said, absentmindedly staring out the windows at the great beyond. I looked in the same direction, but as far as I could tell, there was nothing there except an empty field called Gärdet, where, once upon a time, Swedish cavalry had practiced for wars that never happened. The professor wore a brown tattered cardigan over his anonymous light-blue shirt, and his fingers were stained with color from his own projects: ink and oil. Maybe acrylics, although those stains would wash off easily if he really wanted them to. His jeans had horizontal lines of color, too, across his right thigh, where he apparently wiped his brushes dry after washing them.

"It's a simple exercise," he continued. "All you need to do is to choose your favorite picture from the entire history of art and bring it to me."

"Really? That doesn't sound like *education*," one ambitious classmate said, while others sighed at her and rolled their eyes behind her back. *Come on! Don't be such a bloody do-gooder!*

"Indeed," the professor said, ignoring her completely. "Leave now and bring me your favorite piece of work by tomorrow."

He then exited the classroom, less than five minutes after beginning the lecture. And thus, the trap was set.

At first I thought of bringing something that I really liked, maybe a Suprematist painting by Malevich; or perhaps something that would signal my cool rebel attitude—a costume by a Dadaist? But then I decided to challenge myself and choose a Rembrandt. I picked a painting called *Man in a Golden Helmet*, because I was intrigued by the light, the angry expression on the face of the aging man, and the odd choice of letting him look down rather than toward the viewer or heroically into the far distance.

"Right!" said the professor once we showed up the next day, all of us proudly flaunting a favorite piece of art. "I don't care what you chose. Now copy it!"

"What?!" we all exclaimed in unison. "It's impossible to copy [insert name of ridiculously skilled and famous artist here]!"

"Perhaps," the professor continued with a smug smile on his face. "But this is what the Study of Old Masters is about. Now go to work."

In the ensuing weeks, I embarked on the impossible journey of copying a Rembrandt. I started by applying a grid to the page I had stolen from a book in the library, and then painstakingly began re-creating the painting, tiny square by tiny square, without fully knowing if it would all add up and look reasonably okay in the end. At a slow pace, I began to understand the work behind the painting, brushstroke by brushstroke. From the high-quality print, insights emerged, and I got in tune with what Rembrandt had been up to when he painted his man in a helmet. Trick by trick, material after material, it all began to stand out to me as an advanced palette of techniques that I had never fully appreciated before. My respect for the old master deepened day after day, until I, too, declared him to be a genius, but this time after really understanding the extent of his abilities with my own hands, sweat, and failing color mixes.

The only problem was, even after dissecting the painting down to its smallest fragments, I couldn't find any way to re-create the stunning effect of Rembrandt's work. I *knew* how it was done. I *knew* *every piece of it*, but I still found myself unable to deliver something reasonably similar. *Knowing how it was done didn't make me able to do it.* It was a hard lesson. I hated the realization, and I hated my professor for opening my eyes to the enormous chasm between a young hopeful artist and a fully operational professional at the height of his career.

* * *

In the ballroom, still driven by optimism, Kim and I went through exactly those same emotions. The more we studied the masters of game-making, the worse we felt. For every small hurdle we overcame, it seemed that others were climbing mountains almost on a daily basis. As we moved forward, we were falling behind. The study of the digital masters was simultaneously a study of the growing gap between our dreams and the runaway reality.

7

THE THIRD WAVE

Kim and I were behind the scenes of a movie set in Trollhättan talking to Anders Nilsson, an up-and-coming movie director who was working on a film to which MTG owned the rights. I enjoyed being there, around the cameras, the lights, the microphones, and the set, which was made up to resemble a European city street.

Anders Nilsson had made a name for himself creating low-budget B movies in the style of Roger Corman. I never saw any of those early homemade action movies, but I was told they consisted of his friends running around in the forests outside Lidköping with fake guns, shouting macho dialogue in broken English. Allegedly, the films were hilarious and sort of great if you watched them in an ironic way, but it wasn't clear to me if that was what Anders was going for when he made them. I thought it was more likely that he'd been quite serious about those early projects. Either way, meeting him didn't clarify the matter. He was a big man with a bitter sulkiness about him, and he didn't enjoy talking about his semilegendary B movies. One thing was clear, though: He really *loved* action movies, and shooting combat sequences gave him the biggest rush.

"Here's where the guy will step out and get shot by this guy in the car who has a *giant* Glock in his hands, and he shakes violently as if he's being electrocuted. The blood will splatter in fountains from his arteries over here and over there, and yeah, everywhere, and then he stumbles out into the street uttering his last words. It will be awesome!"

Ta-da! Here we were, finally, in deep discussions about making a game based on an action movie called *The Third Wave* that had a (relatively speaking) large budget! We were promised direct access to the writer, the art director, and the director himself. This was fantastic, and we were pleased to find that Anders was as much a fan of cheap and fast entertainment as we were. He adored the idea of having a computer game created for his movie. He made sure he had plenty of time for us and was eager to show us around the set. It felt like we'd hit the big time. And the good news didn't end there. We'd convinced PAN Vision to finance the production of the game, and they had approved a budget that seemed insane to us: 200,000 dollars! (In comparison, a triple-A game today has a budget of around five hundred times that, between 100 and 140 million USD). We felt slight vertigo thinking about it. Back in Stockholm, Kinna was happy, too, since the new contract with PAN reversed the flow of the money 180 degrees.

Now it was time to get to work. Through the old recruiting game called *Nerdolympics* we'd found a programmer, Niklas, whom we hired to handle the growing engineering needs. There's a lot of code in games, and we'd noticed that he was consistently at the top of the charts playing *Nerdolympics*, but not because he'd beaten it— he'd simply hacked it. Niklas was originally a trained carpenter and looked like a soccer player, easily the most regular dude of us all. In fact, he made the rest of us come across as deeply troubled neurotics.

Kim took on the role of Lead Programmer and Architect, and Niklas was called Additional Programmer (which somehow felt like an insufficient title). Like an optimistic amateur, I was expected to dabble in various tasks, including writing, level design, and, well, uh, that was basically it. I didn't know enough about 3-D graphics to help with the art for the game. Most of my time was focused on keeping MTG at bay, and keeping the complicated network of the project's stakeholders in good shape. I felt like a diplomat most of the time. Clearly, we needed backup.

I imagined that everyone working for Massive back then was a million times better than us, but to my surprise, there were a few people who didn't enjoy working there. They reached out to see if we had something to offer. We picked up a guy named Henrik, a skinny artist who turned out to be the angriest man on earth. We added a guy named Daniel who dressed like a life-hating goth, played artsy, dark music, and, to our surprise, turned out to be quite friendly. And we hired yet another programmer, another Henrik, who came from a local school where he was the youngest teacher on the campus. The arrival of the esteemed gentlemen Angry, Friendly, and School gave us the muscle we needed to create our first major game.

We decided to create an isometric game—two-dimensional, top-down view—in the spirit of *Ghost Recon*. The player would choose a combination of agents to succeed by combining stealth and brute force in a perfect balance. We worked with new complicated technologies like line of sight, which measured what the AI could plausibly see through the maze of objects, thereby creating patterns of movement and vision that the player could use to time perfect attacks. We also decided to include a "perma-death" feature, which punished the gamer for being wasteful or sloppy with the tiny digital agents, and this led to very complicated balancing issues toward the end of the game. It looked simple, but it was hard-core.

In our magnificent ballroom, the six of us worked like maniacs, and we quickly realized that the budget we had first thought was so huge was in fact much too small. It would never allow us to make a game that measured up to those of the competition. We'd learned that studios working on similar projects normally had thirty to forty employees and budgets that were at least ten times larger.

Judging by our burn-rate, our budget would last five to six months tops. I was beginning to think that maybe we were in way over our heads.

We worked in silence like devoted medieval monks. The only thing that disturbed the peace was angry Henrik, who now and then would start smashing his keyboard violently on his desk for reasons that he didn't share with the rest of us. He'd make a strange sound like a twisted seal that was about to explode, creaking and whining, and then walk out of the office without a word. The five of us left behind ignored this, and when he came back, everyone just kept working. Following one of his tantrums he never returned, and after a while we replaced him with Daniel's young and mysterious friend Evelina. A sensitive and fragile goth with a promising music career, she added much-needed diversity to our group of boy nerds. The melancholy black clouds and perpetual silence that followed her everywhere didn't matter, she felt like a breath of fresh air.

As production chugged along, we were all getting more involved in the international games scene. I finally bought my first console to have at home, and it was about time. I had been a die-hard Macintosh gamer forever, but as Apple gradually lost its pioneering status as a platform for games, I simply had to make the switch. I fell in love with my shiny PlayStation 2, which felt like an object from the future, and played as many games as I could get my hands on in the evenings.

In 2001, Microsoft decided to challenge the dominance of PlayStation and launched a gaming console called Xbox, which reshaped the landscape of consoles yet again. Game studios were suddenly churning out games that made the graphics of the previous generations look blocky, clumsy, and garish in comparison. The pile of great games at home and at work was higher than ever, and we could have become lost in playing them if we hadn't been so busy. We ended up splitting the research between us. Daniel played *The Elder Scrolls III: Morrowind*, and as he marched through a

Tolkienesque world, encountering thousands of in-game characters and experiencing a rich canvas of side-quests, the pure size of the world made him dizzy. The game was like being *inside* the story of *The Lord of the Rings*—not reading it. Kim fell in love with *Metroid Prime*, which he played on his Nintendo GameCube, and marveled over the graphics and ingenious combination of skills and challenges. For a while, Kim was mesmerized, living a parallel life as a solitary bounty hunter on the terrifying planet Tallon IV.

As a crisp-and-clean design reference, *Tom Clancy's Ghost Recon* became our favorite game. The developers behind it had taken what they learned from the tight corridor tactics gameplay of the *Rainbow Six* series and succeeded in simulating the challenges that special-forces soldiers faced during missions behind enemy lines, and thus gave birth to a new genre that became known as tactical shooters. *Ghost Recon* was painstakingly slow, realistic, precise, and demanding, but we loved to plan and plot our advancements across the alluring landscapes and complicated indoor areas playing host to our secret missions. Masochistically, we cherished the fact that even the smallest mistake would turn out to be deadly.

Martin Walfisz at Massive was kind enough to invite us to be a part of his studio posse when they went to E3, the biggest industry convention on the planet, hosted annually in Los Angeles. Massive had been acquired by publisher Vivendi Universal Games, which seemed quite disorganized and wealthy because, somehow, we got to stay in the same hotel as all the Massive guys in Beverly Hills.

I felt totally out of place the first time I went to E3. As I walked around the vast show floor at the Convention Center in downtown LA, I felt like an astronaut visiting the rocket assembly room. *So this is how we go to space?* I thought, rubbing shoulders with the best creative gurus and nobody-wannabes in a wild and potent mix.

The entire place was dedicated to celebrating the best games around, and each one had received an insane cosmetic tune-up in order to impress the convention's attendees. I was immersed in videos, in playing demos, in conversations, in weird laser lights, and in deafening sounds from every direction. Eager demoists tried to pull me into their booths to show me their games, and merchandise was handed out in droves as if we were all VIPs.

In 2002, I was nothing more than a tourist on the show floor, an apparent nobody chasing a distant mirage. It was painfully obvious that the games we tried to make at Modern Games were not modern at all. The attention-grabbers at the show were far ahead of us when it came to basically everything—graphics, animation, audio, special effects, and narrative. Kim and I were stunned by the graphics of the racing game *Colin McRae Rally 3*, intrigued by the innovative heights of *Alter Echo*, and mind-blown by the online magic built into *Final Fantasy XI*. There were a lot of rubbish games, too, most of which would be instantly forgotten, like *Aggressive Inline* from Acclaim, and fighting game *Pride FC* from THQ.

It seemed that the world was suddenly filled with publishers looking for great teams in order to feed fast-growing consumer expectations. What did we need to do to stand out? How could we possibly hope to be heard in the midst of all the noise?

In LA we met another great bunch of people from Malmö who were running their own studio called Southend Interactive. They were about to release an Xbox game titled *Deathrow* later in the year, and it was already attracting some attention. At the time, Southend and Massive were competing to be the biggest game studio in Malmö, which in those days meant that Martin had around thirty-five employees and the Jeppsson brothers at Southend had around fifteen. To me and Kim, both studios seemed like superstars, and we felt like little brothers trying to play with the big boys. We convinced (maybe deluded) ourselves that we had an angle because of our relationship to the movie industry.

We wanted to know how big games *were made*. We wanted to understand what made successful projects successful. We were students, looking at creative people who knew more than we did, identifying patterns, taking notes, picking up ideas. We were not fans; we were Padawans. I must admit that we also quietly suffered from our hubris and arrogance. We were identifying ourselves with the global market, with the best games in the world, although in reality the game we were working on would be based on nothing more than a low-budget local movie production with not-so-well-known Swedish actors. We weren't exactly working with Ridley Scott, James Cameron, or George Lucas.

Ten months in, once we were well over budget, we began wrapping up the project. It had been very hard and frustrating, as expected. But in the end, *The Third Wave* was a very good-looking game, rich in detail and almost entirely bug-free. (In those days, we assumed that a game had to ship without any bugs, which meant extensive playtesting in our ballroom.)

The narrative was straightforward and worked as a sibling to the movie; it focused on a bunch of well-organized drug dealers in Europe. The police in the game wanted to take them down, but the criminals were well-connected, protected by big money, and used loopholes in the European Union to establish trade routes for their illegal goods. The only way for the player to stop them was to quietly infiltrate and sabotage the operation. The player would invest in special agents with different abilities and tactically plan and execute missions to slowly break the backbone of the drug syndicate. It all ended with a climactic moonlit shoot-out on the rooftops of Brussels.

The Third Wave was finally released on PC and Macintosh in Russia and Scandinavia, but, despite the generous advertising push from MTG-owned TV channels, to our disappointment it didn't leave even the smallest ripple on the expanding oceans of the booming game industry. Anders Nilsson was still happy as a cat, and that mattered a great deal to us since we wanted to repay his trust with respect. I'm pretty sure he never played the game, but he was able to check off another item on his bucket list.

In the end, no one except the developers cared about *The Third*

Wave. Everyone who worked on the project knew in their hearts that we had outperformed the odds and that the game was an incredible feat considering the conditions we'd been given. The game was our baby, and we liked it a lot. But sadly, no one else did, or rather, no one else *noticed*. What we thought was the biggest achievement in our lives was met by a collective shrug.

It's true, though, that other professionals understood what we'd managed to pull off. They were able to see the mountain we'd climbed from within those difficult conditions, and from them we got the occasional friendly nod: "I see, I see. That is one amazing effort you made right there! Good job." In this we found some consolation, and it also kept important business conversations going.

Everything everywhere felt like unfinished business. I wouldn't say the reviews of the game were traumatizing, but they hurt, and they sure as hell taught me a severe lesson: It doesn't impress anyone that you can make soup out of nails. No one cares about an insufficient budget, bad managers, shitty conditions, strained publisher relationships, or any other excuses. The audience doesn't care if you stayed on budget or released the game on time. *The only thing that matters in the entertainment industry is the quality of the product*. Absolutely everything else is secondary. I have never forgotten that lesson, and it has become the keystone in every choice I've made as a manager since.

8

A MAN DIES, AND ALL I FEEL IS SELF-PITY

I was sitting in the ballroom when I received the news:

DAGENS NYHETER, August 20, 2002

The controversial entrepreneur Jan Stenbeck passed away last night after suffering a heart attack. He died at the American Hospital in Paris after a brief period of illness. Jan Stenbeck was 59.

NY TEKNIK, August 20, 2002

The death of entrepreneur Jan Stenbeck led to chaos on the Stockholm stock exchange on Tuesday. The share price in the companies included in the "Stenbeck Empire" fell freely when trade opened.

I never met Jan personally, but his spirit seemed to be present everywhere in MTG. Those in management devoted their time to perpetual speculation about what he would think once he showed up. No one appeared to have the mandate to act with any real autonomy. Stenbeck also had a reputation for keeping everything in his own head. There was no master plan available in the top drawer of the safe, no documentation—just lots of inspiration and instinct. The general expectation was that he'd carry on leading all the various companies personally until he was seventy. It seemed impossible that his empire could last now that he was gone.

At Modern Games, we didn't expect this to affect us, at least not for a long while. Our guess was that Stenbeck's death would significantly slow down all his companies, putting them in a passive, hibernating state until everything was sorted out. In the meantime, we thought, we'd have plenty of time to develop games. The video game market was growing fast, all over the Western world, and it seemed obvious to us that any media company with self-respect should have a couple of game development teams on their roster. One man's death couldn't possibly change that. Even without the patriarch steering the ship, MTG would need to have a proper game studio at the very minimum, right?

Across the globe, *Grand Theft Auto: Vice City* was breaking all the previous sales records by a gigantic margin. Sitting firmly right behind it on the charts was *Grand Theft Auto III*. Occasionally it had felt as if we were pretty close to the same success, but in reality, we were like a BMX bike next to a Ferrari Formula One car.

Bungie, the makers of *Marathon*, the game we spent hundreds of hours playing at Out There, had shockingly abandoned the Macintosh as their preferred platform, and in 2001 released an amazing game on Microsoft's Xbox. *Halo*, Bungie's new game, was simply groundbreaking. Xbox was using the game as an "exclusive" in order to drive sales of their machines, which meant that it was not available on PCs, Macs, or PlayStations. With *Halo*, Bungie had successfully designed a way to play a first-person game on the hand-held controller that video game consoles like Xbox and PlayStation used for input. It was a revolution, since up to that point, it was common knowledge that first-person games required a PC with a keyboard and mouse in order to function at all. Everyone just assumed that there would never be a way to transfer control from the three central fingers of the left hand to the two thumbsticks on a pad. But Bungie miraculously pulled it off! *Halo* was released with a mapping of the controls that felt natural, smooth, and agile. It opened another door to another realm, and since then, all games in the genre have used a version of the original *Halo* control scheme.

Microsoft's exclusivity deal with Bungie was just another sign of how the economy of the industry was shaping up. Companies like Microsoft would now *pay more* for you to limit the reach of your game to a select group of players through their console. Kim and I could hardly fathom how such business deals were made. Honestly, the content was *that* valuable?

One of the two Stenbeck daughters, Cristina, only twenty-five years old at the time, managed to navigate through an army of middle-aged men and, in just a few weeks, took complete control of the entire corporate empire.

Good news for everyone, except for a bunch of those experimental small companies that old Dad had fired up all over the world. The young queen planned to clean up some of the mess and craziness that had been going on in her father's kingdom.

At least Kinna had the guts and graciousness to fly down to Malmö to fire us all personally. She didn't have to. She could have just sent a lawyer or someone from HR, but she had a good heart, and she felt responsible for us in a strange, emotionally removed way.

After being fired, I cried. I sat at the back of a bus and the tears just didn't stop. I cried for a whole lot of reasons. I'd been incredibly naive. I felt like a failure. Christmas was coming up, and the beautiful lights in the city accompanied by joyful messages seemed to mock me with ironic glee. While I was busy failing, others in the industry had reached the level where their games were advertised on the biggest billboards. This had once seemed like an impossibility, but through the window of the bus and the blurriness of my tear-filled eyes, I saw giant posters pass by: *Battlefield 1942, Splinter Cell, WarCraft III* ... amazing games. *But maybe all of that has nothing to do with me*, I thought as I tried to figure out how to pay for the kids' Christmas gifts and how to put food on the table in the weeks to come.

On one hand, I felt let down by the corporate powers that were in motion around me, but on the other hand, I tried to desperately convince myself it was all for the better. I would never have succeeded as a professional at MTG, I told myself with fragile stoicism. Maybe I needed a taste of failure to mature?

PAN Vision offered me a job after I was let go. The managing director said that his staff "wasn't hungry" and added, with bitterness in his voice, that "people are just too complacent." After listening closer, I thought it sounded like he needed an aggressive salesperson, which was the last thing I wanted to be, so I declined. I was desperate, true, but not *so* desperate.

9

ORIGINAL SINS

I'd failed my friends and I'd been fired. I had no idea how to provide for my family. Not the best way to celebrate Christmas by most standards. Maybe I'd been foolish to believe I could become a part of the exciting game industry that was growing in Sweden. How naive had I really been? These questions kept running through my head as I stood by the washing machine at home, absentmindedly folding laundry in the heart of a city that had once promised to be the canvas for my grand plans. *T-shirt, T-shirt. Socks, boxer shorts, another T-shirt.* Dreams fading away with every fold of cotton.

I thought I should probably call Martin Walfisz. As a game developer in the small town of Malmö, it was impossible not to have some connection to him, the founder and managing director of Massive Entertainment, the "King of the Local Scene" who'd invited me to my first E3 the year before. Since our initial meeting in Stockholm a few years earlier, we'd stayed in touch, and we regularly met for lunch to chat and share management challenges as well as lofty observations about life in general. Talking with Martin, it seemed as if everything coming toward us, day by day from the future, was universally exciting. We came to enjoy each other's company a lot, and over time we developed a close friendship.

I often think about how many of my best partnerships started from a point when neither person actually wanted or needed anything from the other. That condition allows for a different level of honesty and becomes a great platform for building trust.

None of us had formal training in leading people in any professional sense, so we became eager amateur tinkerers who made things up as we went along. Since my own training was from art school, and I had authority issues and an inexplicable mix of low trust and naive total trust, I decided to think of a manager as a tool whose purpose is to set up other people for success. I asked myself all the time if what I was doing was genuinely productive from the perspective of the craftsman, and if it wasn't, I just didn't do it. It was a simple way to look at the responsibility of running a game studio, but I later learned that there are a whole bunch of proper theories around this concept called "Leaders as Servants." The underlying research I'd read validated my choices for me.

After declining PAN Vision's job offer, I asked Martin what he thought I should do. His answer was simple: "Work for me." At first, I said "Yes!" And then, soon after, I said "No."

I did so for two reasons. First, he was too keen and became overly pushy, convinced that he knew how I should operate. I had always had an issue with authority, but this time it was more of a functional reflex: If someone was already convinced they knew how to do something, then why should they hire me? If you hire someone, it should be because they know things you don't. And because of that, you can't tell them how to do their job. You can prepare the canvas, but not steer their hand as they paint. I got defiant, as I tended to do when other people started telling me how to execute my tasks.

As much as I was flattered by Martin's obvious interest in hiring me, my excitement had started to fade. It came to a climax when he laughed at my request to have a Macintosh, claiming that "PCs are better." To be honest, in the game industry, PCs *are* better, but with my perspective on management this was like telling an oil painter to use acrylics, or worse, to use a pony-hair brush instead of a sable-hair brush. The Macintosh discussion could have been trivial, I realize, but it created a deep and fundamental philosophical problem for me. If my potential future manager believed he knew better than I did what I truly needed to deliver my A-game, what value were my own instincts and experience? How was this going to set me up for success? I convinced myself that by folding to his choice of machinery, I would be agreeing to be bulldozed every time we had different opinions, and I didn't want to work like that.

The other reason I said no to Martin's offer was because I was about to say yes to something else. Kim had been working on his own to find financial backing for us to set up a new studio, and he came back with an unexpected solution: *his own dad*. At the time, I had never met his father, even though Kim and I had spent a good deal of time together. It turned out that Kim's dad was just as smart and gentle as his son. Mr. Kent, as I thought of him, was a tall man who looked like an aging actor with a wry smile and intensely piercing eyes surrounded by well-sculpted wrinkles. It was easy to imagine him in an old Western movie as the sidekick to the handsome hero. He'd been clever enough to anticipate the compact disc revolution and bought a bunch of machines that manufactured blank CDs. He had a big plant in Stockholm where his machines were running twenty-four hours a day, providing the world with discs that could contain all sorts of media, not just music. He was competing with aggressively low-cost Asian companies, which had prevented him from becoming silly rich, but nevertheless he had earned enough money to feel relaxed about his finances for the rest of his life. He was happy to spend some of the excess on a company for his boy.

Kim and I struggled, briefly, with the unsettling idea of potentially wasting his dad's money, but Mr. Kent promised us that he fully understood the risk and was okay even if things didn't work out.

We were easily convinced, because we only wanted to be making games. With Kim's dad as our sole investor, we struck out on our own.

Over coffee, I told Martin I wasn't joining Massive after all. With his famous mind-bending conviction skills, this was difficult for him to process. Martin wasn't used to getting a no from anyone, and he didn't like it. But I was firm, and I mentioned the Macintosh snafu as one of the reasons. I felt like a guy clumsily breaking up with his unsuspecting girlfriend as I left him there with his cup of Earl Grey tea. I knew we'd continue to bump into each other in town—Malmö isn't that big after all—but I wondered if I'd burned a bridge for once.

I have a friend named Beardy, an amazing dude with a folksy earnestness who looks like he should be in the Fleet Foxes. He plays the keyboard and the guitar, and he is an excellent songwriter too. When he was fifteen years old, he was asked by classmates who were a year older if he wanted to join the band they'd recently formed. I imagine him as a scrawny teenager, standing in the school-yard in the afternoon sun, feeling validated by the elders, his legs shaking with nervous pride.

The band stayed together for over a decade, first loyally struggling side by side through years of zero attention, dreaming about success in the hot basement where they rehearsed. Eventually, they had a colossal hit and became world-famous, and they remained exceptionally nice and humble to one another through everything that life gave them. It's a story with a happy beginning and a happy end.

Although all of this is true, Beardy once told me that the feeling that he was not *really* an original member of the band was always present. In a subtle way, he was always considered to be the little kid who was invited to play with the rest of the crew. Even though he joined the band just two weeks after it had formed, the difference in time was significant enough to impact the thousands of days that followed.

When Kim and I started working together, we never explicitly defined ourselves as a duo. It was just how things went down in the beginning, and as with Beardy's band, it subconsciously shaped our view of the world. We were the first pieces of a LEGO set. So, when we dissolved Modern Games, it was logical that we'd reboot the next project in the same way: Piece #1 goes with piece #2, and from there you keep building. But what we entirely forgot was that pieces #3, #4, and #5 were real humans and friends. Embarrassingly, it never crossed our minds that they'd feel abandoned by us. But they did. Unsurprisingly, but off our radar, they were incredibly disappointed as we let them drift toward whatever future they could find on their own.

Years later, I discussed this with Kim.

"I didn't once consider that they'd feel let down," I confessed.

"Well...," he said with unusual sadness. "That's it, isn't it? We didn't even think about it. What does that say about us?"

It's never pretty to see yourself in the mirror like that, but at the time we were insensitive enough to be very happy for our own sake and failed to understand why our old mates didn't return our calls when we wanted to have a beer.

As the rest of the global game industry moved forward, we decided to name our new company Bad Robot Sweden. We promptly found an empty room to rent in the corner of the office of another talented Malmö game developer, Upside Studios, which made kids' games.

The studio sat in an old apartment from the 1930s that had been refurbished to function as an office space, and was quite a disaster, functionally speaking. The place consisted of a lot of small former bedrooms, entirely disconnected from one another. There were more corridors and hallways than there was space to work, a little like a map in a shooter, or maybe like the narrow hallways of the USS *Discovery*, the oil tanker from *Metal Gear Solid 2*. It was impossible not to feel as if we were back in our childhood bedrooms again, playing a game called "We Have a Shop Together."

The feeling of dependence was enhanced by the fact that Kim's dad was paying for everything, even though, formally, the salaries were covered by Mr. Kent's CD business and not coming directly from his pocket. But it was the same thing, and we both knew it. We huddled up in the tiny room like kids pretending to be in a moon lander. It was difficult not to feel that our careers were going backward, and we fought the feeling of despair and repressed the shame of having abandoned our friends at MTG. *But hey*, we told ourselves, *this is cool! Let's just remain optimistic!* All we needed was a project, a publisher, a reasonably large budget, more hardware, intellectual property, marketing, distribution, and a group of talented game developers. *How hard could it possibly be?*

10

DISCARDED PAPER CUPS

In 2003 and 2004, the releases topping the global charts were games like *The Legend of Zelda: The Wind Waker*; *Grand Theft Auto: Vice City*; *Pokemon Ruby*; *Grand Theft Auto: San Andreas*; and *Medal of Honor*. All very sophisticated, graphically appealing, and internationally successful games.

Microsoft spent a fortune on advertising *Halo 2*, buying entire front pages of international newspapers, but they had every reason to be confident; the team at Bungie had created *another* masterpiece. They had not been content to create just a sequel that delivered more of the same; rather, they had been dead set on expanding the boundaries of what was technically possible on consoles, and had enabled, improved, and popularized online multiplayer features for a console game, turning it into a necessary component for all games with ambitions to beat the best. *Halo 1* had seemed to reach the extreme limit, but the improvements and additions in *Halo 2* were so advanced, the rest of the industry experienced vertigo.

In just a handful of years, video games had come quite a way since Tamagotchis and the first generation of Amiga software.

I remember playing a lot of *Unreal Tournament*, developed by Epic, with large, multileveled, and gorgeously detailed maps. It seemed that the games had become more immersive, more realistic, and more convincing almost overnight, and entering them took me further and further away into dreamscapes and grand adventures where I was always the hero.

Everyone kept telling me I *really should* play a game called *ICO*, made by an unknown (later legendary) Japanese creator named Fumito Ueda, because, they said, it was so much like *me*. But it was hard to find *ICO* in the shops, and I got lazy. I saw the cover of the box online, and thought, *Man, that is so poetic and beautiful and obviously inspired by Giorgio de Chirico's painting* Nostalgia of the Infinite. It excited me like nothing I'd ever seen in the game industry, but that made me feel too much like an art school stereotype. I hated to be so predictable, and in a childish, defiant way, I decided I wasn't going to play it.

Our *really promising* game development start-up (a.k.a. struggling two-man company with no money) got a break when PAN decided to give us a half-assed chance to pitch for the game called *Dollar* that was penned by author Liza Marklund (famous in Sweden!).

A pitch, but no money, they said. *Up to you if you want to do it. Lots of respect for you guys.*

Really? Respect? How did those words even add up at this stage? But we had nothing else to do, except spend Kim's dad's money and feel guilty about it.

"Fantastic!" I lied. "We'll be in touch."

We decided to build a playable prototype based on a simple mechanic. Point-and-click screens, with images from the crime scenes and other locations. Every scene would contain clues, and once discovered, the clues would need processing and investigating. We thought of the player as a mix between a forensic specialist and Sherlock Holmes. By having different loops on different timescales, there was always something the player was doing and always something to wait for. Add a bit of cool-down penalty, and soon the game became intelligent and tactical enough to generate a smooth gameplay experience. We were vaguely inspired by the classic game

Myst, which had been released ten years earlier when adventure games represented PCs' most successful genre.

At some point, we realized that toggling between 2-D screens became a bit monotonous, and we commissioned a young graphic novel artist to create short sequences of stories that would break the rhythm. All in all, it amounted to a dark, sinister, and—in our own minds—pretty damn awesome little prototype that we proudly wanted to show to PAN.

But by the time we were ready, almost no one we'd worked with previously at PAN was still around. It was hard even to get the meeting organized. Kim and I were in familiar territory: pitching in another unloved meeting room somewhere. Except this one had all the signs of a company in decline. The carpet was riddled with coffee stains, and it seemed PAN had sold their elegant conference room chairs and replaced them with abandoned office furniture. Clearly, they were short on cash, and if these beat-up chairs had made their way to this room, it probably meant the company was shrinking outside our view. On an IKEA cabinet in the corner lay a pile of printouts from some other meeting that were slowly turning yellow thanks to the strands of sunlight that found their way into the room.

"Oh. You *have a pitch*? How?...Eh...good!" the new head of publishing said, barely concealing her surprise.

Apparently there had been several reorganizations amid all the downsizing. We ignored the bad mojo and embarked on a desperate attempt to bend the laws of the universe.

"Yes! We're thrilled about this in fact! We discovered that we can go quite deep on this, and really convey Liza's story in a proper interactive way!"

Kim was phenomenal. It was as if nothing could dampen his enthusiasm.

Meanwhile, the head of publishing was busy looking at her phone. She seemed too young for this kind of responsibility. Was she very talented or was she being set up as a scapegoat? I wondered. No matter which it might be, she didn't respond to Kim's efforts.

"We said we're *excited*!" Kim continued, with a barely perceivable hint of falsetto in his voice. "We can go really deep on the narrative. The prototype proves it—let us show you."

"You have a *prototype*? Who?...Why?...I mean, who asked you to build a *prototype*?" she said.

We were experienced enough to see where this was going, which was exactly nowhere. All that work down the drain. As we walked back to the Stockholm train station to travel south again, our emotions reached an all-time low.

"I don't believe we even got a proper 'No,'" Kim said.

"You're right," I agreed.

The parting had been nothing more than a dispiriting "Let's maybe stay in touch, yeah?"

So why had they even asked us for a pitch? It didn't make any sense. We guessed it came from a mix of guilt and confusion about their own future. They were putting their feet down on the brakes and the accelerator simultaneously. Self-destructing. We were just collateral damage.

A lot of decisions in the entertainment industry simply don't make sense, and as a creative you need to be relentless to survive. Kim and I agreed that we'd seen more false starts than successful ones, but this was just another hurdle to overcome. Or so we told ourselves.

Back in the stuffy apartment, Kim and I embarked on another desperate hunt for a project that would take us to the next level. We looked everywhere, and since we were madly understaffed, we tried to build partnerships and constellations that together would somehow result in a solid deal.

Together with an English writer named Sam Johnson, we created a pitch for a horror game called *Orpheus Rising*. The game was inspired by *Dante's Inferno* and depicted a journey through the bowels of hell. We had plenty of interesting ideas that would probably have scared the hell out of any gamer, but we didn't get much farther than making an expensive-looking PowerPoint. It was at least a good experience to work with a "real" writer, even though we hadn't bothered to check to see if he'd published anything. Great, eloquent words would stream out of his mouth, even in casual conversation. He was a riddle to us. Big, British, bitter, and obviously gravely disappointed with the hand that life had dealt him, but his writing was poetic, delicate, and perceptive.

In the foyer of a hotel, we improvised ideas with a bushy-haired maverick entrepreneur. A Danish businessman who had just acquired the film rights to the Wallander books, grim detective stories set in rural Sweden. The books had become international hits, and he was very interested in broadening his business. He'd heard about us through some distant colleague from Icon and wanted to meet. With his company Yellow Bird as a front, we tried to pitch the game to investors of the film project together, but most of the financiers were already so exposed to risk by investing in the movies that they were reluctant to invest in our game. Our hunt took us to a new string of conference rooms and hotel lobbies in Germany since the books had sold incredibly well there, and we went to London for the same reason, but no matter how hard we sold it, nothing took off. At least we were getting used to pitching, but judging by the results, we were clearly missing something.

We called our old Modern Games client Tetra Pak and pitched them a detective game that would build on their global presence and origin. Imagine: A person (*wait, what? Who exactly?*) visits the Tetra Pak website, where they find a mysterious and complex game that requires them to play as a detective, diving into a world of international espionage and intrigue. It was a dark, elegant, and rain-soaked game in the style of John le Carré. We somehow convinced ourselves that it made total sense, and we were astonished when the Tetra Pak executives seemed confused about the whole thing.

"Yeah, hmm. It seems a bit far-fetched, no?"

"What?" we cried. "*What exactly is far-fetched about this?*"

"Well, I mean, it's not like we have anything to do with any of the themes you propose in your game, do we?"

"Whaaat?" we cried even louder. "The game is *perfect* for you guys!"

But no. Of course it really wasn't. We'd tried to force it upon them because we needed to sign a project, anything. Apparently it's possible to convince oneself of strange things once you spend enough time in a grubby room with a geek.

At one point, Kim and I had the brilliant idea to create a space-themed game funded by ESA, the European Space Agency, and written by legendary Scottish science-fiction writer Iain M. Banks. We set up a few meetings with ESA representatives, whom we found disappointingly gray and academic—not at all matching our illusion of what astronauts made of the Right Stuff should look like. We wrote a letter to Iain Banks and waited.

As we continued to flail, Mr. Kent was most gracious and patient. Not once did he complain, but I began to feel terrible about spending the family money and not catching a break.

Instead of accepting the reality, however, we went the opposite direction and set our targets even higher: We decided to make a game for Microsoft's Xbox! This might have seemed like a good idea, but in practice we'd need at least fifty people to do it. We already had two guys on the team, so why not? Kim and I had pulled off miracles before. I called our old friend Sam the Writer and asked him to refine the story we'd begun working on. Next, we partnered with our friends at Southend whom we'd met at E3 back in 2002, in part because they'd already shipped a game on Xbox and could help us build the game.

"Who'll pay for it?" Mr. Kent asked rationally, without a hint of distrust.

"Yes. Well, that's the problem," I said. "The only one who has that kind of money is PAN Vision."

"What? Didn't they just burn you on the Liza Marklund project?" he said, sounding curious, not skeptical.

"They sure did," Kim and I said with one bitter voice. "But they're the only ones in this market."

"Okay," Mr. Kent said. "Do it."

With little hope, I called whoever was still left at PAN Vision to get them on board. To our great astonishment, they thought the timing was perfect. They had concluded that they'd focused too much on the Scandinavian market when all successful publishers were aiming globally right from the outset. Now they were ready to make a desperate attempt to get into the big league.

"An Xbox game is exactly what we need! We'll pay for the prototype."

We were given 200,000 USD to produce it, but even though it sounded like a fortune to us, we knew the money was going to be spread thin across our fragile alliance. The game we set out to make was called *The System*, a mix between a James Bond movie and the *Splinter Cell* game, spiced up with ideas from *The Matrix* and centered on a strong heroine character. We managed to get the prototype up and running. It was put on a hard drive and sent to Stockholm. The idea was that PAN would then begin pitching it to bigger publishers and somehow remain in the mix to produce.

Well.

It didn't work.

PAN was losing money fast. Behind the scenes they were facing bankruptcy. Their veterans started to leave as hardfisted fixers were hired in a last-minute attempt to save the company. And even though our prototype showed promise, it was too light, too shallow, and promised too little. It was not the kind of thing that could turn PAN's future around, and without any sign of caring, they threw us out again, like a discarded paper cup.

Kim's older sister was working for the family CD company as an operations and finance manager, and she came down to Malmö to have a tough talk with us. I don't think I was fired exactly—

I might have volunteered to leave—but the result was the same. It was logical, and, to some degree, I think I was relieved. It's not easy to catch up with the industry greats even when you have the best of conditions (which we didn't), and, clearly, I wasn't getting the deals we needed to justify a continuation. I felt oceans of gratitude toward Kim's family for having trusted us for so long, but let's be honest: There comes a point when you overstay your welcome, and I didn't want to be that guy. Kim would stay on as an employee of the CD company until he found a new job, but I packed my belongings and cleared the office.

"And the future?" Kim asked as I loaded the last box into my car.

"I don't know," I answered truthfully.

I tried to think of something to say, something that would do justice to our amazing adventures, something about our friendship, *something profound and elegant* that I could maybe one day include in a book about the game industry, but my mind was completely blank. I had no words for this.

II

IN THE SHADOW OF THE COLOSSI

Pink apple blossoms fell to the ground in a slow-motion dance of fragments. The garden lazily soaked up a pale, Naples-yellow sun. The grass and the tall trees looked excited after so many months of the infamous Swedish darkness that begins in September and slowly imposes itself over the land like a gloomy curse, turning us all into worshippers of the first fragile light of spring. The smell of warm stone and vegetarian barbecue hung in the air. I was in a dreamy soap bubble of happiness.

This was my garden, on a special day.

My guest, Fumito Ueda, sipped on a beer while his petite Japanese wife played with the dog, Poppy, a Lancashire Heeler. He put on the special glove that would protect the fingertips of his right hand from the string when he released the arrow from the bow he was holding. I had somehow imagined that Ueda-san had shot many arrows from many bows in his life. Surely the man behind *Shadow of the Colossus* had shot a bow? It turned out that he hadn't, but he was eager to try. I showed him how to ready the equipment, how to aim, and how to draw the bow in a slow, deliberate movement. Steady as a rock he let the arrows fly, one after another, gradually getting closer to gold, the nickname archers have given the yellow bull's-eye of a target.

"I like your bow a lot," he said with a soft smile, and I felt, again, a form of kinship.

He, if anyone, would understand why I had chosen this bow and no other. Mine was not one of the most powerful or user-friendly bows. I had chosen it for the delicate treatment of the wood, the elegant simplicity, and the fact that as an object, it was created with love. This was a craftsman's choice, not a hunter's, and Ueda-san saw it the same way as I did.

It was around the time Kim and I parted ways that I finally caved in and bought Fumito Uueda's *ICO*. I was completely mesmerized by it, just as everyone had told me I would be. The experience affected me deeply, and, yes, I cried, as I had read many others had done when they reached the end of the story. *ICO* is maddeningly beautiful and boldly poetic, like no other game I have played, except of course Ueda-san's other two games, which touched me just as deeply.

ICO is an amazing, unique game, and though many people dismiss it as pretentious and too artsy, what I find so interesting about it is that it explores the boundary of what interactivity might become.

When I played *ICO*, I felt at home. Emotionally, it reminded me of my own dreams, and, visually, it represented almost exactly what I myself had once hoped to create as a painter, but never did. I understood that the unanswered questions provoked by the story, the unexplained, were meant to be just that. They were intentionally designed to leave the audience wondering, thinking, guessing, only to ultimately realize that this game was never going to offer any explanations through intellect alone—it was created to make us rely on emotion as our guide. The only way to get in tune with the game was to let go of rational filters and listen to it with your heart. *ICO* was like an abstract painting, created by a true master.

No surprise, then, that years later, once I met Fumito Ueda, I learned that he, too, came from art school, and that, indeed, he was in love with abstract art. Over dinner, with my large ginger-colored cat sleeping in the middle of all the food, I asked him if his games were intentionally vague, and he said that yes, they were meant to be like a haiku: "Very few words, but a good one contains a very large truth," he said softly.

And he confirmed, also, that his projects weren't born out of a story. He would always start with an image—a vision, a scene that would not stop burning in his mind. As his projects progressed, he would eventually understand the narrative that lay hidden in that first intuitive picture. His games came from the unconscious, from a magical well, just as I had suspected.

Start playing *ICO* and you will experience this:

Trees, bark, branches, and leaves. Birdsong and sunlight finding their way down from the treetops. The sound of the hooves of a horse. No, wait... several horses. Ancient soldiers, with faces hidden behind helmets, bring a small boy with horns on his head through the forest to a cliff. Far below, the water separates the men from a giant ruin.

Rocks and water. A broken black wooden structure rotting away. A boat traverses the sea, and the slow wind sounds like the song of a dying colossus. The soldiers and the boy enter a cave under the ruin and dock the boat.

"Get the sword," one of the soldiers says, in a language no one has heard before.

Another soldier approaches with a heavy weapon in hand. He holds it up to a strange portal made of stone. Black arches of inverted light sparkle from the sword, and the portal responds by opening, reluctantly.

More stone structures.

They move like some kind of machine.

Silence.

Another portal. Inverted light. A giant, aging hall colored in sepia, the walls covered with shelves that hold hundreds and hundreds of large urns. A strange symbol on one of the clay containers flashes in weak, dying blue. It opens. The soldiers put the frightened little boy in the urn and they close it.

"Don't be angry with us," they say and leave.

Silence.

Darkness.

The urn moves just a little. It falls off the ledge and crashes. The boy rolls out on the floor with a helpless cry.

He has nothing.

Nothing at all.

And we know nothing, nothing at all.

That is how *ICO* opens. It is elegant and poetic, mysterious and confusing.

I think of it many times because in traditional games, we are obsessed with making sure that the audience knows where they are, plus why they are there, and we dedicate an enormous amount of time to making sure that they feel successful quickly, or else, we assume, they will lose interest.

ICO is a game that doesn't agree with this design philosophy. *ICO* gives away nothing for free, and it makes you feel exactly like a lost child in a silent, ominous castle. The game forces you to emotionally experience it as the boy, not as yourself sitting on the sofa in front of the television.

Playing *ICO* not only completely transformed the way I looked at games—it provided a new lens through which to consider the story of my entire life. Prior to *ICO*, I believed my life had been divided in half by my own choice to build an unbreachable wall. I believed that I had once reached a crossroads, one that forced me to split my life into a *Before*, which was my life as an aspiring artist, and an *After*, which was my career in game development. As far as I saw it, games offered a career not in art but in entertainment, even though it was taking on a new and exciting form, celebrated by basement hobby enthusiasts.

Ueda's vision collapsed that wall and opened up a whole new

world of exhilarating possibilities for me and an entire generation of game-makers. Playing *ICO* made me feel like maybe I hadn't abandoned art after all. Not if games like Ueda's could be made, projects that were more than a toy, more than special effects and cheap tricks. *ICO* proved that games can, in the right hands, become art.

But I had to face myself in the mirror: failed artist, unemployed game developer. Was there even hope I would succeed with any of my choices? What to make of the *ICO* revelation, now that the game industry had kicked me to the curb just when I had begun to understand what I'd lost? I was aware that it was only by half accident that I'd even discovered the birth of this new medium. Once I discovered how games could be a meaningful form of expression, I embraced them with all my heart. But for what? The results had been underwhelming, disappointing, depressing, and, frankly, pathetic. In a very short time span, MTG Modern Games and Bad Robot had developed and released a total of ten different projects, and it felt as if we'd pitched another hundred, but still: It all amounted to nothing.

Suddenly, a glimmer of hope.

Many weeks after reaching out to Iain M. Banks to propose a collaboration on our imaginary project for the European Space Agency, I received the most pleasant old-fashioned letter from him, written on a typewriter. With awe, I realized that this must be the same typewriter that had given birth to *Consider Phlebas* and his other science-fiction novels I loved so much. My hands shook with anticipation as I opened it, but my heart sank as I reached the end of the note.

In beautiful and efficient language, Banks politely declined to be a part of the project because he was concerned he "wouldn't be good enough." As much as I appreciated the enormity of getting a personal letter from one of my heroes, it felt like a depressing summary of everything Kim and I'd accomplished. We felt *so close* to superstardom, we were *communicating* with entertainment giants like

Banks, but in the very last moment, the world diplomatically turned its back on us with a short and well-written good-bye letter.

Sitting at home as the winter rolled into January 2005, I read in a financial newspaper that the global game industry had been growing an average of 25 percent per year. *But I was no longer a part of it!* It drove me crazy to be so close to this brilliant azure wave without being able to catch it.

I took my two ridgebacks, Maltsev and Sputnik, for a walk in the bitter cold. My feet were on autopilot, and before I knew it, I was at the edge of town. The fields and high skies embraced me like an old ghost. This was where I'd grown up, where the last row of terrace houses gave up and the vast, flat farmlands of Skåne sprawled out on the horizon. Gales carried fine, powdery snow in wraithlike shapes, leaving long lines of white across the dark-brown earth.

Why did I give up painting?

Because I had to.

Why did I fail at making games?

Because I was an idiot.

I returned home, frozen to the core. The bones in my heels hurt as the warmth came back to my feet. Suddenly, the phone buzzed. Someone was calling me.

"Yo, it's Martin. What's up?" a voice said.

"Walfisz?" I asked, squeezing the phone between my ear and shoulder as I took off one sock, wet from the melting layer of snow on my boots.

"Yes, of course! How many Martins do you know?" he said, sounding carefree and upbeat. "Anyway, I thought about the PC thing."

"The PC thing?" I said, confused and one-socked, heading toward the kitchen, where there were dishes to tend to, and maybe some tea to be had later on.

"Yeah, you know, when you declined my offer a year ago?" he asked. "Well, here's how I see it. If you want a bloody Macintosh and you think that's good for you, why should I care? I mean, if I hire you, it should be because I want *you*, and not some version of you that I force you to become. You know?" He was speaking quickly, almost as if he'd rehearsed the words.

"Uh..." was all I could say as hope started to fill my stomach. I stopped in the middle of the kitchen, observing the wet paw-marks from the dogs on the floor behind me. Shit. I had forgotten to dry them off.

"Come see me tomorrow; let's make sure I can hire you this time. Massive needs you. Trust me, it'll be the best career choice you ever make."

"Wow, really? That's really generous, Martin! Thank you!" I said, genuinely surprised and grateful, but apparently still pigheaded enough to throw in a demand on top of the choice of computer. "One thing, though," I added. "You'll have to let me in on the studio decisions, the strategy, and the long game. There is always a good long-play move to make, and I am good at those."

Martin went quiet for a while.

"Right. Exactly," he said. "That's what I mean. I'll hire you to be you, not to be someone I can bend to my will. Excellent. See you tomorrow!"

Four years after *ICO*, Ueda returned with *Shadow of the Colossus*, which took the gaming world by storm. This one I had no trouble finding in stores, as long as the shops weren't already sold out.

Shadow of the Colossus begins like a dream once again: An eagle flies through a steep, moonlit canyon. With great speed, it passes through a tiny waterfall, and then flies by a lonely youngster on horseback riding carefully along a narrow path on the side of a cliff. He is carrying a ghostlike young woman who is either ill, asleep, or dead.

The young boy on horseback exists in a vast, beautiful, silent, and almost lifeless world. There, he confronts the sixteen wandering and voiceless colossi, godlike beings of fur, skin, wood, and stone, so large that they stretch up to the skies themselves. They do not see the boy or care about him, and they have no desire to share their mysterious existence with him. The boy tries to climb on the colossal hair-covered bodies, and the giants shrug in angry frustration, like a horse trying to shake off a particularly annoying fly. The boy gets thrown off, over and over again, not understanding the puzzle they present.

I felt very much like that young man in Ueda's masterpiece, knocked from my mount by a particularly vicious blow.

Now, thanks to the surprise call from Martin, it seemed the colossus had picked me up from the shadows and gently put me back on my horse.

12

MASSIVE ENTERTAINMENT

April 2005: Copenhagen to Los Angeles and back again eleven hours later. It was a killer trip, but Martin had insisted. He said that now that I was going to get hired, we might as well get the publisher/owner invested in the idea, so he set up a couple of interviews in LA for me.

Massive was owned by Vivendi Universal Games (VUG), who had their headquarters in Culver City. Martin had been forced to sell Massive to VUG when he ran into cash problems sometime between shipping the team's first game, *Ground Control*, and initiating work on the sequel.

Ground Control was a gritty, real-time strategy game, played out against a generic science-fiction backdrop. It came with a surprising innovation, combining the slick control scheme from first-person games with the traditionally slow-paced strategy genre. The unexpected combo created a fast and intense connection to the battleground for the player.

Considering that the game was the very first from an unknown studio in a Nowhere Town in Sweden, *Ground Control* was surprisingly mature and had caught the attention of many publishers and investors, but not enough to keep the studio finances in good health, which was why Martin had been forced to reluctantly sell off his baby.

This was very common in those days, and aggressive publishers would hold back on the negotiations with the independent studio until the development team was so desperate that they were forced to give up ownership of the entire studio in order to obtain the contract. On the other hand, the new situation provided financial stability and an opportunity to focus. Having to perpetually worry about next month's salaries is another form of dependence, and, looking back, many of the indie studios that managed to maintain their independence in the early years ran into severe financial problems later on.

VUG was a strange company, part of a gigantic French multi-business conglomerate, and the management for the game division was isolated in California. It wasn't even clear to me if they were really into the entertainment business, or if they'd just been investing randomly. The common perception was that VUG had more money than wits, but in what one would have to admit was one of the smartest moves ever in the history of games, they'd bought Blizzard Entertainment, perhaps the best game developer in the world. Blizzard had just blown the world away by releasing the legendary and industry-transforming game *World of WarCraft*. Vivendi didn't own any other studio. It was just Blizzard and Massive. Nice company to be in.

We arrived at the hotel and slept a few jet-lagged hours, checked out again in the early morning, and got ready for some professional speed dating. I was extremely excited by the whole thing. California has always felt a little bit like home to me, and there I was, embarking on my glorious international career at last.

The reception area of the VUG office was the only nice place in the entire building. We were greeted by a wonderful lady who could have come from behind the counter of a donut shop in a David Lynch movie. She had a personality like a bottle of Sprite: crisp, sweet, and bubbly. Big TV screens displayed endless loops of trailers for the most successful games VUG had launched, either developed by studios they owned or from game titles they had acquired.

But apart from the insanely successful *World of WarCraft*, it was clear that the publisher didn't have a great portfolio. *F.E.A.R.* was great of course, with its time-bending feature and advanced AI, but *Barbie and the Magic of Pegasus*? *Miami Vice: The Game*? *Mashed: Drive to Survive*?

The first meeting confirmed what I'd assumed: The American head office had no interest in my hiring. We met Martin's boss, Peter Della Penna, a cordial chap in a tweed jacket who introduced himself by saying, "Nice to meet you, but I don't understand why you flew all the way over here." His eyes kept anxiously darting around, as if he were expecting someone to barge in and shout at him at any second.

After that, I witnessed something I'd never seen: the Shark Run. This, I observed, was a Martin Walfisz–patented move, and damn, he was good at it!

Deep inside, I'm quite shy and introverted. I always feel slightly intimidated when I visit major publishers—even when I'm not looking for a job. But here was Martin at his best, barging into every single office in Culver City with a big smile like a firework. He'd detect everything that moved, and dive into it with the power of a great white, it didn't matter what it was. Like a shark, he'd bite first, and decide later if it was tasty or not.

He seemed to know everyone, and he seemed to have an endless amount of things to say, no matter which meeting we crashed. This supersocial behavior ran counter to my low-key Swedish style, but soon I realized that I was observing a master at work, and that the Californians really appreciated the adrenaline boost Martin provided. Suddenly Massive's success made a little more sense.

Major-league lesson number one: the Shark Run.

We openly talked about the yes-no moment we'd gone through more than a year earlier, and Martin elegantly apologized for pushing too hard, and followed up with the magic words I wanted to hear: *If I hire you, I have to assume that you know what you're doing, so I'll give you free rein, okay? And, yeah, a Mac.* Deal!

We agreed that my job under Martin would be a combination of marketing, publisher relations, and a general Mr. Fix-It role. Massive was made up of about forty people, so everyone had to do several jobs, including me. I was nicknamed "the Foreign Minister" because I'd usually deal with everything outside the studio, which turned out to be an amazing education.

The fix-it job was interesting, too, because it was a properly open-ended job description, and it allowed Martin to think more freely, while I ran behind like a trouper, trying to figure out how to execute all the good ideas and opportunities he saw. It was the kind of job that forced me to fully understand every part of the studio. What was going on at Massive was a more advanced form of game development than I was used to. I got to know practically every individual in the studio, and I gained an incredible insight into what worked and what didn't.

I needed to figure out why Massive had managed to be so success-ful compared to my own adventures with Kim, and apparently raw talent wasn't the answer. After spending enough time with Martin and the team, I concluded that Massive had two things that gave them a leg up.

The first one was tech. Yes, technology, engineering, engineers, programming, code, software, engines, back end. Mathematical wonders are the beating heart of all good games. Technology was the magic that allowed us to take a vision and make an experience, to make a design into a playable reality. If we could think it, some clever engineer could write the code for it. This kind of hard-core programming was a new experience for me, but I quickly under-stood the power it provided. Programmers are the jet fuel of the gaming industry.

I understood the engineers intuitively, and I found it easy to grasp what they were trying to achieve. And thank god, Massive had a lot of *real* C++ programmers, the kind that didn't use software that others had created. These guys created such things from scratch by themselves!

The second secret ingredient in the studio was Martin himself.

Before I understood him better, I thought he was outrageously ambitious, almost to the point of being out of touch with reality. Imagine a guy coming into the office every day with maxed-out positivity and a big smile, claiming that we were going to make the best games in the world and never, ever doubting himself. This was Martin.

He'd see the talent and the possibilities, no matter how insecure the rest of us were. Some people on the team found him intimidating and frustrating; they saw an impossible boss who didn't know when good enough was good enough. It was obvious to me that Martin's die-hard belief in our own capacity and brilliance was key to keeping everything moving.

My first real task at Massive was to look at a few pitches that the studio had been working on since they released *Ground Control 2*. *GC2* had been moderately successful, but the team had second thoughts about the science-fiction setting and wanted to explore other ideas. The studio was split into several organically formed small teams who worked on a bunch of different concepts. Some concepts were just PowerPoints, while others were playable. What they all had in common, I noticed, was an insane ambition. All sorts of genres, all sorts of art directions—everything looked expensive and sharp.

Out of all the things cooking in the studio, Martin had a pet project, an elegant little thing that seemed more promising than the rest, a tight and intense multiplayer real-time strategy (RTS) prototype. As in a chess game, all players would start with a standard set of available pieces with a rich plethora of available moves and strategies. However, and uniquely for the genre, there was no resource management involved. Traditionally in an RTS, the player would have to establish supply lines and production capacity to be able to build and improve an army that would later go to battle, but as a reflection of his restless personality, Martin had simply decided to skip all such features, and the prototype focused exclusively on the fighting. It was bold, and highly entertaining. He had recently decided to put more development muscle behind it, and he asked me to convince our masters at VUG to green-light it. There was a void appearing in the market as Blizzard had moved on to other genres and the *Command & Conquer* games were growing stale.

Almost all game developers regularly have to ask their publishers (or owners) for money to keep the team alive during the long development cycle when there is no income. This is done in pitch meetings, which can take on a million different shapes, but no matter the format, the core message is always the same: *Give us money (lots!), and the game you get will be awesome (one day).* I'd worked on so many pitches in my life that this was no concern, I just had to adjust to a much higher level of presentation. Privately, I wondered if I was good enough to play on this level.

We called the game *World in Conflict*, and for once I could work on a pitch with more than just a few idle hands at my disposal. Now we were talking trailers! Key art! Budgets!

13

A PLOT

It was still light outside. Martin was walking a few steps ahead talking to someone. The clouds parted and allowed a bit of warmth to find its way to planet Earth. As we crossed the town square in central Malmö after a full day of off-site meetings discussing the pitch, Nils, Massive's producer, took me aside and whispered conspiratorially in my ear: "You know we have to overthrow Martin, right?"

I was certainly not expecting this in my first month at Massive, but here we were: A coup was being planned behind the founder's back, and abruptly it became a large, alarming, unavoidable blip right in the center of my radar. I was expected to choose sides in a civil war that I'd known nothing of until that very moment.

Martin was my friend, and I had already concluded that his drive and never-ending enthusiasm were what made Massive special. And besides... in my mind, it was *his* studio and no one else's. If people didn't like it, they could start their own little company and see just how difficult it was to succeed in the game industry. Personally, I was happy to work for a guy who had at least a slim chance to lead us all to glory. I believed in him. He'd picked me up when I had nowhere to go. On top of that he thought I was awesome, even though I felt more like an industry reject.

Maybe it's because I was so close to my brother growing up, but I have a deep sense of loyalty to those who stand by me when they have nothing to gain, and I was incredulous that Nils would suggest I join him. *Overthrow Martin?* Was he insane?

I looked at Nils, thinking of how to respond. He was not my kind of person. I knew that even before he'd invited me to stab my friend in the back. He was fit, tall, and handsome in a typical Swedish way. People like that always triggered my insecurities. But as I thought about it, I realized that it was much simpler than that: He was just a guy *who didn't dream*, who didn't fight for the (possibly pointless) hope to one day create something *awesome*, and in making that choice, he was at the other end of everything I believed in.

I had a strong desire to join Martin's mad quest for greatness, and I had just lost a bunch of dreams that I'd believed in with Kim. I had nothing to say to Nils about his plans. This was all going in the wrong direction. I had joined Massive to catch up with the industry giants and the studios that I admired, not to wage some stupid office war!

It seemed to me that the game industry was fighting a creative crisis and needed fresh ideas, which a studio like Massive could potentially provide. Looking at the best-selling games was depressing. Every single one was a sequel or an extension of something that already existed. Another generation of impressive hardware was on the horizon, and the hype revolved more around lighting technologies and the creation of truly lifelike characters than anything substantial like genre innovations or new gameplay ideas. It was as if the toys were the same and only the shiny surface became thicker and thicker. Still, the websites and magazines of the day hailed the future and the opportunity to raise the bar even higher. *Doom 3* and *Half-Life 2* were commonly expected to be the new kings of the industry, a promise on which they delivered.

Martin and I were shocked at the lack of innovation and the cowardice of the publishers. We were convinced that it was way too early for the industry to stagnate, and when we said "too early" we meant, like, fifty years too early. This was the gigantic open window we were going to shoot for, a competitive space the size of the USA and as unexplored as Mars! *So, yeah*, I thought. This Nils guy really needed to elevate his focus and stop trying to recruit me for his feud.

It got worse before it got better. I soon realized that Nils had maneuvered in the shadows to build quite a substantial mutiny. I was appalled, but before I had time to reflect, I became seriously concerned that Martin was facing a real risk of being ousted. Nils was not alone.

The theory of the mutineers was that Martin was too far out and was leading us all toward inevitable doom. The right thing to do, they said, was to set *reasonable* ambitions for the studio and start working on *pragmatic* projects. We needed to be *realistic*. Basically, they were hoping to do the same kind of stuff that I'd just spent years failing at: small projects either based on some existing IP (intellectual property) or in collaboration with advertisers. *Lots of good money in that*, they believed. But all I saw was a nightmare of decline, and not for a second was there any question about what I was going to choose.

Nils was crazy enough to share all his plans and the names of his closest supporters before I had a chance to tell him I wasn't interested. I tried to stop him, although it did strike me at the time that I was getting a whole lot of good intel for free.

Once I got a chance to say what I thought, it still didn't end. I was approached by several of the other conspirators, who tried to sway me. How could they not see that this was futile? It was unfathomable. It wasn't as if I played along or gave them any hope that I'd side with them. I tried to explain my point of view, but judging by their reactions, it was clear they felt certain that soon enough I'd understand Martin's *madness* and join them.

The real issue was that Nils had managed to convince Martin that he was his closest friend, and Martin, god bless him, was far from cynical enough to see through the charade. His optimism warped his ability to see what was going on, and he continued to see life through a filter of hope and trust. He just wondered why the studio wasn't always thrilled about his input.

I learned that most of the developers in the studio didn't want to be a part of the coup; rather, they felt uncomfortable being dragged into some alpha-male power struggle, and they wished that it would disappear. If supporting Nils would make the discomfort vanish, then maybe that was one way to go? There seemed to be nothing that could stop the brave revolution leader, so something had to change for peace to be restored. For a short while, I thought that perhaps somehow the situation wasn't my problem, that I could sit things out.

In the end, doing nothing wasn't an option. The worst part of being involved in a secret you never asked to hear about is that (a) either you become a passive accomplice by remaining silent; or (b) you become the snitch. It's an ethical trap. I knew I should probably talk to Martin, but as the *new guy*, I felt stuck in a conundrum. *This was their problem*, I tried to convince myself, but of course, it had become mine too.

I was getting angrier and angrier at Nils for his efforts to backstab the guy who'd given him the chance of his life, and I began to see how the whole studio was plagued by the conspiracies and the secret war going on behind the scenes. All that time we could have spent making great games was wasted on internal politics.

Someone had to break the news to Martin, and I was getting a pretty good idea of who it had to be.

I4

GREEN LIGHTS

I don't know what I expected Martin to say or do when I finally had the courage to tell him about Nils and the mutiny. But once I did, his response surprised me. He made a couple of fast, courageous, mature, and smart moves.

First, he told me that the situation wasn't my problem to deal with. He said not to worry about it and to focus all my energy on the *World in Conflict* pitch. That was making things simple, for sure. No civil war for me!

Second, he didn't jump to conclusions and automatically assume that I'd been truthful or made a good analysis. He wanted to verify things for himself, even though he was concerned he'd find what I'd described. Still, he dove into it alone and started digging. Martin had many discreet private meetings, asking people to be honest. He created a space for serious discussions and patiently listened to person after person. He didn't like what he was hearing, but at least he was beginning to see the patterns. By encouraging the defectors to be open and showing that he understood, he slowly won them over, at least most of them.

Next, he had to figure out how to relate to Nils. No easy thing, since he'd long been convinced that Nils was his closest ally, his chosen number two, his confidant. Martin simply refused to believe that his producer had been staging a coup against him, so he brought in a management consultant, an intense, intelligent young woman with piercing blue eyes, to mediate and gently set the stage for sincere conversations.

While all of this was going on, I kept hammering away at the *World in Conflict* pitch. I became obsessed with it. By focusing on the project, I could stop thinking about all the studio-level drama and settle into my new role.

Massive's two-story office of glass walls and sliding doors was light and elegant. It was also littered with discarded cardboard boxes and coffee mugs, sometimes with scary-looking green stuff at the bottom. At least half of the desks were filled with gamer merchandise. Almost everywhere in the game industry, the desk becomes a shrine that identifies the individual sitting there. It's a code, a window into the personal, and depending on what people put on display (or change as time goes by), you can make a bunch of accurate assumptions about what to expect from that person. Nintendo stuff means "I like fun and playfulness." Figurines from war games mean "I want to be taken seriously and respected (because I'm hiding my insecurities behind my machismo)." Model cars mean "I love technology and fast decision making (unless they're old cars, in which case it's 'I like steampunk')." Tintin figurines mean "I have a preference for elegant, classy entertainment in a slightly academic way." A small sculpture from a Fumito Ueda game means "I'm a sensitive poet at heart, and I think we should invest more in the emotional aspect of our games."

With my ridgeback puppy Sputnik, I shared a room with Björn, another guy who'd also recently joined Massive. He was an online engineering genius and the most pleasant officemate one could ask for. Sitting next to such blinding intelligence, I regularly felt like a child, but he was generous and took time to explain things I didn't yet grasp. Slowly, my understanding of the online world grew. Although Björn and I rarely spoke about the tensions in the studio, we often had a feeling we were like a couple in the waiting room outside a family therapist, and from the other side of the closed door we sensed the anger and the collapsing trust, slowly causing an old marriage to fall apart.

In my dark moments, I had a horrible suspicion that maybe somehow I had misjudged the whole situation, and that I was simply the new guy who'd been jealous of Nils and created a big lie about the mutiny so that I could be the one closest to Martin. These were black fantasies fueled by self-doubt, but then again, what if they weren't? What if I'd gotten the studio into a mess?

The project remained the safe haven, the healthy canvas for a brighter future. Thanks to Massive's engineers, *World in Conflict* was beautiful, with world-class particle effects, so we decided to build the pitch trailer to highlight the graphics. It would be an in-game trailer, showcasing the realistic visuals (this was not always the case, because in-game means you really have to show your hand, as opposed to fake trailers that allow you to cheat and overpromise).

In real life, America wages war all over the world, but it never reaches its own soil. But *what if*, we wondered, this time the fighting took place in America? *What if* the Soviet Union attacked the mainland? It was an interesting thought, and it gave us a wonderful chance to juxtapose quaint American suburbs and landscapes with a full-on military invasion. The scenery was serene and safe, but the violent narrative was original and shocking.

The creative director was a guy I'd briefly met at Southend. Back then he was working with audio, and I wondered what had made him crawl out from his dark, peaceful studio into the bright light of the creative director role. He seemed to be a private character who preferred to avoid all human contact. Everyone called him Soundboy, but regardless of his background in audio and his social reluctance, he was brilliant in his new role. "You can now call me Meetingboy," he proclaimed with a resigned look, because he knew all too well that from then on his professional life would consist of an endless string of meetings.

When thinking about what to say or do next, Soundboy would close his eyes, yank his head upward, and become perfectly still while a pained expression grew on his face. After a ridiculously long and uncomfortable silence, he'd return, his body becoming animated again. He spoke like a sage, and thanks to the framing, everyone took his words as gospel. The silence he wielded helped him appear even more intelligent, and his odd habits gave everything he said a reassuring gravity and sense of finality.

Like many in the game industry, Soundboy dressed in jeans and T-shirts that sent a message. "Yes, this is the same T-shirt you saw me in ten years ago," or perhaps "I like this game/band/beer brand, and I'm willing to endlessly explain why it's *the best* if you'll just ask me about it. Please do!" Everything about him was deliberate. Every moment and every space was an opportunity to impose design, which was a perfect approach for a creative director.

Soundboy and I made sure that the trailer got its final layers of polish. We hired a *real* voice actor to narrate the video. I was enjoying myself like crazy, and I had high hopes that VUG would green-light the project.

Meanwhile, Martin was getting depressed.

His chats with Nils and the consultant had brought out honesty on both sides. But the candor revealed an irreconcilable rift.

Nils admitted that he didn't agree with Martin's vision for Massive. He admitted that he had no faith in Martin's leadership, and he claimed that everyone in the studio felt the same way. Martin had discovered that indeed some people on the team perceived him as impossible. It seemed like a sad standstill with no winner.

I don't know exactly what happened, but one day when I got to work, Nils was gone, and Martin was back to his old self. Well, *more or less* his old self. He'd begun to think further about how to rally the troops, how to gain momentum, and how to ask people for more without coming across as a tyrant. He asked for advice from the team much more often, and then he'd often cheerfully take it.

The whole mutiny experience had brought Martin and me closer together, and he was genuinely thankful that I'd had the guts to be the bearer of bad news. He cast me as his straight shooter, which made it very simple for me to work with him. From that day on, I think it's fair to say that I was Martin's closest ally at Massive. There was almost nothing that happened in the studio that we didn't collaborate on. In general, he was more focused on game development, while I focused on developing the studio's team and relationships.

At last, we were back to business! Which meant: off to Los Angeles, yet again. But this time, VUG wasn't questioning our visit; their response was quite the opposite.

"Where the hell are you? What are you working on? What is all the money being spent on?" We had been flying under their radar for more than six months and they were getting jittery. But we had nothing to worry about. The game and the trailer were polished and convincing and reassured the folks in Culver City. We got the green light from CEO Bruce Hack and flew back to Sweden with a budget big enough to create Massive's largest game yet.

"How large do you think the budget really is? How much will they tolerate?" I asked Martin. Financing had always been a concern for me, and I worried endlessly about how to safeguard the project and the team.

"It doesn't matter," he replied. "We'll make them spend the money we want them to spend. That's my job. Ultimately, they don't have a choice. They need us more than we need them."

15

MAKING THINGS UP

I once made up a game of billiards and lied to everyone about it. I'd been playing various forms of the game with friends down at the local pool hall, a gloomy place filled with alcoholics who had stumbled in through the steel door from a parking lot totally devoid of light and charm. Between the entrance and the pool tables, under the low-hanging ceiling, there was a row of simple one-armed bandits, ready to rob someone of their last pennies. They sang their depressing mechanical tunes as we walked by. As poor art students, it was the only kind of place we could afford to hang out.

Playing pool was frustrating. We simply weren't good enough to generate exciting matches based on the existing, proper rule sets. It made me think of new ways to play the game, where the stakes would steadily increase as the match went along, and result in a great, climactic showdown where the outcome potentially wouldn't be decided until the last ball went in. Once I'd come up with the idea, I wanted to sell it to my friends, but I found it too embarrassing to tell them I'd just made the whole thing up. So I invented a story that I'd learned this particular game one night in Rome. I embellished the tale with some semimysterious Italian friends, a drinking game, and plenty of cigarettes. It all sounded great, and we proceeded to play billiards in my new way. Everyone loved it.

When I was a kid, it didn't really matter if my fantasies were real or not, because they existed only for my own pleasure or, in bad times, my need to escape. It was okay that the line between the objective and the dream remained blurry. I'd watch an empty street corner in a sleepy city in Portugal, and in my mind, it would become a sprawling work of fiction. For me, it didn't matter if any of the ideas in my mind really happened. All the magic in the real world once began in the head of a dreamer. Over time, I learned to be more careful with my moving between portals, in and out of reality and what existed only in my imagination.

World in Conflict forced me to balance reality with the imagined. I took inspiration from many sources, not just the competition. I was acutely aware of the quality level some studios were hitting with their titles. The game *The Legend of Zelda: Twilight Princess* was extraordinarily poetic and effortlessly mixed Japanese haiku with Disney flare and the deep storytelling tradition of the best fantasy literature. Bundled together, it could have been a crazy mix, but instead, it all jelled into a cohesive and epic experience on the same level as *Star Wars* and *The Lord of the Rings*. At the other end of the spectrum, *Gears of War* took cooperative combat and destruction physics to entirely new heights, even though the loud machismo of the heroes made it impossible for me to enjoy playing the game. Overall, I felt that the video game industry was too tech-driven, and that there was a visual and narrative famine. I hoped that my art school background might give Massive a slight advantage.

We had a very promising demo, a good team, a good track record, and enough financial backing to take everything to the finish line. My job was to make all those things look fantastic to the outside world and our publisher, Vivendi Universal.

Apart from supporting Martin on habitual shark runs in Culver City, I began to focus a lot on what VUG called "GPS," the Global Product Summit. This was a meeting held in LA twice a year, where studios showed their games to the VUG executives and the company's salesforce. Traditionally, the event took place in one of the high-end hotels downtown, such as the Biltmore or the Ritz. The entire group of execs would gather under high ceilings and chandeliers that hung like ivy, seated as if in a movie theater. When the lights dimmed, the game developers took the stage one by one. The point of the GPS meeting was probably just to synchronize the various parts of VUG's organization, but it felt more like a cruel Darwinistic survival game that would arbitrarily kill or boost your project. It was an intimidating and dangerous meeting for developers, and we all knew it. We competed with other VUG products like *Scarface*, *50 Cent*, and *F.E.A.R.* sequels, which were developed by other studios that VUG had acquired. Each of us had no more than thirty minutes to protect the future of our studio by impressing a room of indifferent businesspeople.

My storytelling skills went into high gear, and I directed every second of those minutes into a show that made such an impression that every salesperson had no choice except to feel insanely hyped about the opportunity to support our game. I thought of our thirty minutes as a play or a film, where everything needed to follow a carefully designed narrative arc like a classic hero's journey.

At the GPS meetings, I never presented anything myself. I left that duty to people who had more credibility as game developers and a more PR-friendly stage presence. I'd prepare the narrative, the slides, the trailers, the screenshots, the choice of concept art, and the teasing parts of the story. Along the way, I'd learned that working with Americans, you often needed to have a solid answer to the question "What's in it for me?" Part of Massive's strategy became to consciously make sure that those involved in our projects on the publisher side would prosper too. Each point that we touched in the network needed to produce a beneficial exchange.

I worked many angles to make the game look amazing, and a few of them left bruised relationships in Massive. The lead level designer of *WiC* was a talented and soft-spoken guy nicknamed Ludde, who looked like a member of a synth-pop band. He was thoughtful, cautious with people, and deeply motivated by his work. Like many others I'd met in the industry, he was quietly competitive. Although Ludde was not officially responsible for art direction at Massive, he had a very specific vision of how *WiC* should look, and his preference had become the approved art style for the game. Unfortunately, according to me, the direction he was taking was too bright, colorful, and happy. I thought of it as a Donald Duck world, which made absolutely no sense considering the heavy themes and the seriousness of the game, but I decided it wasn't my battle to fight.

Martin was very often involved in a hands-on manner in the development of each game, but he didn't have much interest in art direction, and he didn't seem terribly interested when I asked about the Disneyesque nature of the color palette. Why should a game about the terror of the Cold War, in which innocent civilians are bombed by nukes, look like a perky ad for a theme park?

We were in Whistler, Canada. This time for a management meeting called by Martin's boss. Even though the conference rooms were no different from any other, we were in a fantastic location, right at the foot of the mountains. The large windows gave way to views of the closest peaks, covered in deep, white snow that glittered like a frosting of pearls. Between meetings, we were supposed to enjoy some team-building time on the slopes, but I had no time for it, because I was too preoccupied with my concerns about the visual style of *WiC*.

VUG had suddenly decided that they needed to announce *World in Conflict*. Up until then, no one outside of Massive and VUG knew what we were working on. The announcement was expected to generate a lot of very positive press and excitement across the gaming world.

An announcement usually has two effects for the developer: It makes it very difficult for the publisher to cancel the project (which every developer always worries about); and, in addition, it puts the publisher in a position where it's in their own interest to make the game as good as possible. Traditionally this leads to a higher number of positive "okay-this-can-go-over-budget" decisions. Our only small problem was that VUG was urgently asking for five in-game screenshots that would convincingly sell the game to the press and spark some publicity. We had plenty of screenshots, true, but all of them were still in the comic-book style that I thought resonated poorly with the DNA of the game. I went to Martin and told him we couldn't use the screenshots.

"What? What's wrong with them? The particle effects look stunning!" he replied.

"Well, I think there actually is a problem. The color palette is wrong. Everything looks like it's from a Disney movie, and, in the game, nukes get dropped all over the place. Plus, our story is a serious, humorless exploration that juxtaposes America's international aggressions with the innocence of its civilians. It's not kid stuff."

"So?"

"Frankly, it's bizarre and practically insensitive to make it all look like harmless fun, which is what this art style accomplishes."

Martin thought about this for a while, and then he asked me what I wanted to do. We had only a few hours before we needed to deliver the screenshots to the PR machine.

"The screenshots, and in fact the entire game, should look like oil paintings," I said. "Like classic battle paintings, with big, open landscapes, and large battles fought under heavy, epic skies."

"Okay," he said. "Can you fix it?"

I called a talented senior artist back home in the studio. Rodrigo was a stocky Chilean guy with a can-do attitude. He would have to work late in Sweden to match our US deadlines, but I knew he'd understand what I was looking for. He started to tweak the color settings of the game directly in the engine. Then he grabbed screenshots and sent a few versions to me. I sat in the hotel lobby, and for every iteration I downloaded on my little PC, I would call or email feedback to him. We quickly got to the point where I wanted us to be, because he was completely in tune with the oil-painting look already. I thanked the gods for the slow hotel internet connection that just barely allowed us to pull off the exercise in time.

Armed with Rodrigo's new screenshots, I went to see Martin and our VUG producer, Greg Goodrich. Greg had long been our best ally in Culver City. He was a large, loud, aggressive, and opinionated man who could scare the hell out of people if he thought they were weak or stupid. To me, he seemed like someone who should be cast as a pull-no-punches SWAT team leader in a Hollywood movie. I worried that showing him the screenshots might change his opinion of me.

I nervously pulled up the new images on the meeting room TV screen. Greg and Martin looked at them for a second.

"FUCK YEAH!" Greg looked like he was about to explode. "That's like the fucking most beautiful thing I have ever seen in my entire fucking life! I mean... What the HELL? How did this even happen?"

Martin took a quieter approach, but he already looked happier than I'd ever seen him.

"My god. Can we actually pull that off?" he said, which in developer's lingo meant, "How far have you pushed the graphical settings to make the game look like THAT?"

Martin's question was valid, but as far as I could tell, Rodrigo and I hadn't set up the screenshots in a dishonest way; rather, we'd changed only the overall tonality and palette, so I felt comfortable in reassuring Martin that this was an exercise in art direction, not in cheating with unrealistic settings.

"FUCK YEAH! HOLY SHIT! JEEEESUS!" Greg shouted, louder than ever, making the people at the medical conference in the adjacent room wonder what they were missing.

At the GPS presentation the next day, the five new screenshots were all instantly approved by the entire publisher organization, and then the pictures were paraded all night through VUG emails as an internal hit. Everyone just *had to see* what we had achieved.

And in the next couple of days, once they got their hands on the news, the press was equally elated.

However, I had completely overstepped my boundaries inside the sensitive ecosystem of Massive. Ludde had fought hard for the Donald Duck look, and it took awhile for him to forgive me. And worse, counter to my own assumption, it turned out that Rodrigo and I had in fact pushed the graphical settings beyond what anyone thought was possible for the final game. This was duly and bitterly noted by all the engineers who now officially hated us for creating a promise that would be nearly impossible for them to fulfill.

But sometimes dreamers win precisely because they push the limits and force the real world to adapt and improve. Once the engineers knew the level of graphical fidelity we were aiming for, they eventually found a way to make it happen. When the game shipped many months later, it looked every bit as beautiful as it had in the versions we created that evening in Whistler.

16

WORLD IN CONFLICT

The first time I met Tobias I thought he was a total idiot. He'd booked a meeting with me thinking that Massive was a studio with a fat wallet. He was hoping to sell some far-fetched web service that would broadcast games via the internet and generate millions in revenue.

Tobias had reached out to me because he wanted to sell something, so it was no surprise that I dismissed him as a sales guy, and he promptly delivered on the stereotype. Tobias was from Stockholm and had an air of self-importance that was obnoxious. He just kept talking. I felt that he was taking me for a fool. I judged him harshly for everything: his big skull-shaped ring, the backslick, his hand gestures, the way he paused before he was about to make a particularly clever point. I tried to calculate how quickly I could throw him out without being too rude. I still didn't want to burn any bridges, but this was ridiculous.

While one part of my brain dismissed the meeting as an utter waste of time, another part of it started to drift. God knew I had a lot of other things to do! Massive was keeping me busy. The announcement of *WiC* had beat expectations, and suddenly the demands on my "marketing department" had exploded. The only problem was that the so-called marketing team had only a single employee—me. The lack of staff had turned me into a frustrating colleague. I kept bugging the development team with requests for various assets such as trailers, concept art, logotypes, web page updates, screenshots, events, interviews, developer diaries, time with the audio team, and so on. It never ended, and all the other Massive employees thought of me as a persistent nuisance who would regularly distract them from what they saw as real work. At times I felt my internal credibility was a bit damaged, too, after fighting so hard for those first five screenshots. My only real fan was Martin, who urged me along every day and gave me the permission to remain pushy.

I had completely forgotten that I was in a meeting with an overeager sales guy from Stockholm when I suddenly registered something he'd said.

"We could also help you produce trailers to bump your game to the top of the charts."

My brain returned to the room. *What charts?* I thought to myself, *You have no charts! You have no audience, mate; you have nothing! But trailers? What? Wait a minute now...*

One of my largest challenges with the team at Massive was capturing in-game trailers for *WiC*. I firmly believed that trailers would become our best marketing tool, and anyway, the game looked stunning. But making trailers was too demanding for the team for a lot of good reasons. First, there were too few people in the studio overall; we were thinly stretched everywhere. Second, the maps were incomplete and had severe visual problems like the broken skybox, anti-aliasing issues, and aggressive flickering. Most of the playable units were unfinished, and the few that had been finalized and textured had no animation attached. And every single special effect was "in progress," meaning it looked great for a few hours and then like trash for a few weeks. The individual soldiers on the battlefield had no understanding of collision, which meant that they would walk in and out of all objects as if they were ghosts.

Adding to the hopelessness of the task was that we had no functioning replays, which meant that we couldn't organize a scene and then capture it on camera. All we could do was keep the camera rolling as the disjointed game clumsily chugged along and hope for a few good seconds here and there. This might have been great if we'd had a "camera tool" in our game engine, but we didn't have that either, which meant that even random filming was practically impossible.

At the time, we were working on an in-game trailer with an external consultant who seemed more interested in writing his own feature film about a couple on vacation in Thailand in the middle of their divorce. It was a difficult, roundabout process, and the probable end result was making me nervous. My inner perfectionist's alarms were ringing.

But here was another guy who said he could make trailers. I heard my own voice suddenly interrupt the meeting. It took him by surprise.

"What's your education?"

"Uh? What? Shouldn't we talk about the..."

"What is your education? I mean, what do you *do* when you don't try to sell this web thing?"

"Oh. Aha...Well. I went to film school."

"Right!" I said. "Follow me!"

I ran down the stairs, with my guest on my heels, to where one of the engineers sat. We pulled up the game in its unfinished state. I explained to a confused Tobias what I wanted to do. He immediately had some interesting ideas, but something even more remarkable happened. It was like *another person emerged* through the shell of the salesman. Suddenly, the sales guy was gone, and in his place, a passionate, dedicated moviemaking poet had appeared. I looked at him again, and his entire demeanor was different. It was almost as if he had changed his outfit too. In front of me now stood a sensitive artist in a flannel shirt, with his hair on end and creative intensity in his eyes.

I convinced Martin that I would be able to pull off the trailer production he expected if I could hire Tobias and get some engineering time to build a capturing tool in the engine. He trusted me, and gave me support to move ahead. Tobias, my first proper team member, was able to start the next day. So much for his outstanding career in the streaming business, I suppose.

I asked him what tool he needed. He said he'd need a Macintosh with the software Final Cut installed. I told our IT guy, who immediately fired up a PC and installed Premiere on it. Well, close enough, I guess. Our IT guy always did refer to my Mac as "an illegible interface to the organization." Every other year, when I buy a new Macintosh, I have to promise him it's my last and that I'll switch to PC soon. I don't know if he ever actually believes me, but this dance between us has been ongoing for fifteen years.

Tobias showed up in the office like a whirlwind and began working on his first trailer right away. The trailer was almost complete within two weeks, and it was fantastic. Tobias had to edit and cut in a specific way to cover for the fact that the in-game destruction and special effects were broken. This was common practice, since in the early stages of production, lots of stuff was always missing.

My team continued to grow. In addition to Tobias, I hired a screenshot artist, a copywriter, a test-lab manager, a community manager, and, on the side, I set up partnerships with Nvidia, ESL, and Intel. I noticed that most of the people I hired were bitter introverts. I couldn't tell if this was somehow a reflection of my personality or if the game industry attracted these characters. Either way, we spurred one another on to become an intensely serious and hardworking group. Nothing was ever good enough; everything could always be improved.

We were supporting VUG's PR teams with asset after asset. We were like an ad agency fueled by amphetamines, and we often pushed the sales teams to promote *WiC* even more aggressively in their own territory. *We WILL give you the assets you need! Anything! Just ask for it.*

We did over thirty shows and conventions for *WiC* before it shipped. We spent a tremendous amount of time on the road, wearing ourselves out. Some of us, like me, had kids and families at home, but in general, this was a long tour for young and single nerds who had not experienced much partying in their lives. As one of the first to have had children, I was often the odd man out, trying to find a moment to call back home and say good night to the kids, while the others were heading for the bar and the first cold beer of the day. I couldn't tell if my unrelenting drive to realize my dreams was a professional asset or an enemy to my personal life. But the call of success encouraged me—all of us—to carry on, like sailors in a storm, sailing toward the unknown, enchanted by sirens.

At E3 2006, we finally felt the sweet and addictive taste of global success. Our little prototype had grown into a beast of a demo, and we were richly rewarded by the press and the official judges of the show. We were facing steep competition and winning! Otherwise, the main focus of the show was the increased potential the new generation of consoles offered. It seemed that everyone was talking about the worldwide shift to high-definition (HD) TVs and HD gaming. Sony was feeling the challenge from Microsoft's Xbox 360 and had begun to aggressively promote the quantum leap that the PlayStation 3 would present.

Next to the future heavyweight fight between Xbox and Playstation, expected to last for years, *World in Conflict* was a shining star in the present, not a distant promise. Two hours after the show had opened and our booth had been bombarded by an eager audience, the Vivendis PR guy showed me a text message from the CEO of a competing publisher: *WIC. Clearly the game of the show.*

These were no small words, considering that 2006 was also the year Ubisoft announced the stunning *Assassin's Creed*, a game that had succeeded in re-creating a near photo-realistic version of the Holy Land as it appeared in 1191. In a display of stupendous technical craftsmanship, *Assassins* looked eerily similar to the best landscape paintings of the Renaissance masters Bellini and (the forgotten) Joachim Patinir.

I paid little attention to *Assassin's Creed* at the time. We had our hands full, enjoying that all our efforts to whip up a hype for the launch of *World in Conflict* were bearing fruit at last. We were instantly celebrated as a team among the top players in the industry, and everyone was there, ready to give us the high five: *I always believed in you guys!*

On the show floor, Martin and I ran into Peter Della Penna, his boss, who giggled like a madman and hugged us both in a ham-fisted way.

"I am putting you guys in the Shutters!" he said with a huge smile and ran off.

"Fantastic!" we said, although we had no idea what it meant.

After the first long day in the Convention Center, we finally went back to the hotel many hours later. There, we were promptly informed that all our belongings had been moved to a much fancier place in Santa Monica called Shutters on the Beach. We hopped into a taxi, drove halfway through LA, and checked in just before midnight. There, protected by the posh New England style, the beds were twice as big and four times softer. The gentle ocean breeze blew fine grains of sand from the LA beach into my sheets. My life had become a Hollywood story.

Released in September 2007, *World in Conflict* sold over three times as much as any previous Massive title, close to a million copies. GameSpot called the game "relentlessly fun with an amazing new approach to the genre," and they highlighted exactly what I had intended to showcase in our long, hard-fought marketing campaign: the "large, dynamic battlefields," which they said came "alive with the symphony of destruction." The 9.5/10 review summarized the game with the words " *World in Conflict* is undoubtedly the studio's masterwork. Everything about this game is top-notch, from the addictive gameplay to the amazing visuals." It was as if I'd written the entire review myself.

We had reached a career high point for the entire company. From atop the mountain of success, it felt to me like nothing could possibly go wrong.

17

THE GREAT TRAGEDY

They should have brought their kids and a puppy, I thought. They looked like an innocent married couple from California on vacation, not at all like henchmen on a mission to destroy our dreams.

The legal head of VUG was a pleasant and relaxed woman in her forties, and the global HR manager, sitting next to her, also eerily chirpy, looked us professionally in the eyes without flinching. He was like an android, trained to perpetually broadcast *I-truly-care-about-you. As people, as humans.*

But the message they were delivering wasn't an empathetic one.

We met them in central Malmö for lunch at La Couronne, a cozy French restaurant owned by friends from a band I used to be in. This was supposed to be a safe place. *Yes, outside is FINE!* they said with plastic emotion. *The weather is so nice!* As we sat down around the small table covered with a red-and-white tablecloth, I felt as if I'd accidentally invited demons to my friends' place. Uneasy silence followed.

"Bobby wants to shut you down," the head of legal told us, still smiling as the waiter set water on the table. And then she blinked with one eye in some strange knowing manner, as if we were talking about a little Christmas gift.

"Yeah, he does," the HR manager filled in with an inappropriately reassuring grin.

Martin and I uncomfortably poked at our salads under the summer sun.

"But good news! We told him there's a cheaper way to get rid of you!"

This was the pep talk? This was the future we'd been waiting for, sitting still for almost a year? Martin and I were stunned. *Shut us down?* What on earth were they talking about? *A cheaper way to get rid of us?*

Several months before the horrible lunch meeting, VUG had acquired another publisher called Activision, in what was one of the largest deals ever in the gaming industry. There had been a lot of internal chatter about what VUG really wanted to do with all the money they had made from Blizzard after the success of *World of WarCraft*, and sometimes we'd hear rumors that Bruce Hack, head of VUG, was dressing the company up only to sell it to someone. But instead, VUG ended up acquiring a major competitor, the publisher of the *Call of Duty* and *Guitar Hero* series, two of the most commercially successful game franchises on the planet. The move reverberated throughout the entire industry, and the combination of the two companies was poised to become the largest electronic arts publishing house in the world.

The deal was so large and had such widespread implications that it got stuck in the antitrust machinery in both the US and in Europe, which was a new experience for everyone involved. After two decades of double-digit growth, the video game industry was no longer a hobby for digital dreamers. It had become Big Money, with a revenue that surpassed old gorillas like the movie industry. We were bigger business than we thought.

Waiting for the bureaucracy to churn through the paperwork turned out to be a very frustrating experience. We were told to wait. Do nothing. Don't release any games. Don't discuss any projects. Don't organize any meetings between the two parties. Don't fire anyone. Don't hire anyone. Just freeze. This felt nearly impossible, since we had been fighting like race-car drivers stuck in seventh gear for as long as we could remember, and suddenly, without warning, we were expected to live on one single breath of air until... *sometime in the future.*

Together with another VUG-owned studio called Swordfish, located in Birmingham, we worked on a console version of *World in Conflict.* And we launched a bunch of internal pitches, too, just to fill our drawers with ideas that we could explore further once the corporate dust had settled and a decision was made about the antitrust issue. There were plenty of ideas, including a werewolf game, and a SEAL-inspired diver game set in an abandoned Russian deepsea experimental base where something had gone terribly wrong. A little *BioShock*, a little *CoD*, a little Clancy, and a lot of fresh Massive ideas thrown in on top. Together with a few veterans, I worked on a romantic Philip Pullman–inspired game called *Fauna*, which featured a young girl, surrounded by her pack of wild animals, as the hero.

Martin himself focused on ideas for an ultraquick sequel to *WiC* that was so ambitious and required such a fast-paced development cycle that it was dubbed "*WiC* Crazy" by the team.

There was one side project that received very little attention but would turn out to be most important to Massive's future. Martin had asked the very best engineers to start working on a new game engine. We unromantically called the R & D project "Tech 2." Almost no one had any insight into what the small team was doing, and they were left alone, without supervision.

Game developers are restless and don't enjoy sitting around, so some people decided to leave the studio and move on to other studios that they felt had a better chance of releasing something. Every time someone resigned, we asked to replace them, but we were told we weren't allowed to according to the antitrust rules. The studio slowly shrank in size, lost capacity, and things inevitably slowed down.

Martin and I tried to fight the loss of momentum, but even we felt like we were treading water. At the same time, we were an important financial asset in the megadeal that was going on over our heads. Basically, we were paid to sit around and look like *value*, and I guess we could all have taken a long break without anyone knowing. But we didn't want a break! We wanted to continue our adventure.

Finally, when the antitrust bureaus in both the US and the EU gave their permission for the deal to go through, there was a giant management upheaval at the merging two headquarters in LA. Once the fog of war lifted, it turned out that every single person in the new upper management came from Activision. That seemed strange to us, but we didn't think it would be a problem for Massive. All we needed to do was convince our new masters how great we were. This, we felt, was going to be easy. With *WiC*'s recent success, who wouldn't love us?

The new managers visited us in Malmö for an audit and to see what we were up to. We played all our best cards in an amazing display of a very-good-and-healthy studio. Martin, our producer Petter, creative director Soundboy, and I were all on fire, restless and eager after the long, involuntary break. But the stone-faced and oblivious looks we received told us this wasn't going to be as simple as we'd thought. Clearly, our patented combination of charm and quality wasn't working. This was new.

Upper Management Man #2 started to speak in a nasally voice: "The great traaaaagedy," he began, drawing out the "a" forever to somehow make it sound more definitive. "The great traaaaaaaaaagedy of *World in Conflict* is that it's like a fine wine," he continued.

I thought to myself, *I'd LOVE to be a fine wine. What can possibly be wrong with that?*

"A fine wine is a tragic thing. Veeeery traaaaaagic. Because everyone knows it's great, but no one wants to pay for it."

Oh my god! The realization hit me instantly. *These guys only care about money!* And money was never our forte. We had focused so much on quality. Quality first. Always. Our business strategy was simple: Create quality, and the money will follow. But here was the hard-core opposite: Make money; quality doesn't matter.

After a few pointless and strained conversations, they all left. Audit over. We gave the new company CEO, Bobby Kotick, a wonderful, large sepia-toned *WiC* print on real canvas as a parting gift. We had prepared it in advance as the grand finale, as a celebration of what we thought would be an inspiring first meeting. I had imagined it hanging in Kotick's office, where he'd proudly brag about his Swedish studio every time people asked about the picture. But now that we'd had the misfortune of looking into the souls of these people, the gift felt like a desperate, clingy, and embarrassing act of losers. It made us feel dirty. Kotick seemed to me like the kind of guy who would probably toss the gift in a wastebin as soon as he was out of the building.

We never met any of them again.

A few weeks later, we got the call from the nice folks in legal and HR, the one that led to the fateful lunch: "We're in Sweden. Would you have time to hang out?"

My mind jolted back to the moment. *Shut us down? A cheaper way to get rid of us?* The nice woman from legal continued: "So yeah, we convinced Bobby that it's cheaper to sell you than to shut you down. That way, we won't have to pay any severance or the rent or anything.

"The only problem is that you will have to fix it for yourselves. We really don't have time to deal with all of the logistics involved. Just find a buyer, will you?" the HR manager added, as if it were the most casual thing.

Martin looked at them incredulously. "How long do we have?" he asked.

"That's the catch, though. You have to find a buyer in four weeks," responded the head of legal.

Martin, the man who never gives up, stood up, looked at me, and said, "Okay, time to get to work," and I was instantly on my feet.

We left the table, returned to the studio badly shaken, and began to desperately throw ideas on the whiteboard in Martin's office. I felt strong, prepared and battle-ready, but as I was throwing down some names on the growing list of people we could call to save the studio, I noticed that my hand was trembling.

Four weeks.

We went on a whirlwind tour and met everyone who was someone, and had plenty of very promising conversations in corporate headquarters, in small offices behind the scenes at trade shows, and in airports everywhere. Anywhere. We were like hyperbolic, fueled salesmen, completely ignoring our families on a mad quest to make the impossible Big Sell.

Two weeks down, we had leads. Phone calls. Promising visits. Requests for additional PowerPoints and budgets. A lot of *Let's talk*.

One week to go, and we found ourselves in a hotel lobby getting much too drunk on gin and tonics with representatives of a major entertainment company who practically promised to buy us, but then inexplicably went completely quiet the day after and we never heard from them again.

And then, we ran out of time. Four weeks gone.

Our beloved studio was about to get killed. All that remained to do was to sit in Martin's office with pale faces and black rings under our eyes, waiting for the call of death from California.

Bobby wants to shut you down.

PART II
2008–2016

18

UBISOFT

"Well, I know it sucks, but one of us will have to move to Paris."

The five brothers sat around the kitchen table in Brittany, France, arguing about which one of them would have to take the bullet. None of them were particularly fond of the hustle and bustle of the capital, but they knew that in order to elevate their little video game distribution company, they'd have to win business from the big French retailers. As it stood, the Parisian heavyweights were not interested in working with a seemingly simple family business in the countryside. Businesspeople in Paris preferred to deal with businesspeople in Paris.

The brothers had formed a company called Guillemot Informatique. It was going well, but it had become clear that they weren't going to get the biggest deals unless they had a presence in the capital. After some debating, brother Yves, who was twenty-six, agreed to make the sacrifice and move. They decided he'd start an entirely new company with a different name so that the cityfolk wouldn't realize they were actually working with the rejected countryfolk from the village of Carentoir. The setup was a little bit tricky, but Yves was good at what he did, and soon enough he began winning over the business from all the major retailers, one by one.

There are two different origin stories for the company name,

Ubisoft; one has an intellectual touch, and the other has a subtle rebellious twang to it. Depending on which creation myth one prefers, either the first half of the corporate name was intended as a play on the word *ubiquitous*, or perhaps UBI is an abbreviation of the French Union des Bretons Indépendants (Union of Independent Bretons). The word *soft* comes from "software." Regardless of which story one believes, in 1986, one of the world's most successful game publishers was born, the French giant Ubisoft.

It was obvious to those who already knew the Guillemot family that the brothers' adventure might become a big enterprise.

The five siblings were ready to do the hard work. They'd noticed that the game industry was growing every year, but that it lacked the infrastructure to support an increasing consumer demand. The opportunity was readily apparent. The small company began distributing games across France from the big game publishers abroad. After a few years of growing and understanding the distribution business and developing a tremendous industry network, brother Yves finally decided to make games of his own. In fact, creating games had been something he'd wanted to do for a long time. Ubisoft began looking for local developers, and once they'd gathered a few promising candidates, they rented an old French castle, flew out the team, and worked like maniacs to create something unique. Almost immediately, Ubisoft was creating excellent products of their own.

From there things moved quickly, and the company began to open development studios to create a portfolio of games. They became a dominant force in the industry. In 1994, Ubisoft opened their namesake studio in Paris. The company became publicly traded in 1996, and went on to open several studios around the world. Initially, they targeted countries such as China and Canada, where French was a viable business language, but quickly expanded to become a global presence with studios all across the world.

Thirty years later, Ubisoft's very first CEO, Yves Guillemot, is still in charge.

* * *

The first time I met someone from Ubisoft was when two fine gentlemen from Paris showed up on Massive's doorstep in 2008. It was two weeks before the Bobby Kotick deadline and our impending doom. One of the Ubisoft visitors was a burned-out producer with circles under his eyes, and the other a youngish, red-haired game designer who looked as if he came from an Asterix comic book. They were very nice and open-minded, but both seemed way too junior to signal any serious interest from Ubisoft. I couldn't tell if we or they were more confused about their visit.

To some degree, we'd become used to these kinds of exploratory encounters. There were many companies who just wanted to visit Massive, with no real intent to acquire us. We figured the visit from Paris was out of curiosity or perhaps an attempt to gather some intel. Or maybe they were just being polite to Bobby Kotick by showing pretend interest? I didn't know, and it didn't matter. We fired up the same well-rehearsed presentation machinery, just in case. We still believed in never burning any bridges. But of course, our future was no longer in our own hands, and it was looking more and more as if the industry was about to burn all its ties with us.

Our French guests told us they weren't staying long, not even a full day. But we continued at full speed, regardless of how improvised their visit seemed: PowerPoint bonanza, handshaking, tech demos, cinnamon rolls, coffee, trailers, more PowerPoints, and then some light socializing. *What games do you like to play?* It had been a great year for games, so we ended up making shallow observations about a few favorites: *Portal, Dead Space, Grand Theft Auto IV, Fallout 3, Braid, Little Big Planet,* and *Left 4 Dead.* "Oh yeah, interesting." We all pretended, but the conversation felt forced. I honestly adored some of Ubisoft's games, so there was some genuine pleasure in discussing them with our French visitors who could offer further insight into the games' development. Every game is chaos. Every game has a war story.

The meetings ended up running late, and I decided to walk the two visitors to the train station so they wouldn't get lost and miss their flights. As we half ran through the city, the game designer summarized the visit with a few words that I felt perfectly illustrated Ubisoft's complete lack of interest in Massive: "This visit has been so nice. Thank you. I almost never get to travel abroad for work."

Good for you, I thought, and meant it because I really liked the chap. But of course it wasn't what I was hoping to hear. Massive desperately needed a financial savior, not someone who appreciated a short trip to Sweden as a change of scenery. I waved good-bye, and together with Martin I rushed on to the next far-fetched rescue plan.

Out of the blue odd whispers reached us from the (now almost empty) VUG office in LA. Apparently, Blizzard *really* wanted to work with us, they liked *World in Conflict*, and they had plans to outsource some of their work. That sounded too good to be true. Someone from VUG set up a meeting, and a few days later Martin and I took a flight to Irvine, California, to meet with legendary Blizzard CEO Mike Morhaime. In the game developer community, he was a demigod, a true legend of almost mythological proportions. As far as I knew, he had once started as an engineer (*check:* credibility as a craftsman); moved on to producer (*check:* survived the toughest trenches); and, more significantly, led Blizzard to its being recognized as possibly the finest studio in the world, with brands like *StarCraft*, *Diablo*, *WarCraft*, and *World of WarCraft*. Surreally, every game they'd ever released was extremely successful. Every single one (*check:* divine strategic skills)!

We'd met with the Blizzard guys regularly during our time with VUG, often at the GPS meetings. Although they were always pleasant and polite, they also carried an air of seclusion, like monks who had isolated themselves from the troubles of the outside world and were exclusively devoted to the celebration of their own god—

the craft of their games. They seemed remote, untouchable, and happy in their own magic place.

Mike Morhaime's office was a big and strangely dark room that looked like a mix between a dungeon and an American corporate power bunker. After a cursory exchange about jet lag and the warm California weather, Martin got straight to the point, beaming with hope and optimism.

"We heard you wanted to work with us?" he asked.

Morhaime looked at him and me with a sad expression. Like a doctor about to deliver a bad diagnosis.

"Who told you that?" he asked.

"Al, at VUG," we said truthfully.

"Well, you know Al doesn't work for Blizzard, right?"

"Absolutely," Martin said.

"I'm sorry, but I have no idea why he would have said that. We just don't do outsourcing or codevelopment. Don't get me wrong, I love *World in Conflict*, and I think you guys have a great future, but just not with us."

It hit us like a cold fist in the stomach. Blizzard had no interest? *Al had just made it up?* Why would anyone do that?

"Would it make any difference if it was called Blizzard Scandinavia?" Martin asked, not yet ready to give up.

Morhaime looked at him for a long while in silence, as if he wanted to reward a fellow traveler with a gift, to show appreciation of the ongoing effort. But he had nothing to give, and with a polite amount of regret in his voice he replied, "No. No, I'm afraid it wouldn't make any difference at all."

As supportive and empathetic as Morhaime was to our dire situation, it was clear that the idea that Blizzard would consider working with us was the brainchild of someone not in touch with Blizzard's inner circle. We could only guess why it had even been proposed. It seemed to us that someone about to lose their job at VUG had tried to make themselves part of a significant idea that would put them right back in the middle of an exciting new collaboration. Or maybe it was just a bunch of stupid words that should have never left the bar. Like saying, "Wouldn't it be great to see Tom Brady play for the Cowboys?"

Once we realized this, our visit felt more embarrassing than anything else. It was as if we were Blizzard's younger brother asking for dating advice. But Morhaime was gracious about it all and gave us some good insight during the tour of the extensive new Blizzard campus. It was a wonderful studio with a huge open courtyard in the middle, and a giant statue of a wild orc riding a dire wolf stood in the center. It made me think of Florence, where a different breed of ancient statues had once been erected during the Renaissance. I was watching and processing everything, quietly thinking that the short glimpse of Blizzard's home would turn out to be a good learning experience, assuming I even had a future in the industry.

Walking around the Blizzard office made me realize with amazement that there were other dimensions to the game industry, far beyond my previous knowledge. I had never had access to this part of the stratosphere, but suddenly, there we were, walking in the secret dungeon of the giant, admiring the professionalism and standard they had reached. After shipping *World in Conflict*, I thought we were pretty damn good, but this was on a whole new level. Their online team sat in a huge theater that reminded me of NASA's control room in Houston. The seats were arranged in rows, facing a wall that was covered with monitors from floor to roof, tracking enormous amounts of data. A few of them showed international news programs.

"Why do you watch the news?" I asked Mike Morhaime.

"In case there is something happening somewhere, like a storm or some political upheaval, anything that might affect the running of *World of WarCraft*," he said, as if it were obvious. From the perspective of that room, real world wars, storms, and disasters were only distant annoyances, minor blips in the operation of something bigger; a digital world that invited all the inhabitants of the planet to play together.

"We need to know early, in case we need to adapt," Morhaime continued.

I felt as if we were nothing more than a tiny rock band that had just won the local high school competition for "Best Rock Act" meeting guitar god Jimi Hendrix. It was unfathomable stuff they were up to. The server room was custom-built, the size of a Boeing 747, with cooling and air filters advanced enough to mummify us all if we stayed inside for too long. There was a gym and a museum, a cafeteria and security guards. Somehow it all felt like a Mars colony; all that was missing was the dome on top. Inside, clever people sat in the sun with a fresh cup of coffee, casually solving advanced engineering problems and perfecting designs.

Although I knew I had come far with Massive, this was a daunting lesson in perspective.

Meanwhile, our best buddy Bobby Kotick—the man who did not have a beautiful *WiC* print hanging in his office—extended the four-week deadline for shutting us down. *A few more weeks*, we were told. *Or you're gone.* Maybe they knew something we didn't. But if they did, they didn't share.

Then, almost out of the blue, Martin came to my room and told me he'd just got off the phone with Activision in Santa Monica. I had time to observe: It's Santa Monica now? No more Culver City? Man, they'd really taken complete control of the company!

"We've been bought," he told me without any further ado and sporting an odd smile that I couldn't interpret immediately.

"Wow!" I exclaimed, and started to guess if it was Big Company A or Big Company B.

"No, no," Martin said. "It's not any of them. It's Ubisoft."

Our friend from Asterix delivered after all? This was surprising for sure, but I was about to encounter an even bigger surprise in the weeks to come.

19

MICHAEL COLLINS

It's impossible not to admire the spirit of entrepreneurship at the heart of the Space Race. But I must admit that I'm more of a fan than the average person. In truth, I might just be a little obsessed with it. My living room is decorated with a huge photo of astronaut Ed White on an EVA (spacewalk) in a Gemini XII suit. Next to that is an old Soviet-era poster advertising the upcoming "Day of the Cosmonauts" (May 12, 1961). On my desk at work, I have a bronze bust of Yury Gagarin, one of the greatest heroes of my life, and of course my bookshelf contains a tidy stack of books and movies about the Space Race. Aside from the visual timelessness and the obvious technical feats involved, there's plenty to be impressed by from this time period. But what strikes the deepest chord with me is the mad optimism that the first space travelers possessed; the hope and the fearless desire to go beyond the well-known and the safe. *Do you want to sit on top of the most powerful missile ever built and get blown away from the planet, possibly dying in the process? YES! I do.*

Michael Collins was an American astronaut who traveled to the moon with Neil Armstrong and Buzz Aldrin. As Armstrong and Aldrin became the first men in history to step on the surface of the celestial body, Collins remained in the capsule, alone in orbit. I love

Michael Collins for doing that, for being the ultimate team player and accepting to be so bizarrely, extremely alone. He sat farther away from humanity than any other human, ever, in total radio silence, as the moon shadowed him into black stillness. What was he thinking in his isolation?

Once Armstrong and Aldrin rejoined the capsule safely, the three astronauts successfully returned to planet Earth and etched their names into the short list of unforgettable humans. Well, actually, while Armstrong and Aldrin became legendary names, lots of people quickly forgot about Michael Collins since he hadn't set foot on the moon. Nevertheless, he did write a wonderful book about his journey in which he describes the strange lack of friendship he experienced with his fellow travelers.

On the way back home from the moon, the three didn't have that much to say to one another. Collins realized that, in a sense, they'd never been true friends. They'd just been the most intense coworkers, who for years had spent almost all their time together, working like a perfect team toward a mutual goal. It *felt* like friendship, but once the historical mission was completed, there wasn't a lot to say. Once they were back on Earth soil, they all returned to their families and real friends, making up for time lost. Flying to the moon together was an ultraprofessional relationship. It wasn't friendship, even though it looked like it and often felt like it.

This is how I feel about most of the colleagues I've had: a deep, genuine admiration of who they are and an almost complete trust in their abilities. It's wonderful to work with people like that. As far as I'm concerned, it's even better when they also have complicated personalities. Intense character is good. A lack of perspective can be very interesting, too, because it takes the mind to strange places. My favorite people tend to oscillate between aggressive self-criticism and over-the-top self-confidence. Somehow, the pendulum becomes a creative battery.

On some emotional level, I can understand Michael Collins. As a manager, I feel strongly that it should be the producers and the directors of the games who get to walk on the moon, not me. I enjoy taking care of the capsule and making sure it's fit to take everyone home and then maybe back to space again.

Up until late 2008, my entire journey in the game industry had been a bumpy flight in a close, low-orbit, reliable wingman constellation, first with Kim and then with Martin, both of whom I counted as real friends.

One day, right after we had found out we were going to be acquired by Ubisoft, Martin came with a cup of tea to my office. (One wall was covered with a huge photo of Soviet cosmonaut Leonov, the very first human to walk in space.) After some light talk, Martin suddenly hit me with an information nuke.

"You know what?" he said, looking out the window. "Maybe now is the time for me to leave Massive."

I could not believe what I was hearing. Martin and Massive were synonymous. The two were one and the same, almost to the point that Martin blended his personal thoughts with a demand that everyone in the studio telepathically act as he envisioned. None of us had ever thought that he'd leave. The studio was *his* creation, and it had *his* fingerprints all over it. But there we were. He began talking, more and more openly, about leaving Massive.

He began talking about leaving Massive.

When Massive was sold to Ubisoft, it wasn't actually the whole company that was being shipped off to the Paris head office. Instead, the French team cherry-picked everything they wanted and legally transferred it to a new, clean corporate entity that would hold all the selected assets. This is not unusual, and it's done to make sure that the buyer doesn't accidentally become responsible for some garbage that might be hiding in the closets of the old company. The only hurdle is that you can't sell humans or even their employment contracts, at least not in Sweden. Which means that if the buyer wants all the employees (which in our business is the second-most-valuable asset, after intellectual property), each and every one needs to personally sign a contract that accepts the new owner as a substitute employer. Once an individual signed, the name Ubisoft would simply replace the former employer (VUG) in the contract. Nothing else would change. Seeing as the alternative was to stay behind only to be fired by VUG, everyone signed almost immediately. Massive would basically continue exactly as it had been before, but without potential skeletons in any wardrobes.

As much as being fired by VUG looked like a bad proposition to everyone, Martin saw it differently. He always had the talent to see a unique and innovative perspective in muddy waters. He realized he had an extensive severance clause in the VUG contract, and it would be activated if they let him go. And of course they *would* let him go very soon, since the remaining version of old Massive was turning into an empty shell as everything relevant was now transferred to the new Ubisoft version of Massive.

I was contacted one day by Pierre, a senior manager at Ubisoft HQ, who asked me if he could speak candidly and in confidence. *Sure*, I said (which, by the way, is a really bad answer in most such situations, because you will very likely be corrupted before you realize it).

"We are concerned about Martin," Pierre said. "We really want him to stay, but we can't figure out if he is negotiating really hard, or if he genuinely means that he might leave. We'd like to hear your opinion about it."

And voilà! I was fully corrupted at once, in the middle of yet another loyalty conflict, which uncomfortably reminded me of the days when Nils tried to convince me to join his rebellion.

I did my best to wiggle my way out of it, thinking fast about what to say. I was certain that the best solution would be to convince Martin to stay, and I didn't want to be an unofficial channel of intel behind my friend's back.

"I think Martin is being entirely truthful," I said. "He's negotiating, and you can convince him to stay if there's enough autonomy offered. He works best unleashed. It's not about money, that's for sure. And yeah, he will leave if he isn't excited by your offer, I'm certain of that. But remember, it's about influence, not money."

"Aha. Okay," Pierre said. "What if he *does* leave? Who would replace him?"

"You know, I really don't think I can answer that. I think the best thing that can happen is that you'll convince Martin to stay. Work on that. You'll be happy if you succeed."

The truth was that I couldn't imagine Massive functioning with anyone else in charge. The whole studio was wired around Martin's personality like a neural net attached to a master AI.

The negotiations went on. Formally, Martin wasn't even an employee of Ubisoft, since he was now the only remaining employee in the VUG version of Massive. But the VUG bosses had given him instructions to facilitate the acquisition, so in practical terms he could act as a consultant at the "new" Massive.

One day, not too long after we'd been acquired, Martin stepped into my office. "I have reached an agreement with Ubisoft," he said.

"Yes! Great news!"

But just as I was about to high-five him, he stopped my motion with a discreet wave of his hand that signaled, with some degree of sorrow, *No, please don't.*

"We have agreed to disagree," he continued.

I was stunned. I really hadn't expected this.

"I'm leaving tomorrow, in fact."

"WHAT?! Why...," I started, but then my cell phone rang, and I saw it was a French number.

I held up my screen to Martin to show him it was Paris calling. He nodded in understanding and left my office. I shut the door and picked up.

"David, its Christine," the voice on the phone said.

Christine Burgess oversaw all Ubisoft studios and was easily one of the most powerful women in the game industry. She was in charge of thousands of employees working around the clock to produce Ubisoft's next hits. They said she was a wonderful, warm, and nice lady, somewhere in another part of the universe, but to me she appeared powerful, strong, and dangerous.

"Hi Christine," I said, desperately trying to process what was going on.

"You are taking over," she said.

At once, I felt a rush of adrenaline preparing me for battle, for endless months of severe stress, for fast decision making with too little data, and also for injuries to come. I found myself searching for words in a vain attempt to fill the silence I was producing, but Christine was not one for waiting; she had already made up her mind. In her oil-tanker manner, the rest was only a question of bending the will of oceans.

"I'm not *asking* you, I'm *telling* you. You are the head of Massive now. As soon as Martin leaves the building, call me."

As I began to process it, I had to reluctantly admit that Martin's decision made sense. He'd given everything he had to Massive from the day he'd founded it. He'd spent the last decade steering the Massive ship around dangerous icebergs and through narrow straits. During major stretches of that voyage, he'd been alone behind the helm. He was tired. Very tired. Not of life, but of taming this particular beast. He understood what it would require to start over and prove himself again, and it wasn't a journey that excited him anymore. And temptingly, shining right next to his desire to hang it all up, was the huge severance package from VUG, which would allow him to start a new venture and pursue another dream.

It was true that Martin had negotiated a little with Ubisoft at first, but I think his heart and mind had already journeyed elsewhere. It was perplexing to me, since we'd just hit the big league with the Ubisoft acquisition and would be able to capitalize on everything we'd built. We could finally reach the highest heights possible. *We're in the majors, Martin! This is everything we fought for! This is where it all really begins to pay off!* But where I saw opportunity, he saw too many uphill battles. Where I saw a chance to play with the best, he saw another long and damaging ultramarathon. He had been emotionally out from the start, and now it was official.

So, like it or not, there I was: alone like a bleak and earthbound version of Michael Collins. I had become the managing director of Massive Entertainment.

Hey mister, feel like flying this spaceship solo?
Do I really have to?
Yes, you do.

20

PARIS

It was early 2009, and Sweden was covered in a white blanket of snow. Portentous gray clouds hung over the city.

On a Friday, Martin left the company he'd created. Over the weekend, we transformed his office to a meeting room so that it wouldn't become a monument to the big changes we were about to endure. As much as I'd loved working for Martin, I had to be smart about his departure and signal that the bright future was beginning immediately. A group that owns its own destiny heals faster.

I had discussed the decision to take over as managing director of Massive with my wife, and even though our son and daughter were still young, we convinced ourselves that it would work out just fine, that we'd be able to find a balance. I needed the reassurance, because privately I wasn't so sure about the balance bit. I already felt overworked, as if I had been bouncing around like a pinball in some kind of global game for years on end.

"Let's just rest properly and discuss this all during the ski trip," I suggested. We were planning to go north the following week and teach the kids to ski, with the ambition to build up to future family adventures in the Italian Alps.

Ten minutes after saying that and another conversation with Christine, I found myself canceling the trip altogether.

"We are hosting our annual strategy meeting next week. You will be there," she'd said.

Like a good soldier, I immediately prioritized the tremendous responsibility I felt for the team I'd inherited so unexpectedly. I needed to fight for our jobs and our belief in quality and craftsmanship. Skiing would be for another time, I decided. The mountains weren't going anywhere.

Although I hadn't ever harbored any secret dreams to run the studio, I had in fact spent the last couple of years thinking about how to create internal and external momentum in Massive. This was how Martin and I had functioned for a long time. He'd have ideas, and together with a few other senior people, I'd make sure they became reality. When he hired me, he explained, "I'll just say stuff, and then I need you to make that stuff happen," which was exactly how it had worked.

With Martin gone, I had no time to think about how to replace his vision because I immediately needed to establish a strong relationship with our new overlords in Paris, who were already beginning to wonder if their week-old acquisition was about to fall apart.

I arrived at an expensive-looking restaurant near Les Halles in central Paris, desperately needing a drink, but definitely planning to stay sober. As far as I understood from Pierre, as the new and accidental choice to run Massive, I should "expect some challenging questions." Later I'd learn that this was a typical French version of a pep talk; challenge, frustrate, question, and annoy the hell out of those you love! That way they will take shape, they will show their true form, and the experience will bring you closer to one another.

Once I'd been let inside by the security guards, I shook hands with Alain Martinez, the financial head of the company. He was a good-looking, middle-aged gentleman with a solid, deep voice and snow-white hair styled in a crew cut. Somehow, he was perpetually tanned, like a man who'd been spending all his private time searching for the perfect retirement mansion in the Portuguese countryside.

"Who are *you*?" he asked while his eyes inspected both me and the entire room at once, clearly on the lookout for spies and enemies.

"Well, I'm David, the guy from Massive."

"I thought your name was Martin," he said, his detective sensors noting an anomaly.

I laughed nervously. "You'll have to put up with me. Martin has decided to explore other adventures."

"He left? What a *disaster*!"

"Well, we'll see, I guess," I said.

Three minutes into the strategy meeting, and already I was a disaster? My eyes began searching the room for the closest gin and tonic. It was a closed event, of course, but there were up to a hundred people buzzing around, mostly middle-aged men in suits, many of them hugging and loudly expressing the joy of seeing each other again. *Mon ami! Ça vas? Une autre année de succès!*

I spotted a free bartender at the far end of the long bar taking it easy under the huge mirrors reflecting the room. But before I could go anywhere, Alain Martinez grabbed hold of my shoulder and pulled me back.

"I'll tell you something," he said, looking serious.

He leaned uncomfortably close, as if he wanted to really get under my skin.

"*I never wanted to buy you guys,*" he whispered.

I couldn't come up with a clever answer. He leaned in even closer. I could smell his cologne. He spoke slowly, emphasizing each word.

"You guys have a lot to prove. A LOT."

Thankfully, someone shouted from a table nearby: "Hey! NEW GUY! Over here! Come and join us!"

I didn't know it then, but flatteringly, I was being invited to sit with some of the true superpowers in Ubisoft: Christine Burgess, boss of all bosses; Yannis Mallat, the mastermind behind the wildly successful Canadian Ubisoft studios; and Xavier Poix, the French studio veteran, a charming, fun-loving, resilient man. The three of them were responsible for almost all of Ubisoft's best-selling games. Yannis and Xavier were nonjudgmental about Massive, and smart enough to assume that there might be something to learn from everyone. Christine, though, seemed skeptical, and she hinted that the acquisition of Massive had happened when she was on vacation. She made no secret of the fact that I was seen as a long shot.

But of course, none of this lasted very long. One form of discomfort was soon replaced by another! After a glass of wine, they all switched to French, and as far as I could tell, they had an amazing evening together with fantastic conversation and many great insider jokes. I sat there for hours, not understanding a word, feeling like a distant cousin from Albania.

After what felt like an eternity, when etiquette finally allowed, I began planning to make an early escape to the hotel. But on my way to the exit I suddenly bumped into Yves Guillemot for the first time, and I couldn't just walk out. He was a short, tidy-looking, and soft-spoken man, only slightly older than myself. He had gray hair and was wearing a light-blue, well-ironed shirt. He'd thrown his matching dark-blue pullover casually over his shoulders, and to me, it looked a little like a superhero cape.

"Bonsoir," I said in French, trying to make a good first impression.

"Hello!" he exclaimed happily with a big, warm smile, and for the first time in a few weeks I relaxed a little.

After some casual chatter, each with a caipirinha in hand, I took the opportunity to ask him something I was genuinely curious about and wanted to understand.

"Yves, can I ask you: Why did you decide to buy Massive?"

"What do you mean?" he asked in return, looking puzzled.

"Well...," I continued. "To be honest, it wasn't like you did a whole lot of due diligence. I mean, the two guys you sent to visit us were very nice, but it seemed to me they were quite junior, no?"

"Oh, I see," he said, completely at ease. "My decision was unrelated to their visit; it was much easier than that. I saw that you guys had a 90 on Metacritic and that's all I needed to know. If you have that kind of talent, I want to work with you."

This was music to my ears! The company CEO prioritizes quality! I had become so used to the constant battle with publishers focused on money that I'd stopped believing there were any truly interested in the content. Wow. And it was true that we had an average review score of 91 for *World in Conflict*. I supposed that I agreed with his kind of due diligence. Maybe all you needed to know about a developer studio was that they produced excellent games!

As I walked back to the hotel to get some fresh air, a light rain fell on the streets of Paris. The city was still hectic. Families with strollers were out for late-night walks, groups of businessmen hustled into crowded street-side clubs. Everyone was moving fast, as if the high-energy DNA of the capital was pulsing through them. I shrugged off aggressive glances as I sauntered at a slower pace. I had a lot to digest.

This was an opportunity of a lifetime. A great home for Massive.

The next day, Ubisoft's team-building exercise for the studio managers consisted of racing two-seated go-karts in central Paris, which seemed to be a surefire way to kill off the company's key staff. Yannis generously asked me to be his copilot, and clearly showed some interest in further deepening the ties between us. He drove like a maniac as we shouted over the sputtering engine. The beautiful French capital zoomed by as we bounced over cobblestones between century-old houses and boastful modern buildings that reached for the spring sky. Yannis navigated wildly and expertly through pedestrians, tourists, and cafés, not making any new friends in the process.

In a partially successful attempt to say something more than "Watch out!" I yelled out my thoughts on game development and technology, and in return, Yannis loudly gave me some insight into the inner workings of Ubisoft. The uncontrolled drive through the self-proclaimed home of the Enlightenment movement might have sparked our later collaboration on a big Ubisoft game, but at the time I was just happy to step out of the car alive with all my limbs attached.

As I tried to get comfortable in my new role as Captain Disaster, there were in fact a couple of new friends who appeared along-side in pilot boats, offering help. Perhaps most of all, there was Jason Kaminski, the charming half-Polish, half-American guy with a shock of red hair. He showed up on our doorstep in Sweden with a melancholy smile, ready to help. Like Massive, he was new to Ubisoft but already had a clear idea of what he wanted to bring to the mix. Jason was a free spirit, with no interest in a traditional corporate career, and his point of view was immensely refreshing. I was pleasantly surprised to see that Ubi didn't send a business-person to save the acquisition, which was potentially at risk with Martin's leaving. They must have wondered if everyone in the studio was about to join the founder and start an exodus, but still, no business guy showed up on our Swedish doorstep. Instead, our French masters sent Jason: a media junkie, a rebel, an intellectual, a fan of "cheap" entertainment. Jason simply had the eye and the touch. It was exactly the context and environment we needed to feel welcomed by Ubisoft. He was hired to develop IPs and brands for Ubi, and he had the perfect artistic personality to do just that.

Pierre and Jason kept visiting us regularly, making sure we felt like a part of the bigger family. Jason, in particular, was a pure quality nut, which suited us fine, but certainly didn't make us any easier to manage. We listened carefully and cautiously to what Pierre and Jason said, allowing it all to sink in, and ultimately we felt happy to look inward again and focus on what we loved most: the creation process itself. After all, we wanted to make games, and we had been on standby for a long, long time. *World in Conflict* was released in September 2007, and now it was already early 2009. My first important task as the head of the studio was to get things kick-started; we needed to get back in the saddle. As had become my habit, I used my camouflage of a humble and unassuming person to quietly set my target on exceptionally ambitious goals. I wanted to turn Massive into one of the best studios in the world, even though we were barely able to ship any games at the time.

I asked for a meeting with Christine and presented a five-year plan to her. I told her that I assumed Ubisoft had bought us in order to provide value, and then shared my perspective on how to do just that. My conviction was, and still is, that a good studio has the lead responsibility on at least two large brands, both based on the same in-house engine. The studio should also retain a high degree of control over the back-end infrastructure, as well as the consumer-facing activities such as marketing, PR, and community. As far as I was concerned, this was not rocket science; all you needed to do was look at some of the best studios in the world when they were at their peak: id, Valve, Blizzard. All of them had several IPs in parallel projects based on a shared game engine. When I outlined my plan to Christine, although I knew it was ambitious, I nevertheless felt that I was just pointing out the obvious.

Christine listened. She was hard to read. Clearly, she was not in the same part of the stratosphere as I was with my dream-first-and-reality-will-follow philosophy.

"Mmhm," she said, not committing to anything. "Is that it?"

"Yes," I answered. "Two triple-A projects, one engine."

"So, let's put it into perspective," she continued. "You have no triple-A brands today, and the engine you are talking about hasn't been built yet?"

"Yes," I answered.

"And you are...what? Ninety people today?" she asked.

"Yes."

"And your plan requires almost five hundred people?"

"Correct," I said, unfazed. Not because I had the self-confidence of a great actor, but because I was absolutely convinced I was right.

Christine looked at me for a very long time, apparently at a loss for words. I could hear the ventilation system in the Paris office working dutifully to supply the many floors with oxygen. I looked out her office window covering the entire left side of her room from floor to ceiling. Far below, there was a graveyard dotted with hundreds of crosses and ancient tombstones. As I waited, I thought: *A game developer sees a graveyard from the window at the publisher's office, and it perfectly illustrates the moment: That tombstone represents my project...*

"Mmhm, I get it," Christine said after an eternity. "Lead studio on two projects, a new engine. Well...*good luck with that.*"

I'm pretty sure she said it sarcastically, but at the same time, she was clever enough not to kill the ambition. After all, if Massive could achieve even some part of what we wanted, it'd be great for everyone involved. I decided to stick with one of my basic rules: Don't volunteer to compromise. Compromise has an uncanny way of finding you anyway, so you don't need to make it easier. Compromise is an annoying little animal, a demon that has bad intentions. So why open the window and let it in?

I decided that Christine's answer meant "Sure, go ahead," rather than "You're delusional." I also noted that she didn't offer any direct help, which meant that it was up to us at the studio to prove ourselves, but I already knew that.

I went back to Sweden with nothing except the words that echoed in my head: *Well...good luck with that.*

21

THE SAGE

In the classic hero's journey, the young champion or fool always encounters a sage, a mentor, or a wise guru of some sort. In *Star Wars*, Luke Skywalker meets Obi Wan Kenobi; in *The Lord of the Rings*, Frodo encounters Gandalf; and in the Massive story, we met Serge Hascoët, Ubisoft's chief creative director.

We were introduced to Serge soon after the acquisition. As far as we could tell, he was one of the few who had actually been huge fans of acquiring us. He was (and still is) responsible for the entire creative output of the company. Serge himself came from a background similar to that of Yves Guillemot: once a country boy, but now an entertainment industry legend. He worked on the early Ubisoft games as a game designer and learned the craft in the trenches. At some point, Ubisoft made an exceptionally bold choice to partially separate the creative side of the company from the business units, allowing Serge a huge degree of liberty as he built an editorial team responsible for the content of the games. To this day, during a major part of the creative process the Ubisoft development teams interact with only Serge and his team of strange characters, thus partially shielding them from business considerations to make sure that the fragile visionary process is allowed to blossom properly.

In theory, my boss was Christine, but in practice, I decided to build Massive's future in close collaboration with Serge. This was in no way a politically motivated choice, it was just that I understood him well and felt comfortable, even inspired, being challenged by him.

Serge Hascoët was a fantastic character, an original, a gigantic personality. He was just a little bit chubby, and had a warm, discreet laugh that was supported by twin dimples. He resembled one of those small statues of a smiling Buddha. A very well-dressed Buddha. Serge wore elegant Italian-looking suits and extremely neat leather shoes. He spent his days meeting developer teams with complicated agendas in his office in Paris, a nice, cozy room with a lot of Ubisoft memorabilia on the shelves. In Serge's office teams would spend long hours on the big, comfortable sofa and the elegant Danish chairs facing a gigantic TV, on which the guru constantly played and evaluated the games in production. Serge was a hands-on kind of a guy, not one for PowerPoints, and he stated that it was his *duty* to protect the creative talent of the company. It was clear that he was bewilderingly intelligent, but because of his abstract thought process and broken English, speaking with him could be either perplexing or profoundly enlightening. In his attempts to wake people up from their normal thought patterns, Serge would often break social convention. He'd interrupt a meeting to serve champagne at ten in the morning. Or he'd ask someone to bring a Go board game to him so that whomever he was meeting could spend the next hours exploring the ingenious design of the ancient game instead of talking.

In one of our first meetings with Serge, I was in full presentation mode, talking energetically and pointing at something on a screen, fully immersed by the need to build a convincing narrative in the short moment we had with him. It was not so different from what I had been doing for years: pitching, promising, and sometimes pretending. *Trust me, goddamnit!*

In the middle of a sentence, I suddenly felt Serge's warm breath right behind my ear, only millimeters away, and before I knew it, he growled weirdly.

"RRRRROOAR," he said, in a low baritone, very much sounding like a real lion.

"What!" I cried, jumping forward.

"Rrrrrrrroooarrrr," Serge purred again, with apparent pleasure, like a cat that had just caught hold of a ball of yarn.

I realized he did this all the time. He had developed a million tricks to push people off-script, to force them out of their preprogrammed comfort zones. He was creating situations where everyone had to reevaluate their own patterns, to be in the present, fully and dangerously real. When he was looking for the right words, he'd close his eyes for an excruicatingly long time and make a sound as if his brain were a busy mechanical machine: "*tokk-tokk, tokk-tokk, tokk-tokk*." It would last for a while. When people seemed to doze off, Serge would suddenly fill the room with an ear-deafening Michael Jackson–inspired falsetto scream, as if something particularly pleasing fell into place in his mind at that very moment. It was theater, but a natural version of it. A method to open minds.

I remember a team making a pitch for a shooter game, and Serge's reply was that he was dreaming about atoms. Another time when I showed him an early prototype of the Manhattan we created for a then-secret project, his answer was that he "hated pumpkins." I've heard him try to explain the merits of smoking as a good production tool, and I've seen him throw the controller at the TV screen when playing games, smashing both. After a particularly long and deep presentation that he didn't like, his only comment was that we needed to talk more about *love*. But none of this was as weird as it might seem, because if you embraced his feedback and kept asking questions, you'd eventually realize that he was incredibly accurate and almost always right. The trick was to keep asking and not get confused by the metaphysics.

Serge and Yves had something specific in mind when they acquired Massive. Once they felt more comfortable with us, they revealed their plan.

"Do you think you can modernize Clancy?" they asked. "Maybe turn it into an MMO or an online role-playing game?"

The French publisher controlled all the interactive rights to the name Tom Clancy. In a legendary deal, Ubisoft had sweepingly acquired the exclusive worldwide rights to create and release games with the author's name attached.

There were already several great Clancy-branded games out there, most of them originating from the Red Storm studio, and although they were mostly commercial successes, there was a widespread (but vague) feeling that the brand was becoming stale and old. The very first game Red Storm created in the series was based on a novel by Tom Clancy named *Rainbow Six*, a techno-thriller set in the secretive world of multinational counterterrorism. From 1998 on, there have been more than twenty releases, counting expansion packs and mobile games.

In 2001, Red Storm launched Tom Clancy's *Ghost Recon* (my old favorite game!), which put the player in charge of a fictional squad of US Special Forces that execute classified missions in far-away places, behind enemy lines. The series would march on to the same levels of global success as the *Rainbow Six* series, establishing an evergreen financial foundation for Ubisoft.

Once Ubisoft had acquired Red Storm and all the interactive rights to the name Clancy, a team in Ubisoft Montreal began exploring another, even more innovative game that was eventually released in 2002, soon after the first *Ghost*. The game had been developed as a hard-core stealth game, focused on a single agent called Sam Fisher, who works for a black-ops subdivision within the NSA. The players are given precious few technical and violent tools on infiltration missions, in which often only acrobatic skills or the understanding of shadows was the solution. Tom Clancy's *Splinter Cell* is still recognized as an industry benchmark, and the series became one of Ubisoft's flagship brands.

In spite of the enormous success Ubisoft had enjoyed under the Clancy umbrella, there was a strong feeling that something new was needed, and in a mix of analysis and wild optimism, Serge connected a whole bunch of dots and decided that Massive would be the right place for the innovation. To be honest, we felt that it was far-fetched and perhaps a little too ambitious for us at the time.

Out of respect to Red Storm, we politely asked HQ if they shouldn't ask the Americans to do it, but without any more detail, we were told that this wasn't an option and also to hurry up. Back to our own bunker then. We gave the project the code name Rogue, and I asked the team to start reading Clancy books and playing Ubisoft's Clancy games. In what we found to be a very French use of language, Ubisoft called their request "A Mandate," and as we soon realized, without such a Mandate (capital *M*), you weren't allowed to invest any time in anything in Ubisoft. Project Rogue was our first official Mandate after the acquisition, so it was no surprise we were excited.

We started our exploration for the new game in obvious Clancy territory: stealth, special forces, undercover missions, punishing gameplay, international politics...We read a lot of Clancy books and replayed the existing games over and over. Soon, we began drifting away from the initial ideas and first-day assumptions. "No soldiers" was a phrase that resonated instinctually with all of us, although at first we didn't know what it might mean for the game. Our brilliant writer Christofer Emgård focused on exploring new and meaningful interpretations of Clancy memes. "A nuclear war doesn't feel particularly like a 'clear and present danger' today, does it?; Crime lords in Peru... That certainly doesn't feel like something we should explore," he mumbled. We left him alone, trusting that he'd figure something out, given enough time. Meanwhile, the rest of the small team focused on gameplay that included shooting and looting, lots of it. We really wanted to use strategic positioning and covers to a higher degree than in previous Clancy games, and someone coined the incredibly nonsexy phrase "location-based management" to describe this key feature, making it sound like a game about taxi-driving more than anything.

Once the Rogue team and the development strategy for the project was in place, I realized I still needed another vehicle to carry Massive forward, another Mandate. We caught Serge off-guard when he was visiting us see how the project was progressing. Once we'd updated him on Rogue, we took Serge to another part of the office where we showed him a prototype called Storm. It had nothing to do with Rogue, which was developing into a third-person role-playing game, as opposed to the Storm prototype, which was a first-person shooter. We'd had only enough time to invest in a truly short demo, but it was slick and action-packed, and, most importantly, the controls were perfect and delivered a sense of true mastery to the player. We had utilized an old trick, setting up the player in a confined space while receiving a short (and frankly ridiculously generic) brief: It's the future, you are a space marine, you are being sent down to this place on the surface of [insert cool planet name here] in a small pod. *BOOM!* Crash-land! *BOOM!* The doors to the pod are removed in a controlled explosion! *RAT-A-TAT-TAT-TAT!* Enemies are trying to kill you! Go nuts.

I could tell that Serge wasn't impressed by the backstory, but at the same time, he leaned in as soon as the action began and started firing like a madman. This was the opposite of stealth subtlety; this was fireworks, explosions within explosions.

Apart from a low growling noise, he finished the demo in thoughtful silence, asked no questions, and left without any comment. But there was something in his eyes that lingered on the screen, and we thought we could see that at least we'd planted a seed in his head.

Rogue would be fine, I felt confident about that, but it had all the signs of a slow-burner, like something that would get lost in conception for quite awhile, and in the meantime, we desperately needed something else. Something to keep the majority of the team busy, something for the business, something to *prove ourselves*. I had not forgotten the words from the CFO, Alain Martinez: *You guys have a lot to prove. A LOT.*

22

MONTREAL

One day in June 2009, I found myself in a parking lot outside Visby on the Swedish island of Gotland, supposedly on vacation, speaking to Pierre at the Ubisoft head office about a new and bigger adventure for Massive, in parallel to Rogue. I was sitting in the car with the doors closed to shield out the early summer wind, which made it sound as if I were in the middle of a tornado. Even so, it was a hot day, at least for Sweden.

"Would we be interested in working on *Far Cry 3*?" Pierre asked.

If there was one thing I wanted to change at Massive now that I was in charge, it was our reputation as a studio that could make only RTS games for PCs. Well, it wasn't just a reputation problem, it was a real problem. In fact, all the games we'd released up until that point were just that: real-time strategy games for PCs. We were limited because our own tech didn't even work on the consoles that had become the most important machines for gamers, the Xbox 360 and the PlayStation 4. Our "PC-only" tech strategy seemed to me an obvious and limiting mistake by the "old" Massive, Martin's Massive. And also, as far as I was concerned, the real-time strategy genre itself was in commercial decline, even though some of the finest RTS games had just been released. It was as if this particular category of games had proudly reached a fantastic peak, but now found itself strangely lost, without direction. All the highest mountains had been climbed, it seemed: Relic's game *Company of Heroes*, our own *World in Conflict*, the *Command & Conquer* series, *Age of Empires* by the legendary Ensemble Studios, and of course Blizzard's *WarCraft II* and the aged *StarCraft*. The RTS genre had nowhere to go, and anyway, the general opinion was that complex strategy games wouldn't fit on consoles, due to the difference in how the gamer played the game (pad versus keyboard) and the distance to the screen (three meters versus thirty centimeters). My belief was that in order to adapt to the future and become truly relevant, Massive needed to change both genre and platform, and *Far Cry*, being a solid first-person shooter brand for consoles, would suit those aims perfectly.

When I was at E3 in 2003, before I'd become an employee at Massive, I remembered, I sat in a bus with some Vivendi folks, trying to bring their attention to a game called *Far Cry* that I had seen at the show and that had mightily impressed me. It was in development at an unknown studio in Germany called Crytek. To be honest, what they showed at the convention looked more like a powerful tech demo, but it had truly stunning visuals and an original setting for a shooter game: a paradise island.

"Mmm, no," the Vivendi folks on the bus said with certainty. "That game will never ship; it's just a piece of nice technology. Trust us."

Instead, Ubisoft signed the title and it marched on to become a great success and a benchmark for shooters for years to come. And of course, this required a sequel, creatively called *Far Cry 2*, which in turn was developed by Ubisoft Montreal and built on the CryEngine that somehow had become a part of the deal. The Canadian team had rebaptized the engine and called it "Dunia" for reasons now forgotten.

Far Cry 2, then, was a troubled but incredibly promising title that was released in 2008, around the time when Ubisoft acquired Massive. Behind the scenes, it was hotly debated whether the game was a futuristic leap forward or actually an irreparable mistake, but regardless of internal opinion, the final product had provoked such a mixed response among consumers, it was clear that the future of the brand would depend entirely on *Far Cry 3*.

Ubisoft's creative guru Serge had asked the team in Montreal to work on something nicknamed *Far Cry Redux*, which in essence was *Far Cry 2*, but with all the gameplay flaws and other issues fixed. However, even to the people working on *Redux*, it wasn't clear if the initiative was intended to be released as a product in itself, or if the project was only a necessary exercise that would prepare everyone for *Far Cry 3*.

These were the conditions when Massive came on board with the project. We found it to be a bit of a confused mess. To make things worse, Massive was possibly one of the most annoying codevelopment partners Montreal could have chosen. Sure, we would bring a whole army of talented and professional developers to the project, but it was never a secret to us that our only reason for joining the project was to advance our own agenda. There was nothing hidden or arrogant about it; we simply didn't know how the ecosystem worked, and we approached things in our own naive way.

Far Cry 3 was intended to be our Ubisoft "university" as far as we were concerned. Like school, the project offered a chance to learn a million things in a protected environment, with good teachers and interesting new friends. While Montreal was optimistically trying to figure us out and possibly build a long-term relationship, we were there only to make a calculated statement about ourselves and then move on. We had exactly zero ambition to remain in a role as a support studio to Montreal.

Far Cry 3 was touched by three of the best creative directors I have met in my career. When we joined, we were excited to see that a former Relic employee, Josh Mosqueira, was in charge of the game. He was a short, stubby guy with a low-key and humble attitude. Based on previous competition between the Relic RTS games and ours, we had a tremendous amount of mutual respect and found plenty of inspired and pleasant ways to cooperate creatively. On our side, we had only one established creative director, so it was obvious that Soundboy would be Josh's counterpart in Sweden. Team Petter and Soundboy continued to work in the close partnership they'd established on *World in Conflict*, and to the outside world, they seemed like an inseparable duo. It was problematic that Montreal-based Josh was new to Ubisoft, too, and as a cross-Atlantic team, it seemed we were not following the internal processes as they were meant to be played. We were jazz guitarists who had accidentally joined a pub rock band.

At the time, Ubisoft were the masters of off-line, single-player, and story-based games, but the industry trend was creating an urgent demand for online game modes. Sony and Microsoft had heard the loud message from the PC market: Online was a necessity. The PlayStation 3 and the Xbox 360 had launched with online hardware and software support as an integrated part of their DNA. The prior console standard of two to four players huddled around a single TV quickly morphed into a digital network of connected screens in locations separated by neighborhoods, regions, nations, and continents. The networked machines, headsets with microphones, and built-in messaging systems immediately enabled collaborations, battles, friendships, banter through translation robots, fierce competition, and the helpful exchange of hints and tips. The gamer community became truly global.

The plan at Ubisoft HQ was that Montreal would create an awesome single-player experience, and Massive would add the online components. So far so good. But it turned out to be an incredibly difficult equation to resolve. Our philosophies were very different.

First, we challenged Montreal's game engine, which in comparison to our own tech was slow, clumsy, and actually didn't look all that great on-screen. This was due for the most part to the lighting in Dunia, and we added a lot of improvements on that side, which indirectly became a challenge to some individuals in Canada who thought we were overstepping our boundaries. Second, we challenged the controls, an essential part of a shooter game. Gamers expect perfect control, down to the last microsecond, especially in multiplayer games where auto-aiming shouldn't be used. Auto-aiming is a piece of code that almost invisibly assists the gamer in finding relevant targets on-screen. Well executed, it makes gamers feel skilled, but in multiplayer it feels more like cheating and unsettles the balance considerably.

We built a physical machine called the Frankenstein controller, which allowed us to measure and retroactively map out the control scheme of any game. It was a wonderful-looking piece of hardware, like an oversized steampunk part of an ancient cockpit. By meticulously adjusting the knobs in the various settings, we could get hard data from any game we plugged into. We could measure acceleration and movement, map the code of all our favorite shooter games, and rearrange the control scheme in *Far Cry 3* to suit a multiplayer game. Through this painstaking process of reverse engineering, we eventually designed and rewrote the code for the game's controls and turned them into perfection. This infuriated our partners in Montreal.

Some mornings we'd come to work only to discover that someone across the Atlantic had changed all our settings to better suit the single-player adventure they were developing. Of course we changed them back, aware that it would screw up their workday, just as they had ours.

As much as we were doing our best to improve the game, I have to admit it seemed more and more like we were just being dicks. But there is one thing about Massive that has been true throughout the years: Our loyalty always lies with the project; everything else is secondary. I was infuriating both Paris and Montreal with statements such as "We're not making this game for you. We are making the game for the sake of quality," defiantly making it clear that they had no real way to control us. Which was true. They could influence our decisions only with convincing arguments for how to make the game better.

Yannis Mallat, the managing director of Ubisoft's Canadian studios, flew over to Sweden and bought us an incredible dinner accompanied with a few bottles of excellent wine, trying to understand us better and improve the collaboration. A few years later, once the game had shipped, we met in LA and he leaned over his cup of coffee and whispered, "If I had known you guys were so Alpha, I would never have worked with you." But at the time he didn't know what he wanted to know, and anyway, in our nerd hearts, we had never thought of ourselves as *alpha*.

Ultimately, it was not Yannis's love and attention we craved, even though that was a pleasant bonus. To us, *Far Cry 3* was a project that allowed us to shine and build our own future, not to make friends. But while we'd been busy forging our own paths, it turned out that the entire project was about to fall apart for reasons that had almost nothing to do with us.

23

HIS MAJESTY WANTS TO PLAY

I looked at the email in slight disbelief. (In my head it came with an appropriately elaborate font.)

> Dear Managing Director David Polfeldt, Would you be so kind as to give his Royal Majesty a tour of your company?

The King of Sweden? Really?! When did a video game studio become eligible for an official visit from His Royal Highness?

From about 2010 onward, I started to notice a small change in how people outside the game industry perceived it. We were gradually met with more respect, more interest, more fascination, more envy, and it was eventually impossible for the establishment to ignore the fact that every year, Sweden's largest cultural export product was a video game. If it wasn't DICE's *Battlefield*, it was Starbreeze's *The Darkness* or *The Chronicles of Riddick*, or Avalanche's *Just Cause*. Studios would come and go, briefly hitting the top of the international sales charts, and the heritage of success would eventually give birth to international hit games like *Candy Crush*, *Minecraft*, the rebirth of the *Wolfenstein* and *Battleground* games, and behind them a rich plethora of almost perfectly crafted interactive entertainment products. The masters of cultural export were no longer the musicians behind the Britney Spears singles, the reissues of ABBA albums, or Avicii. Nor were they the children's books coming from the deep treasure chest of Astrid Lindgren, or the modern wave of Swedish crime novels.

It took some time for this to sink into the common psyche. It was hard for many to suspend their belief that computer games were made just by nerds, for a tiny nerd audience, and that they were not only violent but sexist, and dangerous for the young. Eventually, a few local politicians asked to visit the studio and get a tour. They immediately realized we were creating a lot of jobs, and decided they liked it. They would pass the message upstairs, and soon national politicians and ministers showed up at our doorstep too. Sometimes they were genuinely interested, but other times they just wanted to take a photo to post on social media to appeal to young potential voters.

I became somewhat of a poster boy for the industry, due to my commitment to a few charities and my opinions about the responsibility that falls on the corporate world. I believe that we build society together, whether we're private companies, government agencies, or nonprofit organizations. If you have power, you have responsibility; it's as simple as that, and the responsibility grows with your power. Since I managed to voice this opinion while consciously avoiding partisan politics, I was perceived by a growing group of people as a good choice to represent the Swedish game industry. Also, I do enjoy talking and making presentations, so I came with a nice buzz of entertainment value too—like a modern court jester, I suppose. My poster-boy career peaked when I actually had dinner at the Swedish royal castle with the queen herself, but at the time, all I had was an email from a royal staffer, telling us that the king wanted to check us out. *Well, I guess that counts as some form of recognition*, I decided.

The coolest part of the king's visit was the preparation by the Secret Service men, who, I realized, had already done a background check on me and decided I was not plotting to kidnap His Majesty.

The bodyguards/ninjas searched the entire Massive office, looking for anything that could threaten the integrity or safety of the visit. Silent, fit men in black suits, all of them tall and blond. Once they were satisfied with the preparations, they took up positions around the expected route of the tour and stood perfectly still, like statues with a bottled-up capacity for instant violence. I wondered if the king had brought an official taster to drink his coffee and check for poison too. *What an exciting job!* I thought. Eating magnificent food all day, with the added excitement of knowing that every bite might be the very last one.

We made an effort to tidy up our office, but only partially succeeded. Massive, like most game studios, tended to look like a mix between a boring white-collar office and a shy, merchandise-hoarding teenager's bedroom.

The king arrived with his posse, and we did our usual thing: traditional Swedish cinnamon rolls, coffee (no taster, to my disappointment), and a studio tour. I made a presentation that covered Massive's history, our games, and our approach to management. I'd done this many times, beginning back in 2008 when Activision broke up with us and we were trying to find a new home for Massive. I had just kept building and improving on that same presentation until it became an intense explosion of thoughts, videos, and narrative twists that would usually knock the audience over. I was very comfortable. Somewhere in the back of my head I knew that regardless of how I was doing, what the Swedish king thought would make absolutely no difference to my reality.

Suddenly he raised his hand like a schoolboy asking for permission to speak. It felt weird nodding in approval to him, but he seemed to be willing to wait with his hand raised forever.

"Yes," I said. "You." And I pointed directly at him in a strangely demanding way. Then I remembered my manners and quickly added, "*Your Majesty.* Yes?" I'd been told not to address the royal presence by his name, Carl Gustaf, or with a common "you."

"Your *Majesty*! There seems to be a question?" I added with emphasis.

"I might be stupid, but I wonder something," he said, in a classic display of the Swedish tradition of downplaying oneself. *You gotta be humble in Sweden!*

"I don't really understand why games work so well?" the king continued, his statement taking on the tone of a question.

"Uh. You mean technically?" I asked, a bit confused, expecting to explain relatively basic hardware and software stuff.

"No," he said. "As a *medium*. I don't understand why it is more fun than TV or movies. I see that the audiences for the old entertainment forms are shrinking. The young seem to spend a tremendous amount of time playing games. It makes me wonder. Why?"

Such a great question, I thought, and as my unprepared mind began to actually process it, I realized I had no answer ready, just instincts. And then it all came to me, a whole range of insights that I'd never verbalized before. I thought about how the game medium is the best medium ever created, and that the form will overshadow all old forms of entertainment for very good reasons. I finally understood that the industry was not only moving toward respectability, but was on its way to completely dominating the media landscape, maybe forever.

Is it possible that video games are better, more powerful, and even more democratic than TV, movies, theater, opera, music, radio, literature, or any other kind of classic media? Would it be fair to claim that interactive games are fundamentally more pleasing, rewarding, and healthy too?

Thinking about it further, I realized that if nothing else, games have two major advantages over all classic media: (1) the way games engage with an audience's senses; and (2) the role of the hero.

All old media forms engage an audience through one or two senses, hearing and/or sight. Music reaches us only through hearing, but on the other hand, rhythm and melody seem to touch us biologically in such a way that they really engage the emotions.

Literature relies on sight. Radio relies on hearing. Opera, theater, TV, and movies reach us through both sight and hearing and are incredibly powerful media. The percentage of activated senses is in the range of 20 to 40, not even half of the scale. Games, however, push our percentage activation to 60, because they use sight, hearing, *and* touch. It sounds banal, but the effect is tremendous. While the old forms of media are relying on the cerebral, games reach the audience with both the tactile *and* the cerebral, which totally changes the experience in the brain. What the fingers and hands are doing is directly linked to events and situations in the experience, and even the slightest flick of a finger can have a major and instant impact in the game world. Of course, this requires a completely different level of attention and engagement from the audience. It's access, it's being the hand of God, it's *My hands on the steering wheel.* The level of direct interaction with the game worlds becomes more and more complex and satisfying for every year that passes, as the medium continues to emerge and to fundamentally reshape the relationship between storyteller and audience.

Second, games are masterful at delegating the role of the hero to every single person who plays them. Imagine if someone said that they'd write a book and the hero of the book would be every person who read it. How could they? But in games, this is what happens: The designers create a world, a sandbox with some rules and boundaries. As soon as the game starts, the player is the hero. The entire game will revolve around that individual's personal choices, pace, and direction. We don't dictate these things; we just give the player a set of tools and toys and a premise. The rest is created in cooperation. The player gives input through their hands, driven by strategy developed in their brain, and then the game responds with feedback, narrative, and effects. It's an intimate dance, in which exactly every person in the audience has one of the main roles to play.

A good game trusts the player with key choices, like where

to go, when to go there, what to do, and how fast or slow the chosen quest should be accomplished. In comparison, linear media, like TV, books, opera, film, or theater, seem almost unbelievably insulting, narcissistic, and arrogant. It's as if the old-school entertainment forms are convinced that their choices are so amazing that thousands and thousands of people should just passively admire them. Games are the opposite; they assume that each gamer has a valid opinion about key moments of the experience, and they trust the individual to use that power cleverly. Interactivity is largely a democratic, cocreative media.

It's very easy to single out bad games, but the point here is not about the quality of any specific product. I don't claim that games today necessarily deliver a higher-quality experience than opera, I'm just saying that the fundamental DNA of interactivity is much more sophisticated, and that is why I'm sure interactive media will one day dominate all other forms of entertainment. There will be many opportunities for passive media, for sure, but those experiences will ultimately be perceived as someone else's postcard, message, perspective, emotion, or point of view. Compared to that, games will feel personal, privately social, important, close, and genuine.

Ultimately, the brain is a demanding beast. It consumes more energy than any other body organ. Because of that, a large part of what keeps *Homo sapiens* busy is trying to reduce the processing burden on the brain. It's perhaps a sad insight, but I believe that from a biological standpoint, we'd essentially prefer to think *less than we do*! As a side effect, we have excellent systems in place to ensure that we don't actively process a large part of what's happening to us. The "lazy" systems apply pattern recognition and previous conclusions in order to deduce, at lightning-fast speed, what's being sensed from the outside world. What we think we perceive is a very small fragment of everything that's really going on. It makes sense if the plan is to save energy: Imagine if you had to actively see, interpret, and process every single thing you lay your eyes on when walking down a street. Every stone, lamppost, piece of garbage; every person and what they're wearing and how they smell and sound as they walk by. And so on. It would make you psychotic within minutes. It's necessary for the brain to set itself in a passive, automated mode that doesn't cost precious energy. Perception is a construction of our minds.

There is a wonderful experiment, called "the invisible gorilla," that proves how efficient the brain is in reducing signals in order to spare itself from the processing burden of attention. The test subject is asked to watch a short video of two teams playing basketball. One of the teams has dark shirts, and the other has light. Rather than count the number of points, the viewer is asked to count the number of successful passes per team as they play. All right, that sounds easy enough; and hooray, that's all we need to focus on! After watching the video, the test subject reports the number of passes per team, usually successfully, or at least very close. The point is: It doesn't matter, because when the test subject is asked if they noticed the grown man in a gorilla suit who walked across the court in plain view, it turns out that almost no one did. Once told about the gorilla, when the video is replayed people immediately see him walking onto the screen, stopping in the middle, and even giving a little wave to the camera. It seems impossible that we could miss this figure standing there in plain view, but the truth is that almost all of us do!

How is this possible? It seems obvious, then, that the brain naturally gravitates toward *ignoring* input. That poses a difficult challenge for those of us creating media and entertainment, and it is entirely possible that games and interactive media have an extreme advantage over all the classical media. It's not only the higher number of senses involved, it's also the fact that the gamer has a high degree of control and is directly involved in what's going on, which generates ever-changing, new patterns. Interactivity and choice *demand* attention. The level of engagement in a game requires the brain to be fully in the present and to actively engage in the experience. And even though game designers intentionally add surprise and plot twists, almost all games on the market today reward personal choice, exploration, autonomy, and agency. It's simply an amazing form of fun.

Games offer a form of dialogue, as opposed to the monologue of the traditional forms of entertainment. Games are holistic and spiral into a web of alternative stories. Games are Technicolor rather than monochrome. And the game world revolves around each member of the audience, putting them at the center of the universe.

Now, I didn't think fast enough to say all of this to the Swedish king; my observations were better verbalized later. But at least I came up with a simplified version of the same thoughts, and he seemed pleased. A long silence followed. Some part of my brain wondered if I'd simply bored him.

"Well, I don't play games," he said.

I couldn't tell if he was just unimpressed or if he was feeling sad that he was missing out on all the fun.

24

PENROSE

Christian, the former engine team lead on *World in Conflict*, had a project prototype that was coming along nicely, and I thought we should invest more time in it. His passion and enthusiasm were contagious, but thanks to *Far Cry 3* and the Rogue project, everyone at Massive was as busy as ever, and there was no one available to help him. Nevertheless, we sat down together, huddled over his PC, played the demo over and over, and began brainstorming.

Being a programmer, Christian had obvious limitations as an artist, and as a result the world he had built was very simple, consisting mostly of square, clean, 90-degree shapes that resembled concrete. Perhaps seen only through the lens of my art school background, the simplistic design elegantly echoed the gameplay, which gave the player the opportunity to spawn solid blocks anywhere they wanted in 3-D space. Point and click, and presto! A block would appear, and then more! Ramps, disks, magnetic and surfing platforms, long-jump and antigravity blocks, and laser beam reflectors.

Christian had created a lot of variation revolving around the same basic concept, and it was rich, tidy, methodical, and had the trademark of a relaxed but confident designer. Originally, the gameplay made use of the ability to create blocks to produce straightforward one-on-one multiplayer shoot-outs, which quickly became complex and fun even with quite simple rules for the blocks. The large LEGO-like shapes would soon turn into a maze that opened multiple routes of free 3-D navigation for the players, and every match became a new experience. We enjoyed playing the rough prototype—it was as simple as that. Maybe we should have stopped there, but we had too much fun, and as we played and chatted, we discovered a lot of similarities in our personal tastes that spurred us on even further.

Christian was one of those engineers who understood good lighting, so in contrast to the simple shapes he'd used to create his world, the light was phenomenally advanced, beautiful, and gave the prototype a poetic feeling. He'd been using an image from the movie *2001* as a reference, but to my art school eyes, his game made me think of brutalist architecture and the Japanese architect Tadao Ando, who had developed an extremely delicate style based on just concrete and light.

I gave Christian a few reference photos and some texture advice, and, quickly, the demo turned into something special, without any tweaks to the gameplay. He was a one-man show, and it seemed to me that he could do anything. Next, we brainstormed a little with Tobias, my old trailer-creating partner from the *WiC* days, about the context, the setting, and the narrative. What if the game-to-be was single-player instead of multiplayer? What if we steered away from the primitive shooting and created something more subtle? What would it be? Christian and I dove deeper into our personal favorites and discovered that we were both huge David Lynch fans. His surreal movies and TV shows were impressionistic, clever, and intentionally weird, which made us obsessed with understanding and decoding them. Maybe *this* is where we should have stopped, but by then we were on a high and just accelerated.

Christian started doing Escher-inspired mazes with his blocks, and then he created a Magritte-styled portal, where the space you could see through the opening mysteriously led to a completely different type of volume in an entirely different place. Two worlds, joined by only the raw frame of a portal. The effect was surreal and very inspiring. We had never seen anyone do such a thing, even though in engineering terms it was actually very easy to achieve. We called the project Penrose, after English mathematician Roger Penrose, allegedly a master of relativity, cyclical universes, and geometrical objects in the Minkowski space—but I really had no idea what all that meant. Maybe Christian did.

Together with Tobias, we came up with an esoteric story about a girl who found herself on top of an island where she had to enter the strange world we were creating. The girl navigated with her block ability through increasingly complex spatial puzzles. We called her Renard, which is the French word for "fox" (because she was cunning), and gave her a red ponytail that looked just a little like a fox's tail. The *Far Cry 3* art director at Massive took a few hours from the crunch he was in and helped us out with some concept art, and we ended up having Tobias make a small trailer for it.

At this point, my old marketing skills came into use as we started work on a presentation. Still, we had no team available, but we decided it was time to show our work to Serge, if for no reason other than just to get closure and get drunk in disappointment if he turned us down. But of course we didn't *want* to see Christian's fragile dream die; we hoped that at least Serge would allow us to make an Xbox Arcade game, which we estimated would require a team of ten people working on it for a year.

Microsoft had made a bold decision in 2004 when they launched Xbox Live Arcade, a digital platform for downloadable indie games, available through the Xbox hardware. It had become a big driver for innovative game design and a bubbly, inspiring alternative for game developers who found themselves involved in a project that had true promise but perhaps lacked commercial potential. In comparison to the monster-sized triple-A projects, putting ten people on an Arcade project seemed like a small ask. At the time, the largest teams in the industry consisted of between six hundred and nine hundred people, and they might be working at that strength for two to three years. Making games wasn't getting cheaper, that was certain.

Christian made the first trip to Paris all alone. He was extremely excited to go, but nervous, of course. Surrounded by corporate mythology as he was, it took some guts to see Serge alone and show a prototype. But it seemed that there was nothing to worry about. I soon got an email from Serge's assistant asking us to come back with a more developed pitch.

A few weeks later we were in the air again, working on our final slides all through the flight and disturbing our fellow passengers with our constant loud cries of encouragement and excitement. Another visit to Paris, another visit to Serge's office. This was becoming a nice habit. When we arrived, we were told that the man himself was in a bad mood because someone else had made a huge mistake, and *Don't get your hopes up*. But counter to the parade of negativity, once we met Serge it turned out that he was in excellent spirits. Either he was honestly happy to see us, or he was just very good at concealing his frustration, or maybe the stern warning we'd received was just another one of those strange pep talks. We didn't know, and as far as we were concerned, the meeting was starting well.

At the time I'd finally realized a very old dream of mine, which was to buy an Italian three-piece suit, making me feel as if I were a character in the TV series *Mad Men*. Being in Paris made the look feel just right.

"Hello, David," Serge said. "Why are you dressed like the Syrian ambassador?" he asked.

We showed Serge everything we'd been working on, and he spent a long time playing around with the now-expanded demo, filled with puzzles and mysterious spaces, riddled with the heavy symbolism that we'd added. We had been having a good time: Reflections in water pools contained Morse code. Disconnected parts of the rooms would jell into meaningful shapes if you studied them from the right place. Rooms would seem to repeat themselves in repetitive loops, although every time the player stepped into them, they'd be ever so slightly different. In one particular place, you'd see yourself leave the room just as you entered it. And so on. It was packed with intellectual and showy ideas. Christian had really been hard at work, that much was evident. Serge played and played, sometimes stopping to make his *tokk-tokk* sound as he thought about what to say. Finally, he spoke.

"How many people are working on this?"

"It's just Christian," I said, suddenly feeling a bit embarrassed about my pretentious and artsy additions to the project. For the numbers-oriented, the team was twice as large as I had claimed. Serge raised an eyebrow and looked at me, probably calling my bluff, but he was polite enough not to comment on it.

"Good. Rrrroaaar. I like it. It's a go!" he said. And immediately we were ushered out by his assistant to make room for someone else waiting outside.

A *go*! Fantastic.

Now, we faced the challenge of figuring out what a "go" actually meant for this project. We still had no team. No producer, no game designer, no art director, no narrative. Before heading back to the airport, we celebrated briefly with a cold beer and peanuts and began to brainstorm about what to do next. As the studio manager, I knew that we shouldn't distract either the Rogue or the *Far Cry* team by moving people to Penrose, so we would have to hire every single team member if this was going to happen. No problem. Our recruiter was good, and he had a good network of people he'd been pushing me to hire.

Slowly but safely, we gathered a few talented developers around Christian, and in particular we found Basse, one of the best technical artists I have ever met. He, too, understood and embraced the art style, except he was a lot more talented than I was. His arrival meant that my contribution as an artistic mastermind on the project was over, which was just as well. The rest of the studio needed my attention, and as I was getting lost in the Penrose labyrinth, I'd been getting some complaints about favoritism. Basse was a former skater with a wiry build. He had a lot of colorful tattoos, and to our disbelief he actually had real vampire teeth, which showed when he laughed. It felt as if we'd hired Dracula's Californian grandson. The chirpy one.

Christian flew to the Ubisoft studio in Ukraine and came home with a whole bouquet of amazing Ukrainian programmers, who quickly adapted to Sweden and became the backbone of the Penrose engineering team. Apparently, he'd had quite an adventure in Kiev, with black taxis, fur hats, vodka, Communist monuments, and parties. Maybe it was just as well that the trip was short. Who knows what would have happened otherwise?

The team quickly reached a peak of twenty. The group developed the vibe of a proper indie studio, and we all saw the project as a way to explore the meeting between interactivity and art. It was unapologetically pretentious of course, just the way we loved it. That was okay. None of us harbored any dreams about commercial success or even good reviews on this strange project. But back in Ubi HQ, discussions that we were unaware of would soon change everything. Penrose was unexpectedly about to go ballistic in terms of spotlight and commercial expectations.

25

ASSASSIN'S CREED: REVELATIONS

The phone lit up. It was Serge. My adrenaline kicked in. He never called unless it was extremely urgent, and I began indulging in paranoid fantasies, making up more bad news than any reasonable person would dream up in the two seconds it took me to pick up.

"DAVID!" Serge exclaimed, not at all sounding like a man about to deliver bad news. "How are you?"

"Fine, I suppose. And you?" I answered, not knowing what to expect.

"Excellent!" he continued. "Listen, I want you to fly to Ubisoft Montreal and talk to Seb over there. We need you to be the present in the next *Assassin's Creed*, okay?"

I had no idea what this meant. To be the *present*? Like some kind of gift? *Assassin's Creed*? Ubisoft's masterpiece? One of the biggest game franchises on the planet, with millions and millions in sales? My brain was struggling to comprehend.

"Okay, speak soon. Let me know how it goes," Serge said and hung up.

It took us a few days to figure out what he meant, and the reality of it made us dizzy. *Assassin's Creed*, developed by Ubisoft Montreal, had been widely recognized as a masterpiece. The first game in the series was released in 2007. Its success elevated Ubisoft to new heights, and, ever since, a large part of the entire organization had been devoted to developing new entries in the franchise.

Apparently, the next *Assassin's Creed* game, called *Revelations*, was looking good and was in a healthy state, except maybe for the looming deadline. The game was shipping in a few months and something critical was missing. A key staple in all the *Assassin's* games is time travel, placing the player in the world of today and, from there, reliving "ancestral memories" from other ages. This narrative concept was fundamental to the franchise, and it explained why the games could take place in different historical eras and locations, such as Renaissance Italy, the Holy Land, ancient Egypt, or in Paris during the French Revolution.

The time travel feature was the key that guaranteed the franchise would never grow old, stale, or stuck in one particular setting. Thanks to this fundamental plot device, the entire history of humankind was available to the *Assassin's Creed* creators: an endless pool of amazing and appropriate settings. It was simple and brilliant. This was all as it should be, except that the team working on *Revelations* was under extreme time pressure and had been so focused on their historical setting, Constantinople in 1511, that they'd run out of time to create the modern-day sequences that were integral to the franchise.

And this was where Serge thought that Penrose might fit in. Apparently, the modern-day hero in *Revelations* was in a coma throughout the entire game, and who knew what was going on in his head? Even though it was an extreme long shot, the Penrose project was tasked to create the so-called coma sequences so that the player would be reminded that the Constantinople experience was still just a memory accessed from the present, establishing the narrative reasoning that would allow the next game in the series to take place somewhere else. Clearly, Ubisoft's owners were very particular about such details in their franchises, and they didn't hesitate to go to extreme lengths to be consistent. When Serge had said he wanted us to be the present, he meant it verbatim. Not a gift. He had meant the *now*, the *today*.

It was extremely flattering for the Penrose team; Christian and I loved the idea and embraced it immediately. Dudes! Our little art piece was going to the Big Stage! It was fantastic, and I couldn't believe that Serge trusted us to participate in making the next crown jewel for Ubisoft. The idea excited the business-minded people as well, because now it was clear that Penrose would be a profitable enterprise instead of a hopeless self-fulfilling piece of art.

But the next day, the reality of the bold decision struck us hard. First, we had to re-create everything we'd already produced so that it would run on the *Assassin's Creed* engine, called Anvil. It was exceptionally complicated to go from our clean and focused proto- type code to the enormous multibranched beast that was Anvil. It set us back to zero. The Ukrainian engineers took it stoically, with- out even flinching, and hammered on. "Okay. We do," they said in broken English, and apparently that was that. No complaints what- soever. Basse was happy after the initial system shock, because, in all honesty, Anvil gave him access to a much more sophisticated palette, and the game looked a whole lot better with all the tricks he now had at his disposal.

Seeing the *Assassin's Creed* core team in Montreal up close was a dramatic contrast to what we had experienced with the still-struggling *Far Cry 3* team we knew over there. It was like watching a jet pass up a propeller plane. The *Assassin's* developers were in high gear, every single one of them. Chasing the deadlines like Formula One drivers fighting for the win. Their vast floor in the Canadian office appeared to me like a gigantic and efficient machine. The number of people who had loud opinions was way beyond what was needed to terrify any sensitive creative spirit and silence them forever. We assumed that this was truly what the big league was about. Extreme expectations, extreme talent, extremely opinionated people, extreme spotlight, and every single decision put through the aggressive lens of a billion-dollar franchise. I took mental notes for later. *Maybe*, I thought, *maybe one day this will be us*. But I quietly decided that we would build our Massive ship differently, because I wasn't convinced that I liked everything I saw. There was too much machismo there, too much aggressiveness.

Penrose wasn't ready for this vortex, and I think Christian and I realized it in an instant. With only a few months to the launch of the game, and Ubisoft's fiscal year result depending on it, we quickly felt that we were out of our depth. Briefly, we tried to talk ourselves out of it, suggesting some alternative solutions, like maybe putting Penrose on the *Assassin's* disc as a free, vaguely related game that could be ignored if gamers wanted to? We imagined that a free surprise game would invite a much more benevolent reception. But it was too late: The gears were in motion, and all we could do was try to catch up while still preserving some integrity.

Sensing the difficulties only remotely, Montreal sent an amazing guy called Pat Plourde to help us out with a few things, and he added a few touches. But there was no time; it didn't matter that he was one of the best. His quiet off-the-record recommendation to HQ was to abort Penrose from *Assassin's Creed* entirely and let it become something on its own. But no. The franchise required the present.

A writer was tasked with the impossible job of wrapping an *Assassin's* narrative around Penrose. *Well, good luck with that*, we thought as he failed. But rather than giving up, Montreal sent another writer, who was given even less time and harder constraints. He was bitter but brilliant, and somehow came up with a narrative that almost worked.

Christian and the core team traveled back and forth to Canada as if they had the worst weekly commute ever, fighting like maniacs to deliver the high-caliber experience everyone expected. Serge complained that the Anvil version of Penrose lacked "salt," which we assumed meant the raw feeling from the original prototype, which indeed was more organic and challenging to play, but it had proven hard to re-create. There was no time to properly analyze what was missing, try as we would. Christian just battled on in his quiet and polite manner, sticking to his guns. Basse and major parts of the team started sleeping in the office on Fatboys, catching short two-hour breaks between ten-hour bursts of work. That way, they could work twenty hours out of twenty-four. Basse had forgotten to bring a toothbrush but found his daughter's tiny pink kiddie toothbrush in his bag, and that was his only hygiene article for a week. Shipping games isn't always pretty.

On November 15, 2011, the release day of *Assassin's Creed: Revelations*, in spite of all the craziness, the project formerly known as Penrose was properly where it should be: on the disc, included as the present in the main game, as had been mandated. We delivered five strange chapters, called "Desmond's Journey," that chronicled the modern-day hero's experiences while in a coma. We were insanely proud of our achievement and quite woozy from the roller-coaster ride. In the Massive studio, the small team raised champagne glasses and promised one another lifelong friendships, even though we all knew they'd have to part ways soon in order to shift their attention to Rogue and *Far Cry 3*, respectively.

Bad thing: The inclusion of the coma sequences in *Assassin's Creed: Revelations* was madly confusing to the press and the gamers, and very few people understood what the heck was going on. In fact, most people hated it.

Good thing: However, the people who enjoyed our parts of the game *totally got it.* Like Serge, for instance. And Jason Kaminski.

Bad thing: We came across as navel-gazing idiots to quite a few of our new acquaintances at Ubisoft.

Good thing: Christian and I became close friends for life.

Bad thing: We didn't make any new friends in Montreal, except Pat and maybe the second last-minute writer, Jeff. (It was hard to tell with him, because he seemed to be at constant odds with the world.)

Good thing: A while later, we got to release some download-able content (DLC) for *Assassin's Creed: Revelations*, an additional piece called "Lost Archive," which was much closer to our original intentions, thanks to the added development time and lack of surveillance from Montreal. Jeff the Writer had added a powerful narrative that told the story of a lost character from the *Assassin's* mythology, which added much-needed context. The DLC left the team with a liberating sense of completion and defiant pride.

All in all, I guess this was what one should have expected when using David Lynch as inspiration, but it gave us an incredible amount of insight into how Ubisoft functioned when it was in high gear, and, later, those hard-earned lessons proved to be especially useful for Massive when we got closer to launching the project we still called Rogue.

We custom-made T-shirts for everyone who had been a part of the adventure, with a Joy Division–inspired *p* logo (for Penrose) on the front, and an appropriate quote from a happy fan printed across the back:

"Wow. Mindfuck, man."

26

SUDDENLY, AMONG TITANS

Once, right at the very beginning of our relationship, Jason Kaminski from Ubisoft's head office asked me if Yves Guillemot, Ubisoft's CEO and one of the founding brothers of the company, knew who I was. This was only a few months after Massive had been acquired by the French publisher, so it was not entirely evident what Jason was trying to tell me.

"Eh, yeah, well, I guess...It depends on what you mean," I replied. "He knows that I exist."

"Well, uhm, okay. What I wanted to say is that you shouldn't worry if you're a bit absent on his radar. It usually takes him five years to notice someone," Jason said, then puffed out some smoke from the cigarette he'd hand-rolled without looking.

Five years?! I thought. Well, it probably made sense in some big-league way. I supposed that a person in his position would be exposed to a regular stream of individuals who all made big promises, had lots of charm, and came with great, game-changing ideas. Yves knew that the game industry is not about making promises, seeing opportunity, or having new ideas; it's all about execution, and, unfortunately, most people simply aren't cut out to deliver. If you even got a chance to visit his office in the first place, I imagined you'd have to be pretty damn good at *something*. Five years. No problem.

But in the end, it seemed I was on a get-noticed fast track. In 2012, only three years and nine months after the acquisition, I got my first personal email from Yves. "David," he wrote mysteriously, "I don't have your phone number. Can you please provide me with it? I need to call." I dutifully replied with my cell phone number and waited. At the time I didn't speculate much about what any of this could mean, but judging from my experience, bad news usually came through HR or the legal team, so I wasn't too anxious.

A few days later, I was in a design review meeting for Rogue when the phone buzzed, a French number. Though admittedly self-aggrandizing, it still secretly pleased my ego to flash the screen at everyone and walk out of the room, moving quickly toward the elevator, signaling I had *very important stuff to deal with*. But regardless of my own vanity, this particular phone call was actually from Yves, as I had expected, and I had no intention to keep him waiting.

"Hey, you're coming to E3, right?" Yves asked me.

"Yes, I am very happy to," I said. I'd always loved E3, and I wanted him to know that I appreciated being sent there by Ubisoft. I rushed through the cafeteria in the Massive studio, headed to my office, which was filled with memorabilia and cherished high-end merchandise, both our own and from those I admired.

"What are you doing on the Wednesday of that week?" the boss asked.

"I honestly don't know yet," I replied. "The schedule keeps changing all the time, but I can make myself available. What do you have in mind?"

"I want you to come to a meeting," Yves said.

I hadn't even reached my office yet, and we were already at the important part of the call.

"Sure, no problem. What's it about?" I asked, intrigued.

"I can't tell you now. Just make time. I'll fill you in later. Got to go now."

He hung up.

Not leaving a single clue.

For a while I could hardly think about anything else and was impatiently trying to figure out how to get more intel. A meeting with Mr. or Mrs. X.?

But I didn't hear anything more about the mystery meeting. When I finally boarded the plane to fly to LA, I wasn't even sure if it was still going to happen. Nevertheless, before I set foot on American soil, I'd developed a theory about whom X might be, and if I was right, everything in my career was about to be taken to an entirely new level. Back home, both Rogue and *Far Cry 3* were keeping us busy, but I started sensing that this meeting would potentially lead to something completely different. This was shaping up to be a defining moment for Massive.

I don't believe much in luck. Sure, there are those moments in elite sports when the ball bounces off the post and off a defender's foot into the goal, but still, luck is not supernatural. Luck starts many, many years before scoring a goal that ricochet's off a defender's foot. Luck started when that player was seven or eight years old and began playing football several times a week, and it accumulated over a decade of practice and intense dedication before the person had a chance to play with the best. My opinion is that it takes a large part of your lifetime and a fantastically long string of personal choices to even be in a position where you can experience a few seconds of good luck.

Sadly, and for the record, I don't believe that bad luck works in the same way. Bad luck seems terrifyingly unreasonable, arbitrarily striking anywhere, out of the blue.

At E3 in 2012, we showed the *Far Cry 3* co-op mode at the Sony press conference. It went reasonably well, but it was a close call, and we knew it. Tuesday passed, and just as I was beginning to accept that the meeting wouldn't happen, I got a text from Yves, telling me when and where to meet him the next day. To my surprise, I found that Serge would be joining us too. Serge made everything better; he always brought a pleasant creative dimension to a meeting, even when it wasn't expected or necessary. It was as if he couldn't allow any moment to be devoid of pleasure, and he was very good at seeing the fragile beauty of almost everything and everyone, everywhere.

We traveled in a shiny black car with darkened windows toward Manhattan Beach.

"Well," said Yves, "you know we made a couple of games with Hollywood, right?"

"Yes, of course," I replied, and thought of the elegant *King Kong* game Ubisoft had developed with Peter Jackson a few years earlier. In the back of my head I couldn't help but embarrassedly compare this with the game Kim and I had once created for *The Third Wave*, light-years removed from big budgets, fame, and international success.

"We don't normally like to invest in IP that we don't own, but if the opportunity is very good, we sometimes engage in collaborations like this," he continued.

"Makes sense. And this is one of those opportunities?"

"Yes, correct," Yves said with a discreet smile, as if he was about to give me a gift that he was particularly proud of picking out for me. "Do you know who the most successful movie director of all time is?"

"Yes, I do," I said, but as the words came out of my mouth, I realized I'd mistakenly thought of George Lucas and the *Star Wars* movies. I stopped myself before I said anything else. *The most successful movie director of all time?* Hang on, it'd have to be James Cameron, writer/director of both *Titanic* and *Avatar*.

"So, then you can figure it out: We'll be meeting James Cameron soon," Yves said casually as he turned to something important happening on his cell phone.

Those words were the sweetest ones I'd heard in quite some time.

We still had a bit of a drive through the never-ending highways of Los Angeles, so I quickly began reading up on Cameron and speed-watching YouTube interviews with him. Cameron talked about processes and work ethics. I needed to understand his thought process—fast.

Cameron this, Cameron that. Fast-forwarding through the crash course. I genuinely liked what I was hearing and reading, and I was particularly impressed with his uncompromising focus on quality. He was almost aggressively pushing the quality-first agenda—indeed, much harder than anyone I'd met—and it was clearly a bit intimidating to some of those around him. In one of the interviews I watched in the backseat of the limo, Cameron almost absent-mindedly dismissed the idea of working with anyone who wasn't world-class. It was elitist, but his reasoning made sense and echoed some of my own emotions: We *already know* it's hard to make the best games and the best movies in the world. In fact, I'm fully aware of that realization even before I get out of bed and have my morning coffee. So why on earth would I need colleagues who tell me something I already know? *It's difficult?* I know that, even without anyone's input. *I know that, all the time.* The only people I really want to work with are those who offer solutions, especially to the hardest problems.

In one interview, Cameron stated that he couldn't work at all with people who expressed the obvious. I quietly admired his ability to be at peace with himself and so hard-core. He didn't ask his team "How do you feel?" or "What can I do to help you?" He simply stared people right in the eye and asked "What do you bring to the project?" And of course, he seemed to ask himself the same question, relentlessly whipping himself to deliver far above expectations, even when he'd already written and directed the two most successful movies in the history of humankind. Not an easy man to satisfy.

We parked the car in a three-story garage right next to the Lightstorm office. A tough-looking guard let us in after some scru-tiny and suspicious eyeballing. Once the elevator bell announced our arrival, we were led to a conference room, passing some of Cameron's private memorabilia along the way. Original props from *Aliens*, *Terminator*, *Avatar*, *The Abyss*...I saw the original sword from *Conan the Barbarian*, which Arnold Schwarzenegger had once given Cameron as a gift. It was impossible not to feel excited, and I allowed it all to sink into my memory. *This might be the closest I'll ever be to Hollywood*, I thought. As a fan, it was priceless, but of course we weren't there to be fans.

Jon Landau, the producer of both *Titanic* and *Avatar*, greeted us as we entered the typical American conference room, with the air-conditioning turned to "Arctic" and thick blue carpet that muted our footsteps. As I've since learned is typical in Hollywood, there were a few unnamed hang-arounds present too. It seems that famous people in the US attract a posse wherever they go. Is it because they want to? Or is it needed? I don't know, and I haven't attracted a posse myself, so I'm not able to tell.

Landau seemed incredibly nice, but I found the mood strangely tense. The famous director was late, and the small talk stuttered and spat like an old truck on a bumpy road.

"You guys having a good E3?"

"Yes."

[PAUSE]

"Yes, it's good."

"Okay. Fine. Okay."

[PAUSE]

[PAUSE]

[PAUSE]

"How's *Avatar 2* going?"

[AWKWARD SILENCE]

[PAUSE]

"Let's wait until Jim is here, okay?"

[PAUSE]

[AWKWARD SILENCE]

[CLOCK TICKING]

Normally, I'd have helped to warm the social climate in the room, but I was the new kid on this particular block, and I was convinced that it was my role to remain quiet until I'd tuned in to everything. As a Swede, I have very limited interest in etiquette, but shutting up seemed like the polite thing to do even to me.

A baritone broke the uneasy silence.

"Hey, I'm sorry I'm late. You guys got coffee?"

Cameron had arrived and immediately took charge of the proceedings.

In 2009, when the *Avatar* movie premiered, Ubisoft had released a game based on Cameron's space saga. With the luxury of hindsight and reading a few postmortems, it's easy to understand why the first *Avatar* game was a complicated project that left a mixed bag of possible interpretations on the table. Lightstorm had drawn their own conclusions, while Ubisoft had come to others. But no matter how anyone viewed *Avatar: The Game*, the contract between the companies contained a clause that gave Ubisoft the rights to make a second game based on a movie sequel, assuming one was forthcoming. In Yves's and Serge's minds, it was a good moment to introduce a new Ubisoft studio (Massive!) to Lightstorm, hoping that this would lead to a fresh start on a collaboration that had a slightly frayed history but simultaneously a lot of untapped potential.

The contract clause had an end date that was slowly approaching, so the question of when *Avatar 2* was expected to release was critical. If the *Avatar* sequel was very, very delayed, it would mean that Ubisoft's contract would not cover the interactive rights. But a straight answer was not offered, and it seemed to me that Lightstorm was just meeting with us to be polite. It felt as if they were nowhere near knowing any dates for their next movie, and if so, they already knew that the contract would expire and release them of any obligations to make another game with Ubisoft. Or, I realized after some further thought, they might be planning to shop around for new partners as soon as they were liberated from the existing contract, exploring all the available options regarding studio, technology, publisher, and cash. If I was right about this guess, it would put us in direct competition with basically every good developer in the world. *This might not be looking too good.*

Yves and Serge did a great job of pitching Massive to Cameron, highlighting the many benefits of our engineering skills, which was the only part that made Lightstorm a little excited. But the famous director and the producer were guarded and opaque. Very difficult to read. The director powerfully in charge, driving the meeting to where he wanted it to be, almost directing us all as if we were actors. The producer jovial and warm, taking the role of the easy-going partner, but fully in control of every single beat. I could see how they made such great movies together.

I watched it all, feeling like a voiceless bride being offered to a skeptical prince.

Just as we were about to leave, Cameron suddenly looked me straight in the eye and asked me the first question that wasn't related to technology.

"*You.* What do *you* think *Avatar* is about?" he asked.

Hooray, I thought. I'd been preparing for this since the minute I realized who we were about to meet: James Cameron is a person who really cares about quality, ethics, and the creative process itself—not money or business. The question he directed at me was my cue, and in the back of the limousine I'd spent some time thinking about clever and unexpected answers to a million different questions about *Avatar*, although perhaps not this particular one. Nevertheless, with great self-confidence and pride, I answered him. I was waiting for the words to come out of my mouth, elegantly framing something philosophical and profound. All that was needed was for the internal copywriter to come up with the right words, but he seemed to be on a break...

"*Avatar*...," I said and paused dramatically to gain time, and also to make sure I had everyone's attention. "*Avatar* is about *peace.*"

Cameron held my gaze for a second and then (as I began to panic) shrugged disappointedly. He was not impressed.

"No," he said. "No, it's not. *Avatar* is about *fighting for what you believe in.*"

Shit, shit, shit, I thought. *I'm such an idiot.* And immediately I started the long emotional descent from the stratosphere of my imagined Hollywood career to the floor in the editing room, cut away like a piece of bad footage.

Before I knew it, we were back in the garage in the rear seat of the limo. I beat myself up for failing the most important audition I had ever been to. To my surprise, Yves didn't seem worried or disappointed at all. He was busy looking at his emails on his phone, already moving on to the next thing, whatever it was. Almost absentmindedly he said, "Looks like you will have to win the confidence of those people, huh?"

I couldn't possibly have agreed more.

27

FAR CRY 3

Montreal-based creative director Josh Mosqueira was fighting his own battles.

His soft-spoken, rational, and highly accurate way of working wasn't gaining traction in a company where creative directors are expected to be emotional, dramatic, loud, and extremely opinionated. In a meeting in Paris, the French team blasted an explosion of tough feedback, and all he did was take notes and say, "I'll think about it," which made perfect sense for a man who wanted to digest and process information before jumping to any conclusions. But in the eyes of the French HQ, the thoughtful silence was perceived as weakness, and the gossip in Paris began to mount: *Josh Mosqueira has no balls.* Observing as I was, from the background, this taught me an important lesson: In France, everything can be (and probably is) a negotiation. Even when someone opens a conversation with statements like "This is not a discussion" or "This is an order," the expectation is still that you will (and should) make a counter-demand. And if you don't, it's likely that you will be perceived as a pushover. The sad thing is that sometimes it doesn't matter what is right or wrong, it's just a layer of positioning that exists independently, on top of analysis. To get what you want, you have to be a tough negotiator *and* right.

Josh's main issue with Ubisoft HQ was on the narrative side, where his ideas were constantly challenged, and it was stalling the rest of the production. In game production, story is less important than most people believe, and to a certain degree the narrative doesn't affect the development pace, because many features in a game remain independent of story, such as controls, rendering, back end, dev tools, and world generation. On the other hand, plenty of critical parts of a game are directly and inseparably affected by the narrative *tonality*, like location, AI, art direction, and, ultimately, practically everything. After almost two years on the project, the original idea of releasing the massively improved version of *Far Cry 2*, called *Redux*, had been completely abandoned, but it was proving difficult for the development team to move on to a full-blown sequel due to the lack of alignment on the story. The team was hurting. Once a game spirals into troubled waters, a lot of people will want to abandon it.

On the Montreal side, we started seeing aggressive staff turnover on the floor, and then the producer himself was removed abruptly. Without warning, Josh resigned in disappointment. After all, he'd left his job at Relic and relocated his entire family specifically because he was in love with the *Far Cry* brand and had dreamed about making a legendary contribution to it. Being questioned and stalled was not what he had dreamed about.

And the turnover continued, which in turn gave fuel to a rumor in HQ that the entire game was about to be canceled. No senior staff wanted to be part of a spectacular failure. When Activision threw us into the ditch, we had experienced firsthand, with horror, how easily a large organization can distance itself from what they perceive as a troubled child. But in Ubisoft we had observed with admiration that the last people to abandon hope were Serge and Yves, who would sometimes end up challenging the rest of the executives with their undying belief that the team would eventually pull through.

Note to self: Don't get intimidated when the canary birds start dying off. Just make sure you know what Serge thinks.

Josh left *Far Cry 3* when it was an unpolished gem, but in the final product, his groundwork would still shine brightly as a key ingredient. Soon after, he landed a job at Blizzard and was asked to turn *Diablo III* into a console game. It seemed he'd finally found a home for his exceptional talent.

We kept going on the ruin that was *Far Cry 3*. For a while, Soundboy was the only creative director on the project, and briefly we floated the idea that he move to Canada to take over the whole thing. But he wasn't willing to move west, and the idea fizzled out.

Somehow the game-with-no-captain was beginning to look good, and the flow of the core loop became rock-solid. We could see the promise, somewhere in the fog, but the team was beginning to wear down. Petter was spending way too much time in the office at the expense of his personal life and health. To survive, we needed to clarify for ourselves why we were accepting these punishing circumstances. The three of us made a list of what we expected in return for shipping a great game, assuming we eventually did.

When/If *Far Cry 3* is released:

1. We will only work on our own tech.
2. We cannot be a partner studio.
3. We would like to have our own IP.

As Petter and Soundboy stayed in the *Far Cry 3* trenches, it became my job to manage the ecosystem around us and set the stage for our newly established wish list. Admittedly, our requests made up a tall order, but I genuinely believed it was based on insight and self-awareness. I told Serge that we felt like a racehorse who wasn't allowed to run. He nodded and grunted mysteriously.

And then, seemingly out of the blue, we were told that Montreal was shifting their producer for the third time, and a new creative director was coming. There was something about the way Paris talked about this particular director. It was with reverence, with awe. *Pat is coming; Pat is coming.*

And before we could say "Plourde," all the hype translated into our new reality. Almost magically, on the development side, these staff changes quickly translated into major improvements across the board. The new 180-degree story reboot made sense! The weeding out of bad features made the healthy parts of the game shine, and lo and behold, apparently there had been an excellent game hidden under all the weirdness this whole time! The fun experience had been there, but hidden in the code, drowned by doubts, conflicting agendas, misunderstandings, pointless debates about meaning, bad chemistry, and infighting.

As much as we missed Josh, we truly loved Pat Plourde, a Ubisoft veteran with solid experience from *Tom Clancy's Rainbow Six* and *Assassin's Creed*. And he liked us, too, especially after our brief encounter during Penrose. And, of course, he understood the Paris psychology extremely well, and began navigating the muddy waters cleverly, allowing everyone else to get to work and focus. We were gaining momentum fast, and ten months before the game hit the shelves, I was finally feeling confident that it would be a hit.

Pat Plourde is one of the few people I've met whom I'd be happy to call a genius. He has the perfect mix of ego, skill, and self-doubt. This results in a creative battery that propels him into an intensely high gear of precise decision making. He'd pump himself up every morning with aggressive hip-hop and then spend every minute of every day fully focused on making the game fantastic. He flew in from Canada, and performed a major part of the game-to-be in front of the entire development team as a weird piece of one-man theater: jumping, shouting, running, waving madly, hiding behind imaginary palm trees, and improvising dialogue. He moved effortlessly in and out of all the various characters, and before we knew it, all the dynamics and inner workings of the game were crystal clear. It was tremendously entertaining and almost surreal, but more importantly, after his stand-up performance, everyone who'd attended understood what they needed to do. With Pat's talent and political clout within Ubisoft, *Far Cry 3* took a final turn toward excellence.

As much as the entire endeavor had been plagued by dysfunctional narratives, Pat simply boiled it all down to a relatable and instantly immersive story. "Imagine you're on a backpacking trip with your girlfriend, your brother, and a few friends. You're having a great time, partying, taking selfies, and bumming out in Asia somewhere. One day on an adventure, you carelessly end up on an isolated island, and due to bad weather, you're separated from your girlfriend and friends. To your utter disbelief, you find that you are suddenly in the hands of a drug-crazed criminal who is running the island as his private little empire, living out dreams of power and violence. You still can't take it seriously, but when your brother is executed in front of your eyes, the carefree tour to paradise becomes a shocking one-way journey to a savage hell."

Pat threw this premise at the gamer within the first minutes of the game, and immediately set the stakes for an adventurous exploration. So simple and direct, and it solved a billion issues. Pat always knew how to cut out all the fat and focus on the right things. It wasn't just witchcraft, though; he was spending a tremendous amount of time studying playtest data, and he'd developed an incredible ability to dive deep into the reports and find the answers for his design dilemmas.

The final piece of the *Far Cry 3* puzzle was the extensive wildlife that was added late in the game. Of course, the nightmare island should be full of wild animals who were as detrimental to your survival as the local pirates. The dangerous animals added unexpected action, and the wildlife became a centerpiece in the franchise.

"Man, you are really good at what you do," I told Pat over coffee, during one of the rare moments when he would sit still for longer than two minutes.

"Well, you know," he replied with an angled smile, "they say I'm a great creative director, but honestly, I'm just a clever parasite."

"What do you mean?" I asked. It was unusual for a creative superhero like him to take down the protective shield of a confident ego.

"I just play an enormous amount of games," he continued. "I ask people on the team the right questions, I dive deep into playtest data, and then I listen very carefully to the white noise these things create. All the answers are there. I just see them, pick the right ones, clean them up, and use them. In essence, that makes me a parasite."

Or perhaps a brilliant, curious genius, I thought to myself. Every facet of a game project adds risk. Removing as many dangers and unknowns as possible by careful study of the old (and current) masters seemed more like a move by a truly mature creative director than a parasite.

We were supposed to release *Far Cry 3* in September 2012, but everything was falling into place so late. At the very last moment, the marketing teams had finally begun to show interest and asked for time to adjust their campaigns to what was now beginning to feel like an important release for Ubisoft. We postponed the release to November of the same year and began a final sprint to the finish line.

If there was one thing we were learning the hard way during the Ubisoft university course called *Far Cry 3*, it was the importance of close collaboration and sticking together no matter what. We'd been fighting about so many things, but they weren't necessarily the right fights or the most productive approaches. Disagreements covered basic things as well as high-level design topics. We had once thought the clouds looked horrible, and we changed them to something that looked epic, only to come back the next morning and discover that someone in Canada had changed them back to the old versions overnight. It was silly, but as teams, we were simply not able to find a good rhythm. At Massive we were deeply frustrated with player animations because in multiplayer, the audience would see one another move, but Montreal didn't prioritize this issue. They were working only with single-player, where the gamer would see only AI animations, which are controlled and smooth in comparison to player movement, which is jerky and twitchy. They literally didn't see the problem.

One of the most significant design challenges we faced when starting to work on console games was the allocation of different player inputs to the small handheld pad that the player used to play the game. As opposed to the multitude of keys available on a normal computer keyboard, a console controller had only around twelve buttons and two thumbsticks. This made games easy to play, and an experienced player didn't have to look at the controller when playing. The difficulty, then, was to decide what action was controlled by which button, and, inevitably, the designers had created way too many features to fit the limited number of buttons. It was always a struggle to find clever solutions that accommodated all of the actions while making the game feel intuitive and comfortable. On *Far Cry 3*, we worked with different button layouts on the controller, in that Ubisoft Montreal had a preferred layout and we had our own. This escalated into an ugly fight.

But all infighting aside, in a large part due to Pat's guidance, the game managed to hit the market on November 29, 2012 (December 4 for the US), and it became an instant hit with critics and gamers worldwide. We jockeyed with *Mass Effect 3*, *Borderlands*, and *Diablo III* for the top spot on the charts, and in many cases we beat them all, hitting #1 in significant markets. The release transformed Ubisoft's fundamental two-horse-carriage economics into a three-horse model. Up to that point, Ubisoft had relied heavily on the sales of *Assassin's Creed* and *Just Dance*, but *presto!* Here was a third megabrand to bank on. We felt we'd paid Ubisoft back for trusting us when Activision threw us under the bus. Now, we were finally ready to move on with our own plans.

A few weeks later, my boss, Christine, called.

"Hey, I have a great idea for you and your team. Why don't you work on *Far Cry 4* with Montreal?"

My answer didn't make her happy: "I'd rather be unemployed."

28

SNOWDROP

Saying no to *Far Cry 4* was a real faux pas, and I knew it. I had to ask myself: Was I putting the future of the entire studio at risk because I was a diva? The answer that echoed back from the rational part of my brain wasn't the one I wanted: *Yes, you probably are. You fool!* How could I pull myself and Massive out of the grave I'd just dug for us? My brain went into hyperspeed mode. I was terrified. A true scholar of the paranoid, I imagined bureaucrats in Paris already preparing to fire me over my disobedience. Maybe I should just beat them to it and hand in my resignation? *Yeah, that'd solve the issue. Great job, man.* The office chair squeaked as I leaned forward with my head in my hands.

Before I could even begin figuring out a way to bounce back, things got worse.

The phone rang. It was my former officemate Björn.

"I think we're under attack," he said.

Piracy, the habit of illegally copying and distributing games, had become a gigantic problem, particularly for PC gaming, and we learned firsthand what a handicap it had become after releasing *World in Conflict*. We knew from our own data that almost 80 percent of the people who played the game hadn't paid for it. And it was far from just a thorn in our side alone. Analysts estimated that the problem amounted to accumulated losses of up to 100 billion USD worldwide. No doubt about it: This had become a huge, pressing issue that had to be dealt with yesterday. If we couldn't stop it, it was possible that Ubisoft would implode like a record label.

Maybe we were irrationally attached to the idea that gamers should pay us for the job we did, but to us it seemed entirely fair that we be permitted to add some software that made it impossible (or very hard) to copy a Ubisoft game and play it without paying for it. Björn was picked to lead this mission and had recently transitioned into a new role as Lead Programmer of Orbit, a clever little piece of antipiracy software we'd developed for all of Ubisoft.

No matter how innocent and straightforward this might have seemed, the addition of antipiracy software was perceived as exceptionally hostile and rude by gamers. Every publisher that tried to solve their piracy problems inevitably attracted the intense hate of internet bullies.

We knew all this, and yet, there we were, launching Orbit, a direct insult to pirates on the digital seas across the globe. Of course, they'd lash back with the most aggressive weapon they had in their arsenal.

"Under attack? What is it?" I asked.

"It looks like a DDoS," Björn said, and went silent for a while. I heard him type something on his keyboard.

I didn't say anything, but his words made me feel cold and sick. Orbit was a major project for us, and a distributed denial-of-service attack would potentially impact all Ubisoft's PC titles. We were about to become responsible for a devastating, company-wide failure.

We'd never experienced a DDoS attack before, and our assumption was that there was no way to defend against it. Björn had a few tricks up his sleeve, though, and it was evident that they'd be rapidly tested in live conditions. A DDoS attack... *the ultimate fury of the net.*

A distributed denial-of-service (DDoS) attack is a brute-force method used to bring someone else's computer system to its knees or potentially break it completely. It's a simplistic but efficient form of sabotage. To explain it in layman's terms, it's like blowing up a dam to instantly flood a valley. This is achieved by completely overflowing the traffic to the targeted system with meaningless and consistent rapid requests for a connection. It's like gathering a crowd of a hundred thousand people shouting simultaneous questions at the same individual. It completely blocks and breaks the functionality of the system under attack. The system becomes incapable of responding to genuine requests from real people who wish to access the service, in the same way a human hearing questions from hundreds of thousands of people at once would be unable to respond logically.

The challenge for a hacker group organizing this kind of attack is that in order to reach sufficient volumes, they need to control hundreds of thousands of PCs that will create the synchronized wave of digital requests. Gaining that kind of control is achieved by constantly spreading invisible viruses that are planted on unsuspecting private PCs all over the world. Such a small virus is fast asleep until the hacker decides to activate it. When someone has angered the hackers enough, as we had through Orbit, the planted virus allows them to take simultaneous control of the vast net of PCs and use them to generate a tsunami of pointless data traffic directed toward the target.

I knew Björn was sitting a few floors away, perched in front of his triple-screen setup, watching an impossible number of windows and programs simultaneously. The data and code that scrolled across his monitors made it look like he was piloting a spaceship. Color charts and diagrams, live-updated lines of accumulated statistics moving like gentle waves. Björn in the middle of it all, a true digital zen master, taking it all in, and somehow analyzing every single piece of information in mere seconds.

The phone line was still open, but Björn remained quiet. I listened to the white noise and the sound of the occasional keyboard stroke. In the background, as in an echo chamber, I heard the rest of the team: agitated, worried, carefully calling out important observations to one another across the office. Computers made soft sounds like *ping*, *boing*, and *blip*, humming out alerts, sounding professional, unaffected. But the Orbit team was facing a frightening load increase right in front of their eyes.

"Hmm," Björn said.

"Yes?" I replied, still clinging to the hope of good news.

"It's the Russians. And from Ukraine. Yes, confirmed. It's a full-on DDoS attack."

"Aha," I said, feeling utterly useless.

"I need to deal with it," Björn said.

"Yeah, good. I'll take care of my side of things," I said, referring to the internal political nightmare and the external PR ordeal that I knew was coming.

Russia, Ukraine—the best hackers in the world were involved. It meant that someone had opened the gates to Hacker Hell. Someone had unleashed an unstoppable army of hijacked PCs, all connected in a robotic net. Every single one of them dancing in perfect coordination to the scripted tune of a central server with a single focus: destruction. Like sharks in a feeding frenzy, the machines had turned into an efficient hive-minded beast that would find—and kill—its prey.

The DDoS attack on Orbit lasted a few days. Other hacker groups from the rest of the world joined the effort to shortcut our system. At the end of the week, the intensity began slowing down. It seemed that the group of hackers who had launched the DDoS were gradually losing control of the hijacked PCs. Perhaps various locally installed antivirus programs were kicking in? Or maybe the hackers didn't bother to keep everything going at full strength.

There was no way for us to know; we could just observe the steady load decrease.

Björn and his team had battled day and night, like maniacs, surprising everyone with their successful strategy to redirect the millions of repeating access requests to a bottomless digital hole somewhere. Their magical tricks were beyond my understanding. They talked about proxies and a web of hundreds of satellites, and I heard that somewhere along the way we accidentally shut out most of the entire nation of Ukraine from the internet.

The launch of Orbit as Ubisoft's new antipiracy solution had become big news indeed, and everyone hated it. It was a PR nightmare, both internally and externally. The entire concept of adding software that prevented illegal copying and redistribution of a game was challenged by a righteous, entitled, and unified internet. It was as if it were a human right to steal digital copies, and we were denying people that right.

But soon enough, the internet and the international hacker alliance decided to move on to other battles and leave us alone, but scarred, traumatized, and publicly shamed. The age of pirating PC games was reaching a logical end anyway, especially as more and more games went online. It was basic: As opposed to off-line games, an online game made each individual player dependent on the connection to the developer's server, which as a consequence gave studios and publishers a tool to limit piracy. An illegally copied version of the game would be detected immediately when it tried to connect to the server.

Massive moved on, but Orbit lived a quiet life for quite some time in the hands of Ubisoft, running silently in the background on a bunch of games. Due to the excellent work Björn and the team had done, Orbit occasionally became a toy for hackers who wanted to test their skills. The system was like an advanced game of chess, and only the best hackers could even scratch the surface of it. One hacker in particular made many sophisticated attempts to crack our antipiracy solution. He called himself Raw Spoon, after an obscure heavy metal rock band with the same name. He left traces and messages to the Orbit team as he tried to break in, like graffiti from a failing invader on a castle wall. One day, Björn left a little message for this hacker buried deep, deep down in the digital trenches: "Raw Spoon, we see you." The words lay hidden in the code, ready to automatically pop up on the screen if the hacker tried to break in through a particularly complex Orbit loophole.

Six months later, Björn received a message from an untraceable sender.

Hey Orbitman. Thanks for the message.

For me, watching someone like Björn work through endless rivers of code on a computer screen is like watching a surreal matrix of logic and emotion broken down into impossibly small and fragile strands of information. As with all forms of abstract art, it might not appear to make any sense at first, but as you keep watching obsessively and zoom in and out of the various layers of digits in the software stratospheres, patterns will begin to emerge. After a while, it becomes possible to instinctively understand what's going on: It's like using spaghetti to re-create a sculpture by Michelangelo, or LEGOs to re-create a cathedral. I find it strangely comforting that we as a race have this ability to use mathematics and logic to build amazing worlds and simulations.

Apart from Orbit, the programmers at Massive had been working on another majestic piece of technology: a full-sized modern game engine we romantically called Snowdrop.

The term "game engine" encompasses all technology used in a game studio to create a video game. But if you could look under the hood of a game, there'd be no single engine. A game engine is a mix of multiple, almost independent solutions, which, in coordination, solve completely different problems, such as rendering, performance, physics, saving/loading, AI, animation, patching, branching, and scripting, to mention just a few. In addition, the team of developers needs to have custom-made tools to apply their design. These are the access points to the underlying systems.

Behind it all, the game runs on an online ecosystem that needs to be sturdy enough to support millions of layers, and perhaps to survive the occasional DDoS attack. If you pack all this into a connected whole, it becomes what we call a game engine.

In Sweden, the snowdrop is the first flower of spring, a sign of early hope that promises brighter times. It was a perfect name for our engine. Our ambition in creating Snowdrop was to have technological independence and to create our own array of production advantages stemmed from the very origin of the studio. This was one of the goals we had set for ourselves when we were painted into a corner with *Far Cry 3*. All the early Massive games had been built on in-house engines, and it was hard for us to imagine any other path.

Although Ubisoft offered several game engines that were much more advanced than what we had created for *World in Conflict*, we had a strong desire to write our own code entirely from scratch. We wanted to get rid of all legacy code, because even the virtual decays over time, just as the physical world does. The long year we spent waiting for the VUG/Activision merger had freed up time for some of the studio's most technically sophisticated talents, and they'd begun building a range of new software. In particular, Snowdrop was created with a focus on enabling artists and designers, essentially liberating them from dependencies on engineers. The creation of efficient software tools is exceptionally underestimated in the video game industry, often leading to projects collapsing under the weight of a thousand small imperfections and bugs. We felt that the tools themselves were the most underdeveloped side of game engines and began to create a suite of powerful levers and knobs that were easy to use, even for people who had no clue what was going on in the invisible code.

The climax of this philosophy was the real-time updating that Snowdrop became capable of, in effect making any change by any developer on the team instantly available in the game itself, without any overnight "baking" or complex updating processes depending on the approval of a risk-averse associate producer. *From inspired idea to playable reality in seconds.* Simultaneously, on the player-facing end of the spectrum, we began to write code enabling us to render an insanely high number of polygons on the screen, at lightning speed. This would allow for photo-realistic worlds and pitch-perfect light, coupled with sophisticated particle effects for fog, smoke, clouds, weather, destruction, and weapons. We were building game worlds that covered up to ten square kilometers of fully playable areas in which the player could see up to four kilometers in the distance. The goal was to ultimately create a world-class game engine that would set free our creative minds.

I remember one of the engineers saying that their goal was to build tools that were so open-ended, agile, and efficient that no one would ever need to ask for assistance from a programmer again. I suspected that some part of that goal was a private ambition to be left alone and to avoid interaction with other humans, but even if it wasn't, the result was fantastic. Snowdrop gave artists and designers amazing powers to develop a game at a very high speed, without being blocked by their inability to write code.

With *Far Cry 3* disappearing in our rearview mirror, I felt confident that we'd found the perfect recipe for our future: Snow-drop was the vehicle for the top secret project Rogue that would revitalize the Clancy brand for the next generation of consoles.

After fighting off the DDoS attack, I got lost in dreams about Snowdrop for a few days. But soon enough, I remembered with a cold shiver that I had just put the entire studio at risk by declining to work on *Far Cry 4*, probably insulting a whole bunch of important people in the process.

29

THE PARATROOPER

"Shit, man! Don't step on my glasses!" I cried to Cece as he stumbled around clumsily in our tiny camp.

To be honest, it wasn't much of a camp; it was more an assembly of sad sticks pathetically posing as a shelter. It was embarrassing. As if two depressed slacker children were playing Robinson Crusoe. But we were trying our hardest, honestly!

Nicklas "Cece" Cederström, the first creative director on Rogue, and I were lost somewhere deep in the Swedish forest, with a steady rain pouring down from the dark clouds above. In every direction, the fir trees stretched out in endless dominance. The fir is a tree that slowly and methodically kills all other plants and spreads out like a virus until it creates a vast, gloomy forest, firs-only. We honestly had no idea where we were, and night was falling fast.

Cece was a large, slightly red-haired guy, with (when not lost in a forest) an optimistic attitude and a loud, charismatic personality. Cece was always full of ideas and naturally gravitated toward pleasure. But behind his fun-loving facade, he was a complicated figure, with an inability to completely connect with people. I was looking forward to getting to know him better. I was hoping to find a tormented artist behind the shield, the kind of person I trusted more than the easygoing jokester I knew him to be.

Cece had an almost reckless habit of coming up with new concepts for the projects he was working on, making him particularly useful in the early stages, but a real nuisance later when execution was more important than innovation. He had been responsible for the abandoned Shadow World project (a madly ambitious fantasy RPG, heavily influenced by *World of WarCraft*), and together with that entire group, he'd been switched over to do some hard work on Rogue. But here we were, two thoroughly unprepared office workers in survival training in the middle of an endless Swedish forest. We were supposed to keep watch over the fire, boil tea from fir-tree needles, eat ants, avoid poisonous (or hallucinogenic) mushrooms, stay dry, and ideally catch some fish to cook. There was plenty of water around, thanks to our nemesis, the everlasting rain, but we learned that before drinking it we had to filter it through antiseptic white moss. As far as I could tell, we were doing an amazing job of failing at absolutely everything, except the tea, the taste of which we detested.

"How many days do we have to stay?" Cece asked in a weak voice. "Maybe we can cancel the rest? The guy said it's okay. I think we get the point now."

"Shut up, dude. Just be careful with my glasses and keep an eye on that fire," I said. "We don't even know where the guy is or how to contact him," I continued, desperately in need of some sleep.

We'd been told that this would happen: We'd fall in and out of despair. We'd experience wild mood swings, and we'd occasionally feel some kind of high, only to suddenly get angry and frustrated again. The key to everything was to adapt. *Embrace. Don't fight it.* We'd been promised that eventually, we'd find a rhythm where we were extremely caring for each other, because dependency does that to you. *One will support the other when he is down. Your biggest worry will be how your friend is sleeping and eating.* Well, I had to admit it seemed we weren't quite there yet.

Back at the studio in Malmö we'd finally given our top secret mystery project (a.k.a. Rogue) a real name: *Tom Clancy's The Division.* I once described working on *The Division* as like living in a very small apartment with a perpetually angry teenager. The journey was a very challenging experience, and it created a lot of frustration for everyone involved. It almost didn't matter what we did in the studio or on the Ubisoft side; all in all, it was just always difficult.

In defiance, I chose to see the opportunity instead. It became somewhat of an obsession, and I kept saying things like, "If it were easy, anyone could do it. But now it's super hard, which means that only the best can do it. And that's us." I wasn't lying or trying to create good PR; I was absolutely convinced that it was true. And why not? I trusted the team. I trusted that the obsessive quest for greatness would be the right choice.

When we began working on Rogue, we were stuck in traditional Clancy stereotypes: SWAT teams, military specialists, global politics, stolen submarines, nuclear weapons, secret weapon factories, drug cartels…It was all horribly boring and nowhere near the modernization Ubisoft had requested. For lack of better ideas, we built an ambitious prototype that started on a hangar ship with an army veteran giving a mission to the player. The player was then flown off to Peru in a military chopper to conduct some fishy military stuff. Mostly killing. The short prototype looked amazing, and it played well, so even with the lack of innovative ideas for the Clancy franchise, we managed to keep the project alive for a while longer.

But then the small team had an epiphany. They asked themselves, What would happen if all the typical Clancy heroes failed? *What if those heroes weren't even a part of the solution?* This provoked several exciting new ideas, and at the same time, we asked ourselves what the old Clancy slogan "Clear and Present Danger" would mean in the world of today. Those two questions combined led to a host of answers that became *The Division.*

Imagine: In the near future (maybe even next week), a smallpox virus is unleashed on Manhattan, intentionally placed on dollar bills on Black Friday. Soon after, those infected fall ill, and promptly begin to die in large numbers. Trying to contain the lethal infection, the authorities close all the bridges to Manhattan and refuse to send in any help, knowing that almost everyone would catch the disease and die. After a few days, the city falls into chaos, and those trapped fight for their lives while trying to stay away from the virus. What would we do if we were there, any one of us?

Modern society collapses within seventy-two hours. This is not fiction; it's a fact and an uncomfortable truth, one that governments all over the world are aware of and prepare for.

And imagine this too: The player is part of a sleeper group of agents ready to jump in as a backup if every other government entity fails. They train and prepare, but under the assumption that there will never be a scenario that would actually require them to be called into action. They represent the Strategic Homeland Division, which consists of engineers, doctors, policemen, firemen, plumbers, drivers... literally anyone who could protect the continuation of civilization as we know it. In the game, we sent the most courageous Division agents to the sealed-off city to save what remains, to fight the criminal chaos on the streets, and to investigate the nature of the outbreak.

We got extremely excited by the premise, and immediately set up a call with Serge and his team. It was a slam dunk. They got it right away, and we felt like superheroes going back to work. *Just don't make it a game about sick people*, Serge said, and off we went! It seemed almost too easy to get the green light, but we all knew that this was a major accomplishment, and that perhaps other parts of the organization would not be so easily convinced. We decided to worry about that some other day.

Fully supported by the guru himself, the team began deep-diving into a dynamic digital version of a collapsing Lower Manhattan. The gritty realism and the big canvas we required for the story we had in mind were pushing Snowdrop to the extreme, but even our most cynical engineers admitted it sang like a fine-tuned engine. Everything began to fall into place: the cover-based mechanics we had toyed around with from the very beginning, the looting (more importantly: the narrative *reason* to loot), the rich variation of weapons and modifications, the player hubs enabled by the shared multiplayer areas, the pseudoclasses from the RPG genre, and, finally, a story that was based on a hero who really didn't want to kill anyone if given a choice. *No soldiers*. It finally made sense.

The team attacked the scenario with a newfound optimism, and we all started reading up on urban survival and the fragility of society. We became very interested in preppers, the people who spend a huge part of their lives preparing for impending doom. Some of the developers on the team got so paranoid after studying a potential collapse that they became preppers too. They started buying canned food, water-purification tablets, and all sorts of clever gadgets that allow a person to survive after a catastrophic event. I, too, thought about getting ready for the apocalypse, and ever since the research phase of *The Division*, I've been convinced that any sane person should be prepared for at least seventy-two hours of solo survival, but in reality I've never got around to buying all the necessary stuff. I guess I should.

I also became intrigued by the psychology of humans in stressful situations, and I followed real-life disasters and societies at the brink of collapse with interest. I thought it was obvious that we needed to research disaster scenarios further, and I proposed to the core team that they sign up for some real survival training to better understand what it does to the psyche, and thereby maybe add some spice and credibility elements to the game. To my surprise, no one felt that it was a good idea, and the team dismissed it quickly. But after a few weeks of ignoring the proposal, Cece, ever the curious kid, came out of the blue and told me that he'd have a go at survival training on the condition that I join him.

After a quick online search, we found an old Swedish paratrooper who hosted weeklong courses for anyone stupid enough to try. I tried to imagine what it would be like to run a business like that, but as I continued reading, I realized that the only thing he needed was a forest and some bad weather. Plus a few gullible cityfolks ready to experience it all. Cece and I fit the bill perfectly.

Before leaving Malmö, we received a list of everything we were supposed to bring, and of course I didn't own any of it, so I went shopping. A light backpack, terrain boots, a sturdy water-proof jacket, outdoorsy pants with many pockets, socks made from fast-drying material, ignition steel, small dry sticks, and water-purification tablets. Once I had it all packed in my new shiny bag, I felt confident that this would be a walk in the park. I hid a big piece of Marabou chocolate in the backpack, which I imagined eating on the top of a mountain with a nice bonfire casting a beautiful yellow-orange light on my perky cheeks. What could possibly go wrong?

After a long drive in high spirits to the center of Sweden's deepest forests, Cece and I got out of the car and stretched our legs. We'd arrived at the abandoned shed the paratrooper used as his office. The sun was shining, and all we needed to make the moment perfect was a cup of coffee!

We secretly rolled our eyes and exchanged meaningful glances when the paratrooper came out to meet us. He was at least 140 years old. His face was covered in deep wrinkles, and his back was stooped over, making him look as if breathing itself was too great a burden to bear. Right after he said hello, he went on to tell us that he'd suffered a stroke a few weeks earlier, but that it "shouldn't be a problem." We laughed nervously. In comparison, Cece and I were young, fit (sort of), and exceptionally well prepared. How was this guy going to keep up with us?

We sat on simple wooden chairs in the shed as the paratrooper fired up his overhead projector. An *overhead projector*! Cece and I laughed even harder as he tried to figure out what was up and what was down on his transparent plastic sheets. This was hilarious, but we soon got bored by the lecture, which was long and detailed. My mind started to drift.

The shed looked like something from a Chernobyl photo, and there was no traffic on the gravel road outside. I noticed that it would get dark early, since the tall trees covered such a large part of the skyline. We were taught a lot of stuff about knives that we forgot almost instantly. We heard about mushrooms and lost track of which ones we could and couldn't eat. We asked for coffee but were told to be quiet in a surprisingly rude way. But we'd just been taught that the key to all survival is *acceptance*, so we shut up.

"You have to embrace everything that happens and just accept it," the man said. "If you fight it, you will fail. Now, did you pack everything I asked you to? The stuff on the list I sent?"

"Yes!" I exclaimed, a bit too loudly and eagerly, I realized. But I was so happy about my stuff, and I wanted him to look through it all and admire my good shopping choices. Somewhere in the middle of his lecture he'd casually mentioned that he'd spent ten years of his life entirely outside any known civilization, and this had made a huge impression on me, so I was hoping to get some validation.

The paratrooper suddenly leaped up from his chair in a surprisingly agile manner, and said, "Well, leave your bags and everything in them there in the corner; you won't be bringing them."

"What?!" Cece and I cried in disbelief.

"What did I just tell you?" our new tyrant continued. "Accept change, embrace it. If you fight your situation, you will fail. So just leave your bags; we are heading out now."

Before either of us could object, he added, "Lucky for you both, you're wearing the right pair of boots and not those sneakers I saw in the car. Otherwise, it would have been hell. Hell. As in: for you. Let's go!"

A few hours later, we were soaked by the pouring rain, hungry, and lost. The old paratrooper was annoyingly chipper, running around like an athletic leopard filled with energy, bouncing from rock to fallen tree, trying to make us see the hostile forest as he saw it: an endless, self-healing resource where one could survive easily and forever. We must have been bad students, because all we could think about was what a prick he was. We'd been marching for hours and hours, to "simulate exhaustion." Cece and I were getting grumpier by the minute, but we still looked forward to the evening camp we'd soon set up for the first night. We speculated that the paratrooper would surprise us with something to eat—we hadn't had a single bite of food since we were on the road and had pulled into a highway rest stop to eat. Surely he wasn't planning to completely starve us? We were expecting a nice, native-looking camp with a cozy fire and entertainment in the shape of war stories from the old pro. With a steak.

The old man stopped suddenly, still looking like he was ready to win an Olympic triathlon.

"Well, I guess this is as good a place as any," he said.

We looked around suspiciously.

"Okay, then," he went on, "set up camp here."

"Yeah, cool. But how? What kind of camp? How do we stay dry? Will we get a fire?" we asked. "Do you have food?"

"Do what you want; it's up to you. I'm leaving now. Cheers!" And to our disbelief, he just wandered away into the pitch-dark wall of trees and left us there alone.

"Asshole," Cece said, and pulled out an ignition steel he'd hidden in his pocket. "Let's get a fire started."

Aimlessly, we tried to build a shelter from fallen branches, and then we tried, and failed, to light a fire. The useless pile of sticks didn't provide any cover at all, and everything we tried to set fire to was soaking wet. We sat down on a few stones, cursing the old bastard. Neither of us slept at all that night, and the next morning, when the paratrooper showed up dry as a desert and happy as a cat, we were ready to fall into tears and go home.

"Right!" he said. "Let's go!" And off we went for day two, deeper and deeper into the forest, realizing that the rain would fall forever.

During the next couple of days, we marched and starved, marched and starved, in a loop set to repeat. But the old man gradually gave us small tips for how to build a better shelter, how to keep the fire alive, how to manage constant hunger, how to keep the mood up, how to navigate in a dense forest, how to get rid of mosquitoes, and how to take care of wounds when we cut ourselves on branches in the unwelcoming terrain.

We built homemade rucksacks from materials provided by the forest, and kept our few new and precious possessions in them: the ignition steel, some drying grass to light a fire, an empty can of beer filled with white moss to filter water, a nail that could be used to pierce things, a rusty tin can we'd found and used to boil the awful tea, a thin nylon thread that maybe we could use to catch some fish. *Fire* and *water* were essential. It was fascinating how quickly our lives had become reduced to the elements. Gathering kindling was important. Drying wet logs became important. Counting the burning logs at night when you were on watch duty became the simplest way to keep track of time. Distributing the logs in an even pace became important. Large parts of our brains were occupied with fire management.

After nearly freezing to death the first couple of nights, I was particularly happy about the paratrooper's lesson on how to keep warm at night. It was simple: "Dig a small trench under the leafy branches you sleep on. Take one or two of the stones from around the fire once they're hot. Put the stones in the trench, and you'll feel as if you're sleeping on a radiator. When you change the fire watch, change the stones." Once we knew this, keeping warm was simple.

After a while, the brain and the body settled into this new reality, and my only interest in life became staying warm and safe, and keeping Cece warm and safe. The best sound in the world was his snoring as I kept the fire burning at night. *What a peaceful noise*, I thought. *He is doing well.* I couldn't imagine anything more important. Hunger was a constant source of obsession, but remarkably, it mattered a lot less than I'd thought. Often, the old pro abandoned us without any warning, and we'd never know when he planned to come back or where he was in the meantime. We assumed he just went off and killed a bear with his hands and enjoyed a great steak on his own. Nevertheless, he remained filled with energy and in high spirits, while Cece and I were dirty, lost, had no sense of time, and stumbled around like zombies.

Once, by a lake, we were supposed to learn how to catch fish and failed miserably. But before we set up camp that night, the old man gave us a fresh fish that he must have caught behind our backs. We cleaned it with our six-inch nail and cooked it on a hot stone without any spices, but to us it tasted as if we were eating in a 3-star Michelin restaurant. We huddled together in the rain and almost cried with joy and relief.

After what felt like months, the paratrooper suddenly told us to stop and create a majestic smoke signal so that the imagined rescue helicopter would find us. We did as we were told, lit the right kind of fire as we'd been taught, and out of nowhere the man's friends suddenly appeared in a four-wheel-drive Jeep.

"Your 'chopper' is here. Congratulations," he said.

All that time when we'd been walking around feeling lost and entirely off the grid, we'd been mere feet from a hidden road? *The bastards!*

The paratrooper and his friends drove us to a small cabin with a cozy fireplace where they started making coffee and frying pancakes. In the meantime, I showered in HOT CLEAN WATER— *who'd ever dreamed of such a luxury?* Once we regrouped in front of the fire, I smelled of exotic things like soap and shampoo.

"Eat slowly," the paratrooper said. "Your stomach will need to get used to it."

After the first bite of food, my brain exploded. I *totally loved* everyone in the room, and I was *so, so, so fantastically grateful for my life.* The anticipation of seeing my kids again soon made me want to cartwheel through the small cabin. In some sort of double exposure of realities I saw Cece as my younger brother, playing with my real-life big brother and not with me. It was a game of survival and adventure, much like the board games we had once created. I suddenly missed my brother sorely; *I totally loved him, too*, and I decided love was an amazing emotion. It was as if the entire meaning of the universe had been condensed into that moment, and for once, I was absolutely, perfectly at peace with everything.

The pancakes were made by angels.

Before we ran back to the rental car and escaped our abusive warden forever, we took the time to ask him some questions about the scenario in *The Division*.

"If you were stuck on Manhattan when the virus broke out and they closed the bridges, what would you do?"

"I never travel to places with a lot of humans. They are the most dangerous creatures of all. Avoid them at all cost," he said with a happy smile.

"No, come on. Play along," Cece said. "What would you do, really?"

"Okay," he said. "I'd hide in Central Park. I could survive there for as long as I'd want to."

"Hmm, interesting," I said. "What if you couldn't go there?"

"In that case I'd seal off an entire apartment building and make sure it was empty," the paratrooper said.

"What? An entire building?! Why would you need that?" Cece asked, while I wondered what he meant when he said he would "make sure" it was empty. By now, I had no doubt whatsoever that he was capable of killing anyone and anything, anytime.

"First of all, I need stuff for my fire so I can keep warm, and all that furniture is going to last for quite some time. But more importantly, every toilet in the building contains several liters of fresh water," he said.

"Fresh!" We laughed.

"It's clean," he said factually, before continuing: "And then I'd loot all the Dumpsters around nearby restaurants within the first twenty-four hours. I'd take everything I could eat and bring it back to my building."

"Why twenty-four hours?" I asked.

"Because after sixty hours, everyone else will have realized that there's food in those trash bins, and I don't want to be anywhere near them, especially when they are desperate and probably have guns. I told you, there is nothing more dangerous than a human. Everything else in nature is fine. Just fine."

And with those joyful words of encouragement ringing in our ears, we hopped into the car, still feeling high from being clean, fed, and free to go back home to the magnificent comforts of modern society. Cece turned on the radio, which immediately filled the car with popcorn commercials and disco as we headed south. We switched on our cell phones and watched as hundreds of work-related emails and text messages dropped in.

"Free at last!" Cece said and laughed, sounding just a little bit crazy.

It felt amazing, it truly did, though I couldn't help but think that maybe we were missing a profound philosophical point somewhere.

The passenger seat was warm and cozy. Through the car window I saw an endless procession of black and green fir trees pass by. Slowly, they began to take on a familiar, friendly shape instead of the looming threat they had represented only hours earlier.

Survival.

It seemed to be a shadow that followed me everywhere.

The survival course had allowed me the freedom to step outside my life for a moment, to be someone else experiencing a new story and new circumstances. Being at the center of the adventure, as painful failures progressively led to increased understanding and the development of new skills, had been profoundly rewarding. Like a game.

Cece began talking about going back to the office and getting to work on Rogue again, applying his new insights. He started to mumble incomprehensively about "explosions within explosions." I wasn't really listening. The humming of the car sounded like an army of satisfied cats. I was in my own version of a Russian nesting doll, seeing patterns of *survival within survival*. In the simplest of terms, life itself is a fight for survival. So, too, were my desperate attempts to build a career, to establish relationships with others, and to save Massive from doom. My homegrown management and business skills had been developed purely so I wouldn't get swindled in the world of international bigwigs and real money. It was as if my whole life were shouting at me: *Don't drown.*

Suddenly it was obvious to me: *The Division* was a game about the same thing—survival. My perpetual companion was at the center of the project we were betting our future on.

Since I was a child, one of my main coping mechanisms, a key survival strategy, had been dreaming. But I didn't indulge in just aimless, naive daydreaming. Instead, my fantasies had an intentional quality to them. I made up things that I actually expected to happen, one way or the other. And even though I sometimes felt like the King of Failed Starts, I had in fact achieved many of the magic moments that had once been nothing more than a fantasy in my head. Like becoming a painter. Like publishing artsy (and unsellable) children's books. Like making the album cover for a childhood pop idol. Like making games. Like seeing major parts of the planet. Like falling in love and having babies. Like meeting the most successful movie director in human history. Like running a marathon. Like having dinner with a queen. Ultimately, experiencing all those highlights had opened my eyes to the wondrous songs of the mundane. Life bloomed like a spring flower, and from the fragile petals came the beauty of small things. Seemingly insignificant and trivial moments emerged as the true peaks of my life.

Coming back from the earthbound, analog version of survival training with the paratrooper, I yearned for me and my team at Massive to go beyond mere survival. To be at rest and to dream new dreams. To stop fighting; to rise to a higher aesthetic level as craftsmen. To create games that were not just entertainment but also aspired to a kind of poetic beauty, a playground where others could find a home and inspiration for their dreams, and maybe one day, turn them into their own realities.

30

E3

When I told Christine that we didn't feel like working on the next *Far Cry* game, it inevitably resulted in quite a bit of drama. Some felt that we still owed Ubisoft a favor for saving Massive from inevitable doom in 2008 and that we were in no position to demand more than what they'd already generously offered us.

Before I went overboard with attitude and bravado or made any further knee-jerk decisions, I stopped and thought hard about how far I was willing to push. I asked Petter and Soundboy for advice. The meeting turned into a mutual pep talk, and we decided to stick to our own assumptions. They want a good studio? Well, let's give them one! Working on *Far Cry 4* was not the way to go. We asked ourselves if we were genuinely prepared to lose our jobs over this, if we were just being stupid and obstinate. Soon enough, we agreed that we were ready to go all the way to the bitter end. For Soundboy and Petter, this was particularly brave, since the core team of *The Division* was built around Cece and would not offer them any positions; all the key roles were already filled.

In the Swedish culture, negotiations are often seen as unnecessary and a waste of time. Why not just say what you want from the start, and then take it from there? The French, on the other hand, seem to enjoy the gameplay of negotiation, and are very good at it too. We had no clever strategy, and we came across only as being blunt. "I'd rather be unemployed," I'd said, because I truly meant it. Christine went through her entire playbook of French negotiation skills, but she was savvy enough to realize that there was no leeway. We simply wouldn't budge, and it infuriated her.

"Well, what on earth would you be doing then?" she shouted at me.

"We need to focus on *The Division*," I said.

"Well, that's not going to cut it! What are you going to do with the core team from *Far Cry*?"

"Something else!" I shouted, with just a hint of falsetto. It was a horribly insufficient answer, but there must have been something in my desperation that made her convinced I was really going to push this to the point where she'd have to fire me.

She went silent for a while, probably throwing things in anger at the wall in her elegant corner office in Paris, a thousand kilometers away.

"OKAY, FINE!" she shouted. "But for the record, you are really *such a prima donna*!" She abruptly hung up on me. The heat of her anger burned through the ether. I sat there with the phone glued to my ear for a while, lost in thought.

I'd never been called a prima donna before, and I truly didn't like it, but at the same time, a great sense of victory began to spread inside me. I'd promised the team many times that they'd be given the chance to prove themselves on *something else* if they just stayed focused on *Far Cry* and delivered an awesome game, which they had. Part of my stubbornness stemmed from the simple fact that I couldn't stand the thought of facing them and having to admit that I couldn't keep my part of the contract. Apparently, the thought of that shame contributed to my brave willingness to get fired.

But suddenly we had what we wanted, and it tasted sweet. On

one side of the studio, I began preparing the ground for Petter and Soundboy and their trusted core team, and on the other side, I shifted a lot of production capacity from *Far Cry* to *The Division* so that the project gained a much-needed boost. In the middle of those two (fragile) projects, we had the Snowdrop core of technology to build on. We'd put ourselves in a great position, but obviously with a lot to prove—again. Autonomy is freedom, but it's also responsibility and loneliness.

The Division team went into high gear, and momentarily it felt good, but only a few months later, in the early winter of 2013, we'd exhausted Ubisoft's patience.

One way to look at *The Division* was that it had been in production since early 2009 and had all the signs of a project that would never ship—constant narrative reboots, ever-changing core mechanics, major disagreements on art direction, impossible tech challenges, and a thinly disguised lack of trust from major stakeholders at the head office. But another way to look at it was that it had been a big ask from the start, one that required a huge leap from us as a developer, and, in addition, the project had been starved of staff until we shipped *Far Cry 3* in November 2012. Depending on which perspective one took, *The Division* had been in development either for three years or for only a few months. Either it was forgotten, hopeless, and past its prime, or it was exciting and new.

On the studio floor, we felt that we were making amazing progress. We found it difficult to understand why Ubisoft thought we were being slow. Nevertheless, we benefited enormously from the long preproduction and the intense collaboration we'd enjoyed with Serge's team. While we were constantly being challenged on the financials, the project itself had matured well and was ready to go into production. In most cases, the opposite is the problem: Game projects suffer from a rushed preproduction and they enter full production with large teams way too early.

Even with the boost from the *Far Cry* team, we began hiring more people, and sometimes I felt like we were in the recruiting business rather than in the entertainment industry. We had originally occupied the bottom two floors of the six-story brick building where the Massive offices were located in central Malmö. Slowly, we spread to the rest of the structure, first to the third floor, then the fourth, then the fifth, and finally the sixth. The fast growth coupled with the rising pressure was hard on the team, and some of the problems we faced later were caused by this sudden rise in temperature. *This is how dinosaurs die*, I couldn't help thinking.

Personally, I was way too busy and began showing early signs of burnout. No matter how hard I worked, I felt perpetually insufficient. I was double-booked, triple-booked, and quadruple-booked on my calendar, regularly pissing people off by not being able to attend meetings that were important to them, and probably to me. Since I didn't attend, I didn't really know. I was hard at work trying to accomplish what I'd once managed for *World in Conflict*, which was to convince the publisher to support and prioritize our game. In the Vivendi days, the group of people we needed to convince was limited in number, and we faced them all at the unified annual summits. If we did well at the summits, a lot was achieved. But Ubisoft was a much more complicated company, with an incredible salesforce distributed across the world. It seemed impossible to win them over one by one.

In an attempt to focus, I began making a straightforward list of everything I did during my workdays, and it didn't take me long to realize that Massive needed a proper brand director if things were going to work. Over half of my daily tasks were related to brand-building, both internally and externally. It had originally been a significant portion of my job for Martin Walfisz, and when I became managing director in 2009, I and everyone else had assumed that I'd just continue working on publisher relations, brand, PR, and marketing. I vainly enjoyed the fact that my colleagues considered me to be the best at these things, but it was obviously no longer possible.

I made an important decision: I was going to hire a brand director for the studio, and it was going to be someone from deep within the Ubisoft business teams. That way, we'd gain instant access and establish our own connection to the business network. If I found the right person, it would be one elegant stroke, and we'd have someone who understood how to position Massive and *The Division* internally. Removing me from these tasks would be more than problem solving, it felt like it would constitute an organ replacement. I hoped the benefits would kick in swiftly.

One fine evening in Paris, in a dark and busy restaurant where they allegedly served the best tiramisu in the world, I had an after-dinner drink with a Frenchman named Eric Moutardier. He was intense, funny, and openly ambitious (which made my Swedish psyche nervous). Eric was tall and gangly, with a French nose and small, lively eyes that were flanked by wrinkles from laughter. Many years earlier, he had enjoyed a semisuccessful career as a rock guitarist, but finally, after some time in Ubisoft's licensing team, he'd ended up on the company's European business team, also known as EMEA. I liked his charm and energy. He was a forward-leaning guy with a strong desire to win, and a chip on his shoulder. I tried to convince him to come to Sweden.

Although we'd never met during the launch of *Far Cry 3*, I discovered that he'd played a huge role in the marketing of the game. In fact, Eric had even more in common with Massive and me. He was a former entertainer with big dreams, and once he came to the conclusion that he was never going to be a famous rock star, he'd turned to the gaming industry. He had a reputation for being pushy and uncompromising (a prima donna!), and after having been overlooked for an important promotion, he felt he wanted to prove himself. Relocating to Sweden and Massive at the time was a big leap of faith on his part, since it was extremely difficult to gauge what *The Division* was about to become, but Eric decided he was willing to give it a dedicated shot.

"If I join you, will you promise to make it worth my while?" Eric said.

"I promise to make it the best decision you ever make in your career," I answered, only vaguely aware that these were almost the exact words Martin had used when he convinced me to join Massive many years earlier.

Eric proved to be crucial to our ability to anchor *The Division* within the broader Ubisoft organization, and he had an amazing ability to condense all the ideas the team had into an elegant and cohesive brand. He embarked on an ambitious journey to make our marketing colleagues fall in love with our project. The internal promotion was like running a simulation of how to bring the game to the market later on. With incredible speed, Eric and his growing team of artists and product managers refined and polished the facade of the project until it shone like a true jewel. The game itself had always been promising, but with the clarification of the stakes, the setting, the tone, and the premise, it began to look like an amazing package.

Despite the last-minute and increasingly successful efforts to gain support, we were also being highly criticized and challenged by many, and doubt was spreading like wildfire. This only spurred us on and boosted our self-image as outsiders, and ultimately the sole effect it had was to make us even more determined. The doubt was rocket fuel. Quietly, Jason and Serge kept an eye on us and rooted for us with their everlasting support. More and more they felt like our last remaining champions at Ubisoft.

Finally, we had to face reality. We were out of time to make promises, and now was the time to deliver. But a live demo? The project was still a fragmented mix of great ideas, good writing, and promising prototypes that had meaning only to us in the know.

The team had just recently become large enough to deliver anything that was able to survive a public showing. Nevertheless, we were told to produce something awesome for the upcoming E3, which was only a few months away. The team scrambled desperately with last-last minute calls and began piecing together a demo. As soon as I saw what they were creating, I was convinced that we had something unique on our hands. The team entered a seamless state of flow, the finest form of creativity.

After jumping through a million hoops and meetings, we came out of the tunnel suddenly facing the spotlight of Ubisoft's annual press conference in Los Angeles.

We were in an old Art Deco–style movie theater downtown, the clock ticking down toward the start of the global broadcast in which we were expected to be a surprise highlight. It was a beautiful place, painted in red and gold, with magnificent balconies high above. People ran around with all sorts of equipment, cables trailing them like octopus arms. Outside, California lived on, the sun shining on surfers, pedestrians, celebrities, and a billion cars on the highways. Here, many before us had faced their verdict as creators at various premieres. The scent of nervous sweat and many months of hard work hung heavy in the air. I couldn't stand it; I had to leave.

I went outside to breathe some air. It didn't matter. I had no stage duties. I was planning to stay in the background, as always, leaving the stage to the core team. I took a deep breath.

Suddenly I felt a gentle pat on my shoulder. It was Jason Kaminski.

"Are you okay? Aren't you going to go in?" he asked. "There won't be any seats left if you don't watch out."

It was fantastic to bump into him just minutes before the big moment. He'd played such a crucial part in the journey. He wore a pair of strange black pants with large holes that made his underwear visible. I gave him a brotherly hug, acknowledging what was at stake, sharing the moment.

"Yeah, I'll join you in a minute," I replied, feeling dizzy with trepidation. "Cool pants," I added with some hesitation, and wondered if there would ever be a time in my life when I would be comfortable wearing something like that.

"Okay, buddy. See you inside," Jason said through a puff of smoke, and disappeared.

The air was still, and the busy street felt like an illusion.

As the giant doors to the movie theater were about to close, I squeezed in and found a seat, not noticing anything except the dimly lit stage in front of me. As the other projects were touted in slick and well-rehearsed presentations, I found it hard to focus. My hands were growing numb and I desperately needed some water to get my blood pressure up. After a long while, the press conference seemed to reach its logical end and Yves Guillemot made a good show of wrapping things up, but then, as I knew he would, he threw in the magical words that would be the cue to defining Massive's future: "But, oh. Wait. I've got something more to show you," he said with a confident smile.

My heart stopped. Half of me blacked out and my limbs went cold from the sudden adrenaline surge, while the other half became ultra-alert, noticing every single speck of dust.

"This is a game from one of the best game developers in the world," Yves continued, going off-script. The room went completely dark, and an intense, moody trailer that I knew well began outlining facts about modern society. Fast-paced edits, perfect tempo, leaving no time to think. I heard journalists in the room posing questions to one other: *No logo? Nothing? What is this?*

The trailer highlighted the fragility of society, our dependence on infrastructure far removed from our control, and then introduced the idea of a virus being intentionally planted on dollar bills on Black Friday, on Manhattan Island. *What would you do if you were there as the collapse began?*

Blackout.

The dim blue lights shifted to a soft orange.

Out of nowhere, Cece came onstage like a magician, majestically standing alone in the middle of the stage with nothing but a PlayStation controller in his hands. In a few words, he introduced himself and began playing the demo we'd carefully crafted.

Still no logo? Nothing? What on earth is this?

As our elegant in-game rendition of New York came to life on the giant screen behind Cece, I heard the audience waking up, getting genuinely excited. One by one, cell phones lit up as the crowd began tweeting and texting about what they were experiencing. The demo flawlessly ended exactly where it should, and inside a glowing orange circle on a pitch-black background, the name of the game was finally revealed: *Tom Clancy's The Division.*

The audience went ballistic and cheered like maniacs. No one had seen this coming! Everyone who knew anything about games recognized in an instant how big a game this could be.

Our segment had been nine minutes long, and it closed the Ubisoft press conference with a loud bang. I wobbled out, slightly shocked, on an all-time high. In the street, I searched for the team as I ran into a shock wave of love and a storm of journalists. I hugged everyone like an idiot and thought with deep gratitude about the folks back home who'd made it all possible. Without delay, we continued down to the show floor at the E3 Convention Center and basked in the glory of industry admiration. The most important form of recognition we got was from other game developers whom we truly admired. They kept coming to our booth during the entire show, asking for a private walk-through, and their delight and honest praise were the best forms of validation we could have ever received. For a few days, we were the kings of the world.

Once E3 finally wrapped, we ventured into LA for dinner, exhausted and happy. We were giggling over drinks, and, almost telepathically, we agreed that every single person present had to make a speech. We were high on alcohol and success, and as the night went on, the speeches just got funnier and funnier.

We were the proud architects of *The Division* announcement at the Orpheum. We'd consciously crafted a specific string of emotions, a web of connected dots, that had cast a spell over a global audience. And our dreams had only just begun to reshape reality.

31

OREGON

As a part of the studio surfed the wave of success brought about by the announcement of *The Division* and turned their attention to the complicated production of the game, I was still struggling with another difficult challenge: How were we ever going to convince James Cameron that we were the right game studio to develop the future *Avatar* game? The first meeting in Santa Monica hadn't given me any discernible clues.

The world of Pandora offered exactly what I was looking for. It was a rich, colorful, and insanely well-crafted universe, with a billion stories to tell. The attention to detail fit us perfectly. And, oh! We soon realized that they were not just planning a single sequel, but in fact, *four*! If it worked out, we might have a decadelong partnership with one of the most successful teams of entertainers on the planet.

Lightstorm's clear focus on a meaningful message being embedded in *Avatar* was intensely attractive to me, Petter, and Soundboy. Behind all the traditional entertainment one expects in an epic Hollywood movie, there was an important narrative that we felt strongly about. In addition to *fighting for what you believe in*, the *Avatar* movies are about ecology and balance. Seen through that particular lens, the *Avatar* stories are a provocative reminder of the unethical liberties we humans take with all other living creatures on earth. In comparison, everything we'd worked on until then felt shallow and light, like pointless exercises in special effects, vehicles, simple narratives, explosions, and weapons. We were ready to make a game that subtly focused on something more important. To some degree, *The Division* was already a step in this direction, with its underlying question of what any one of us would do if we faced a collapsing version of modern society. Who would we become in the face of starvation and fear? But *Avatar* was taking it all further, perfectly wrapped in the most accessible form of traditional fun. We were irresistibly drawn to it.

Massive had come halfway with the self-imposed, long-term goal of establishing two parallel core teams with a central engine. *The Division* was the "new" core team, and they were already pushing our engine development to the extreme. Simultaneously, a small remaining group of the "old" core team who'd shipped *World in Conflict* and *Far Cry 3* were available to experiment with something new. Together with Petter, Soundboy, and the blessing of Ubisoft HQ, we decided to launch an exploration that might impress the cautious folks in Hollywood too.

Meanwhile, Cameron's company, Lightstorm, had moved to an awe-inspiring studio in Manhattan Beach, near the Los Angeles Airport, and we visited for a few follow-up meetings. We felt like kids when the guards allowed us on-site. *Hollywood, baby!* This was a childhood dream come true. We were given a tour of the extraordinary premises, allegedly twice the size of any other. As we walked around in awe, we bumped into some of the least known but best talents in the movie industry, the team behind Cameron's creations on the silver screen. They were low-key, intensely focused people, proud of their work, and surprisingly shy, like many of the best game developers I had met. Almost casually, some of the famous director's props had been placed in the studio, but to us this was true magic. The Alien Queen from *Aliens*, the actual full-sized model! Two enormous models of the *Titanic*, before and after the accident. A full-scale mech suit from *Avatar*! Our heads were dizzy.

During those visits we outlined the broad strokes of what we wanted to do in an *Avatar* game. It was madly ambitious but caught Lightstorm's attention enough to keep conversations going. In the corner of the meeting room we noticed gifts from competitors who'd left promotional material behind, trying to establish a friendship, just like us. Considering that the merchandise was left to collect dust on a drawer in the meeting room, we assumed that others found it as difficult to impress the demanding celebrities as we did. Still, between the lines, we picked up that we were probably not the favorites in this particular beauty contest.

We were introduced to the new team at Lightstorm: Brooks Brown and Kathy Franklin. Apparently, these were the people we'd have to convince, since Cameron and Landau felt that they personally knew too little about video games and wanted someone to evaluate the various proposals while they themselves focused on the future movies. We turned our attention to the newbies.

Brooks was called the "Game Expert," and over the course of several meetings we got to know him well. He was a tall guy from Colorado, always wearing cowboy boots, no matter the weather. His hair seemed to grow longer every time we ran into him, and the hippie look was soon supported by a beard that together with his round glasses made him look like John Lennon's giant brother. He spoke in an unusually loud baritone voice that made people listen. Brooks seemed angry, always. In long rants, he was outspoken about the many faults and flaws of basically everything in the world and the people in it. He reminded me of my brother somehow, and quietly I sympathized with many of his frustrations. I realized that I agreed with most of his rash and blunt judgments, except my upbringing made me filter my words through polite and careful choices, from which he apparently felt liberated. Perhaps, unlike me, he was convinced that he was always right and that drove him on. A big part of my life has been spent thinking that

I probably don't know enough, and that every individual I meet offers the potential to learn something new. Brooks had no such patience, and as a result most people would certainly perceive the two of us as very different, but somehow, there was a seed for a genuine kinship. Brooks blustered on about the worst games he'd ever played, and it didn't escape me that he had a very good eye for what makes games work and what makes them fail. *He should be a creative director somewhere*, I thought to myself, but there he was, looking at others who were pitching their dreams to him.

Kathy had been hired to oversee franchise development for Lightstorm, and in contrast to Brooks, she was soft-spoken, rational, precise, polite, and the most pleasant person one could possibly run into. But no one underestimated her, because it was evident that underneath the perfect manners, there was a sharp and exceptionally efficient businesswoman. It was no surprise to hear that she came from Disney. She meant business in the utmost sense.

Unfortunately for us, the most essential part of what we were pitching to Lightstorm was very difficult to grasp for someone with limited experience producing games. We wanted to create an enormous rendition of Pandora, larger than anything anyone had ever seen in a game. We felt that the epic nature of the movies deserved a sister product that was of equal scale. But when attempting to build such vast worlds (or a moon, in this case), a development team runs into unsolvable problems. It is insanity to hand-tailor every strand of grass, every branch of every tree, every drop of water, and every animal that should live there. So how does one approach it, unless there are thousands of people on the team? Our theories for making the game were based on the fact that nature in itself can be described in mathematics. Flora behaves rationally and predictably, as do fauna, geology, ecosystems, and weather patterns. Everything in the real world, except perhaps the most advanced mammals, behaves in foreseeable patterns. But what if we could re-create those algorithms and make our game engine build the world by itself? Video games had finally reached a point where a vast world sprung from the imaginations of the artists and engineers at Massive was within reach.

I loved the idea of teaching Snowdrop the mathematics of nature. Apart from the daunting task of doing it, this was a fully plausible approach that no one had ever used, at least as far as we knew. We could teach the digital herbivores what they preferred to eat, in logical locations where elevation and weather would ensure that the right plants would grow. Over the course of a year, seasons would force them to move to where the plants were plentiful, and they would mate and have puppies in a pattern that enhanced their chances of survival. We'd build similar logic loops for the predators, who would hunt, mate, and migrate, depending on the world conditions around them. If we could make it work, it would be a perfect sandbox in which to place a gamer, and not only would every player become an agent of change, but also, the side effects of their choices would be profound. It would all boil down to the mathematics, which would appear as knobs for a god to adjust to control everything.

It was incredibly exciting, but we must have done a poor job of explaining it, or perhaps more likely, a poor job of appearing like people who could pull it off. We left Hollywood over and again feeling more like a surreal dance act performing at the Super Bowl halftime show than convincing craftsmen.

"We need proof," Petter said matter-of-factly.

"Yes," Soundboy added. As usual, he didn't waste many words.

We began exploring the tech in earnest and gave the project the nickname Oregon. The official Mandate described it as "a Snowdrop-based exploration into procedural generation of worlds and ecosystems." Exceptionally cool, for those who understood the true meaning of the words, but ambitious to the point of being less likely to succeed than humans setting foot on the moon.

32

LIKE DROWNING IN CORSICA

A major triple-A game like *Assassin's Creed*, *Far Cry*, or *The Division* is developed in a colorful blur of great assumptions and prototyped failures until it Darwinistically takes on the best form it can. The game itself is like an unborn child in a dream world, yearning to be launched into being. During the process of germination and fermentation, the team and the publishers identify key moments in the process, called milestones, each one with its own specific definition and goal.

"Green light," for instance, means that the publisher is impressed with your pitch and is ready to spend money on it (Hooray!). "First playable" is another milestone, where the name tells you all you need to know. (Celebrate! Things are about to become difficult.)

Later milestones come with secretive names that don't really reveal what they are about, like "alpha" and "beta." On the triple-A level these are exceptionally complicated affairs that require several hundred talented developers to reach. But to make it simple, alpha is the moment where everything that is eventually expected to appear in the final game is, or should be, included in the software, in some shape or another. At the alpha stage, individual features can be in terrible shape, as long as they are included. It's like going naked, unfit, and unshaven to a party where everyone is completely okay with it. All that is expected of you is to show up, as you are. No makeup required.

Once alpha is approved, the team begins to focus on turning all the unfinished systems into something functional, and they fill the feature buckets with all the content and fun they were originally intended to support (like being able to hunt *all* of the animals, not just the warthog). After struggling like maniacs to make all these miracles happen, the developers finally reach beta stage, which means that no feature or content can be added. The following weeks and months are spent on fixing bugs, on purely mathematical tweaks in the code, and on selective super-polishing of the game's flagship features.

Or, well…so we claim. What is described here is the theoretical alpha and the theoretical beta. Predictably, in real life, no one has the ability or the discipline to follow such healthy guidelines, which means that the gates of feature-creeping hell open up at alpha and grow worse between beta and the (theoretically speaking) final milestone called Gold Master Candidate. If crunch magically didn't occur earlier, it is guaranteed to make an ungraceful appearance after alpha. ("Crunch" is the nickname game developers have given to periods of excessive overtime. The epithet literally refers to getting physically and emotionally crushed by pressure, lack of sleep, bad food, insanely long hours, and a complete resignation of your entire life to the Great Cause of Shipping the Game.)

Late in 2014, after our successful announcement at E3 in 2013, *The Division* was approaching a delayed alpha, and we'd again strained the seemingly endless patience of our dear friends at Ubisoft HQ. Maybe the game was in acceptable shape. But if it was, we couldn't tell. As is always the case with open-world games, things were falling into place very late in the process. Linear and session-based games are much easier to control during development, because the boundaries are fixed, and the number of choices delegated to the player is finite. But in open-world games, one of the core design principles is to maximize unconstrained player choice. This leads to a focus on systems and features that can be interconnected and interact in multiple ways anywhere in the vast world.

Developers of open-world games try to give as much liberty as possible to the player. If it works, it's a fantastic piece of entertainment with a generous set of player options. The problem is that during long periods of development, the multitude of underlying systems are disconnected and seem to appear in silos. The sensation of playing such a game before it jells into a cohesive whole is like eating all the ingredients of foods that make up a three-course meal independently and then trying to guess the chef's intended recipe.

Trying to judge the development velocity through fragments was impossible for all of us, and it seemed we were unable to break through. *I bet the studio on this?* I thought with fear and sadness one day as I tried playing the latest version of the game. It was horrible. Unplayable. Paris felt the same way, and they didn't hesitate to let me know. We were getting a bad reputation at HQ, and there were plenty who hadn't forgotten how I'd acted like a prima donna.

Perhaps in panic, and to the frustration of the Oregon team, I put their project on hold and made sure everyone in the studio was working on the upcoming milestone for *The Division*. Personally, I thought this made sense, since we were staking our entire reputation on Snowdrop and the ambitious Clancy game. But for the individuals involved, it created friction. Those on *The Division* who'd become used to making decisions suddenly had to adapt to a host of additional and opinionated colleagues who were given a slice of their empire. For those coming from Oregon it was painful, considering they'd fallen in love with their new project and the perceived freedom they'd earned through their hard work on *Far Cry 3*. Now, instead, they were forced to give up their labor of love and bring their A-game to a project they'd long been disconnected from. To a degree, this meant I'd broken my promise to them. In my mind, it was a necessary sacrifice to achieve our long-term goals, but this kind of rhetoric is always thin ice for a manager. I felt lonely, but on the other hand, I was not personally in the trenches taking bullets. I felt very much like a traditional boss, sitting behind a desk, making cold whiteboard decisions without fully appreciating the potential human cost of my self-perceived elegant strategies.

And honestly, the game looked like shit. It was terrifying, and still, no one was able to tell when things were going to fall into place. None of us had ever made a game this complex before. Eric went to Paris for a meeting and came back telling me that he'd been asked many questions about me, Massive, our ability, and the game. The words thrown around in Paris hurt like a dagger: David is not *stellar*, he is just a *seller*. What a perfect way to wrap an insult in a few words.

Right after Christmas 2014, I visited the head office, located in Montreuil, on the eastern side of Paris. It wasn't far from the cemetery Père-Lachaise, where the legendary Doors vocalist Jim Morrison is buried. Ubisoft had a great discount at a hotel called Mama Shelter on Rue de Bagnolet, and at breakfast I ran into a bunch of colleagues from all over the world. It was a bit like a camp for a secret society, which enhanced the family feel that Yves nurtured so well. The interior decoration of the hotel had been designed by Philippe Starck, which gave the place a weird retro-'80s vibe. It looked like a tiny nightclub with the black walls, neon lights, corny metallic details, and a stage ready for a Pet Shop Boys performance. In the foyer there was a shop selling wrestling masks, Starck souvenirs, expensive motorcycle helmets, and designer books. I wondered if they ever saw any business.

The hotel was close enough to offer a morning stroll to the office, through quiet backstreets and across the highway that separates the *real* Paris from Montreuil. This distinction is important to the French, but to me it made no difference to be in one part of the big city or another. It was all Paris as far as I could tell. The day ahead offered a few uncomplicated meetings: a discussion with central IT about purchasing, a follow-up on a couple of HR topics, and a meeting about *Just Dance Now*, which we were involved in as a side project at Massive.

During my promenade I got an email from my boss, Christine, asking me to make time to see her ASAP that day. This had not been scheduled. My mind immediately snapped to attention. Over the years I'd realized that she actually had a really difficult job: to be the skeptic among romantics. She'd always be the one to ask the hard questions and to follow up on unpleasant topics. An email from her requesting an immediate meeting likely didn't mean good news.

The weak winter rays of the January sun felt a lot colder all at once. My mind drifted to another time and another place, years earlier, when I was sinking into black waters.

I once took a diving license test in the murky waters of Stockholm, where there is nothing to see. All you can do there is learn how to dive well. Otherwise, it's a lot like submerging yourself in a brown sauce. Certainly not what diving looks like if you google it.

At the time I had a girlfriend who was passionate about everything underwater, and she'd just returned from working as a diving instructor by the Red Sea. Her former boyfriend was an ex-military Israeli, who, in my mind, sounded like a well-built Brad Pitt with a Land Rover and an advanced diver's license. How was I supposed to match that? Well, I decided to try, so I booked a surprise holiday to Corsica for the two of us, where, I promised, we'd dive together in the azure-blue waters of the Mediterranean. The diving course in Stockholm was only preparation for my rock-solid plans to be the Best Boyfriend Ever.

After a few weeks I had my license ready, although I found the whole thing confusingly casual. Wasn't diving supposed to be dangerous and very serious? Meticulous and precise? No, apparently not. It felt more like what I had imagined surfing to be: cool people sitting around on beaches and rocky shores, in cool professional-looking gear, with a beer in one hand and a war story hanging in the air, building a brotherhood of bravado.

When we eventually sat on the boat headed toward the beautiful French island, I felt that diving was a lot easier than I'd imagined. We found a nice beach somewhere in the south where there was a diver's club that perfectly matched my idyllic expectations. They operated from a garage close to the water, and everyone who worked there looked like a body-building sailor with sun-kissed skin. Trés *cool*.

The confident dive instructor looked at my manual and grunted.

"Hmm. I see you are new to this? Oui?" he asked in a heavy French accent.

"Yes," I said, feeling like a disappointment. "I just got my license."

"Okay, okay, alors…," he said, hesitating before he continued: "In that case we will only go to eighty meters, oui?"

"EIGHTY?" I said as my eyes popped out. *Eighty?!* As far as I knew that wasn't even possible unless you were a professional diver breathing strange mixes like Nitrox or Trimix.

"Oui," he said. "Or wait. Zut alors! NO! Actually, I meant that we go to eighteen meters maximum. EIGHTEEN, okay? Not eighty."

Well, that certainly made more sense. Eighteen was supposedly a safe and beginner-friendly depth that should be good for me. *Brad Pitt, prepare to be dethroned!*

A short boat ride later, we jumped in and began the dive next to a set of Corsican cliffs. The bubbles from our exhaled breaths floated upward. I was surrounded by the magical scenery of a whole underwater world, filled with small miracles and exciting life-forms. This was nothing like the Stockholm experience. Six meters. Ten. Fourteen, Sixteen. And, finally, eighteen! It was unbelievably exciting, like some sort of unexpected homecoming. I signaled that I was okay and happy to my diving buddy, a.k.a. my girlfriend. It was hard to see her face behind all the gear and the breathing regulator, but I imagined that she smiled lovingly at me.

I looked at my depth meter again: Twenty. Twenty-four. *Twenty-six*…What? WAIT, WHAT? This was not what we'd agreed upon!

I'd never been deeper than twelve meters before, and this was getting scary, but everyone else in the group seemed oblivious to my fears. It was as if they'd all reverted to their own private bubble of consciousness. *Twenty-eight. Thirty. Thirty-two.* I felt my heart pounding and reached out for my buddy to get some reassurance, but she was too far away, swimming elegantly like a dolphin.

And then.

I faced death.

Literally.

I tried to take another breath, but all I felt was the solid resistance of my regulator flaps. Full stop. The vent was closed. I knew that this could have been caused by a few different things, but the cause was not important, because all the possible explanations would result in the same thing: no air. *I had no air!* I looked upward at a roof of water above. Thirty-two meters to the surface. Indeed, it looked like the promised cathedral of light, but unfortunately for me, also impossibly far to swim without breathing at least once or twice. From my training I remembered that a human can survive without fresh air for a few minutes at best, and then the inevitable will happen. Drowning seemed like a horrible but suddenly very real proposition. It was no comfort that Corsica was a beautiful place to die.

My brain zoomed out to a safe distance, and all I could think was: *Hmm. Interesting.* I became my own experiment, detached to the point where I thought of myself in third-person. *How curious! What will he do?* It was like watching a movie, admittedly very close to the end, in which the brave hero tragically dies. I could imagine my girlfriend in tears on the beach, shouting in anger toward the gods and the setting sun. *Why? Oh why did you steal my love from me?*

For a few seconds I just hung in weightless stillness, surrounded by underwater beauty. Instead of the pleasant sound of my own bubbles rising toward the surface, I heard only an eerie silence. I waited for a reaction. Would I panic? Would I cry? Would my last action among the living be flailing my limbs ridiculously in embarrassing desperation?

But...

Nothing.

I felt nothing at all. My brain started analyzing what was going on in a cold and rational manner. What had I learned about running out of air? What was the correct procedure? What were the few solutions still available to me?

Okay, I thought, *this is how I react under extreme pressure. Good to know.* And I saw my body doing the right things, unemotionally.

Swim to my buddy (even if the speed burst would cost me more of the precious air I still had in my lungs).

Make the right hand signs.

Start cobreathing from the buddy tank.

Take two breaths each.

Then switch.

Abort the dive immediately.

Resurface.

Live.

My visit at Ubisoft HQ in the early days of 2015 turned out to be way too similar to that memory.

When I entered the front door of the Paris office, I got another email: "The meeting will be in Yves's office." *Jesus,* I thought. *Going down. Eighteen. Twenty-two. Twenty-six.*

In the elevator, I ran into Nicolas Schoener, who oversaw all the production processes at Ubisoft. I absentmindedly tried to make small talk.

"Hey, how are you doing?" I asked. "Did you get anything nice for Christmas?"

Nicolas was usually a friendly and talkative guy, but he remained unresponsive and silently stared at the elevator doors. Clearly, he wanted to get out as soon as possible, and I realized my company was tainted; I was dangerous goods. I was *That Guy.* Someone that people needed to avoid if they still cared about their careers. I realized this was going even deeper. *Thirty. Thirty-two.*

I stepped into the office of the CEO and found myself facing what could be described only as an intervention. On the other side of the big table sat more than a hundred years of experience: Yves, Serge, Christine, and my elevator buddy, Nicolas. They stared at me in silence. It was clear that I was out of air to breathe by now, and that I could only observe what was going to happen next. As in Corsica, I zoomed out and thought rationally about what was going on, already looking for the few remaining solutions. If they were planning to fire me, they wouldn't have bothered to waste their time like this, I decided, and felt a slight sliver of hope.

Yves began explaining his concerns to me. He was furious, agitated, frustrated, and disappointed in a way that I'd never seen him before. Once he was done, Serge continued with another scorching lecture that hurt me to the bone. If we had lost his trust, we were truly at the end of the line. Like an improvising jazz band, the four of them took turns playing their solos. All of them had the same melody, though: This is it. Your last chance. We are exceptionally concerned, angry, and disappointed. *Do you realize what's at stake?*

Of course I understood what was at stake, but this was not the time for smart and smug replies. It wasn't even the right time for a dialogue, because anything I might have said was going to sound like a bad excuse or like a coward's attempt to put the blame on others. I was drowning, careerwise. My mind was racing, and I couldn't digest everything that was being said on the spot. *Forget the shame and fear. Focus on fixing the problem, the project. Get to the surface.*

I took up my notepad and began writing down everything I was told. During outbursts of anger or pointless ventilations of bitterness, I just pretended to write it all down to at least signal that their words were being noted and taken seriously. In my head, my imaginary hands were already reaching for my trusted diving partners, Petter and Soundboy. I could not save *The Division* any other way.

Much later that day I finally left Ubisoft HQ, with quite a few new gray hairs and feeling woozy. It was the first time in my career that I'd experienced a proper scolding. My biggest problem, though, was that they were partially right. The project was in a complicated state, and something needed to change for us to deliver on the majestic promise we had created at E3 in 2013.

I decided to fire the last bullet I had and bet Massive's future on it. I was going to replace the producer and the creative director of *The Division* as soon as I got home. I'd give the roles to the old dependable hands, the only people I felt certain would make a real change: Petter and Soundboy.

33

FROM A MOSS-COVERED STONE

I went home to Sweden fighting the onset of depression and desperation. My brain wanted to escape into fantasy to find hope somewhere, but I knew I had to confront the harshness of my reality.

I fell asleep on the airplane, exhausted, and began dreaming.

In the dream I found myself running, as if I were lost in a forest. It was sometimes frighteningly dark, sometimes very beautiful, always very busy. But I found a glade among all those trees where I could see the sky above, and there was thick and healthy moss on the rocks. I stopped there, to rest, to breathe, to feel, and to hear myself better. As my heart slowed down, I decided to enjoy the things that were close to me. It felt peaceful. It was introspection, not isolation.

I liked it, and I wanted to stay and swim in the moment, soaking it in fully.

But then, in that rare pause of sober breathing, something else dawned upon me and hit me like a bolt of lightning. Out of the depths, a dark, strong voice said, "David, it's time to stop running now." And suddenly, I felt that I was utterly done with the game industry. I felt worn-down. Tired, hunted, and spent. The gigantic and marvelous labyrinth that I'd spent more than fifteen years navigating had finally led me to a path and a place where my inner voice said, *That's it. It's finished now.*

I took a step back again and looked at the emotion. Was it just a ghost that was trying to scare me, or was it a real instinct? Was it just this particular job that was an insurmountable death march, or was it the entire game industry, or was it simply all the jobs in the entire universe? It was hard to tell. The feeling spread like a freezing lake inside me.

"Get out," the dream whispered, with long shadowy fingers and tired old eyes. "Get out now, before you break."

And then the dream faded away.

A long time had passed since Oskar at Out There Communications had shown me his little Java-applet game, but it didn't escape me that in some bitterly ironic way, I was back at square one, as a beginner, a noob, the guy who was *only watching* while others delivered the real deal.

Once upon a time I had huddled over Oskar's screen, marveling at his creation, staring through the magic door that made me dream of a career in games. Seemingly limitless possibilities had beckoned me to join them, like digital sirens calling me to become a full-time maker of stories.

But now, this.

Broken. Ready to quit.

The words had such a bitter taste.

What had brought me to this point?

As is the case with any complex relationship, it was a combination of many things. But perhaps the most apparent reason was that for every year my career had progressed, the projects and teams became bigger. I'd added a layer of emotional hardness to my psyche in order to cope with the ever-growing expectations and demands that inevitably followed. I had been desensitizing myself in order to remain strong on the journey. When I finally admitted this to myself, I knew that if I went back to the same survival strategies, the years that followed would not be good for me.

All my life, I'd dealt with difficulties by just working harder. If a situation was challenging, I would just tell myself, *Work harder*. When I felt tired and alone: *Work harder*. When I ran into disruptive idiots: *Work harder*. I always fought quietly. I defended my inner child and his right to dream; I fought for my friends, my colleagues, and the quests we embarked upon; and I fought to provide for my family. Working harder was the answer to everything, always. And it worked, except...I didn't realize what it was doing to my soul. By focusing on working harder and harder, I was slowly becoming unable to *feel* anything at all. Now, something had to change. For my own sake, I needed to take a stance, and I decided to protect the childlike sense of wonder that had been the core driver in all the important decisions I'd made in my life.

There must be other ways, a voice whispered from within.

In that inner glade where I stopped to think and breathe, I realized with sadness that I'd brought my life to a point where I was gradually forced further and further away from all the wonderous things that heal the soul. But to see magic and miracles and to reach out and touch them requires a delicate hand and an eye sensitive to the hidden beauty of the world. If I was running, I couldn't see a thing.

Slowly it became clear that no matter what was going to happen to *The Division* when I came back to Massive, I had verbalized what truly matters to me: I believe in those who stubbornly hold on to fragile ideas, who protect them in the face of the cynics. I believe that a strong narrative can shape reality. I believe that life is ultimately about being generous, curious, and honest with ourselves and others. I believe that when we inevitably fail and make mistakes, we need compassion and love from our fellow travelers— particularly from those we have hurt. And in return we will be happier in our own lives when we choose to understand and forgive those who have hurt us. The world is truly a magical and quiet miracle if we allow it to be.

Once I got off the plane, still feeling low, I unexpectedly got a text message from my old art school buddy Jonas. It had been several years since we'd actually spoken to each other, although in our imaginations we were timeless friends who could pick up the thread any time we wanted to. Until the reunion, we were consumed by our respective journeys into marriage, parenthood, and careers.

I read the words on the tiny screen:

I was thinking about you the other day. My kids were playing a game, and I told them I knew the guy who made it.

I felt a wave of gratitude for this gift of warmth and empathetic support. Jonas! *My friend.* He had always cheerily supported me at every turn back in art school, no matter if I deserved it or not. It was wonderful to be reminded of what loyalty felt like.

Hey, that's cool. How are you nowadays? Any plans to travel south soon? I wrote back. But he wasn't accepting my change of topic.

Dude, the game! They went ballistic! They were so impressed!

Remotely, I felt a keen sense of pride that stopped me in my tracks. Was Jonas pulling my leg?

Really? I texted back.

Yeah man. You're a superstar now. The coolest. You're making me look like a cool dad just by knowing you!

Was the timing of this conversation arranged by some benevolent deity who wanted to comfort me? It sure felt like it. Either way, it was the kind of medicine I needed, and at the right time. No time for my inner insecure artist—I had to be the confident leader Massive needed. The severity of the situation demanded it.

So: *Yes.* I was going to take care of the project, with a clear and sharp focus on what truly mattered. *No time for crying or self-pity,* I stoically told myself, but before I knew it I spiraled into an unexpected vortex of something much worse.

* * *

Without any real warning, in absurdly painful slow motion, my marriage began falling apart. Frame by frame, the emotional damage splattered all over my life like the blood from a violent accident. Except it was no accident at all; it was *my own failure*. Profound, horrendous failure that pushed me over emotional borders into a land of eternal black. I fought the journey into darkness with the energy of a dead fish, slowly sinking toward the deep.

I regretted everything I had ever done and didn't know what that meant. I just wanted to run around like a maniac screaming *I am sorry!* to everyone alive.

I became a highly limited version of myself, capable of expressing emotions only from a menu offering nothing but hopeless anger or the plain pathetic. I was furious inside, at everything. I wanted to fight someone. As if I were addicted to speed, I'd fall asleep at 2 a.m. only to wake up again at 4 a.m., erupting out of bed, ready to take on a new adrenaline-filled day. Like a drug, the despair fueled my ability to work harder than ever before, and I did. *The Division* was a painful, extended fight to stay alive anyway—it suited me just fine. *So what if the project seems hard?* I shouted at people. *We are just GONNA MAKE IT! Don't you fucking complain.* Anything that numbed my ability to experience real life was welcome medicine.

Consumed by guilt, I desperately wanted to blame someone else for the breakdown of my private life, and for a while I tried to blame it all on work. The Division *destroyed my marriage*, I tried to tell myself in an attempt to rearrange the narrative. *Crunch destroyed my marriage*, I tried, too, but neither had the ring of truth. Well, *someone* destroyed it! In what direction was I supposed to direct my fury?

Slowly, with great pain, the realization dawned upon me: I had no one to blame except myself. My marriage had suffered from my obsession to express myself as an artist, to become a great story-teller, to realize my own self. My personal life had been obliterated by my stubborn refusal to give up on professional challenges. Accepting that I had only myself to blame gave birth to an agonizing self-hatred.

Further away, behind the layers of pain, I felt suicidal fantasies stir like a poisonous ghost. And then I knew I was in really bad shape.

But I did the only thing I knew how to do.

I worked harder.

34

EVERYTHING IS MADE OF STARDUST

In a divorce, there are no heroes. But in wrapping up a game, there actually are.

At the end of the development of *Far Cry 3*, we had been exposed to a Ubisoft concept that was entirely new to us at Massive. "A *closer* is coming," they said ominously, and we imagined professional hit men or shady lawyers showing up at our doorstep. In fact, these fantasies weren't completely inaccurate, because, apparently, Ubisoft considered it to be a well-known truth that a development team can't wrap up their own project. Someone always needed to come in with a hammer and nail the doors shut. The assumption was that we game developers were too attached to our project and wouldn't have enough perspective to make tough decisions. Of course, for a team who was used to autonomy and who was fiercely proud of itself, this was bordering on an insult. But we decided to play along until we knew more. In good old Swedish tradition, Petter was furious but kept his clenched fists in his pockets.

"Shipping a game is MY JOB!" he said to me. "I don't need anyone to help me do *my job*!"

He felt robbed of the ultimate climax, the culmination of many, many months of dedication and hard work. Delivering the final Gold Master to the publisher is the producer's finest moment, like the hero's chance to hand over the Holy Grail to King Arthur—but now it seemed that this important and symbolic finale would be hijacked by a stranger. It was difficult and frustrating to accept.

A few weeks later, a tall Romanian guy entered Massive. His name was Cristian Pana, and he was the first closer we'd ever met. Initially, he delivered on our expectations of a trained assassin with a quiet and expressionless demeanor. It was as if he alone carried the eternal melancholy of the world on his broad shoulders. Behind the wire-rimmed glasses, his eyes were tired but revealed a very active intellect. No doubt he was clever. Too clever, in fact. We'd have to abandon Plan A. We quickly decided that there was no way we were ever going to be able to bullshit or sideline this guy. We'd have to accept him on the team. Enter plan B: Make him one of us.

At Cristian's request, I joined him outside in the parking lot next to the back entrance to Massive soon after he'd arrived. He was a smoker, the kind who smokes with no guilt, as if to signal *I am killing myself and I like it*. He was huge and confident. In a parallel universe, he might have had the nickname Chewbacca, but he was way too intimidating for cuddly talk.

"Listen," he said through a puff of cigarette smoke. "You have a great game. It will be very good. But I will have to do damage here before you can ship it, okay?"

"Why?" I had to ask. I was never a fan of the idea that suffering is necessary.

"Because...," he said, and paused before continuing, "Because it's always like that. Before I go, you will all hate me."

Man, this guy has been a closer for a really long time, I thought. His words genuinely piqued my interest, though, and a plan for an alliance began to form in my head. *What if we managed to wrap up* Far Cry *together and become friends in the process? What if we didn't do any damage to the team at all, and what if we didn't end up hating him in the end?* As a matter of principle, I refused to accept the finality of his expectations. And besides, in inner defiance toward my own predictability, I'd begun to really like the guy, and I thought that he was beginning to like Massive too.

After his smoke, we left the parking lot with a sense of unspoken brotherhood. *You close the game, and in the meantime, I will think of your future, after the trenches*, I thought. Cristian was like a loyal soldier who needed to come home.

At the end, all games need closing. At some point everything simply needs to be wrapped up and packaged into an experience for gamers everywhere. This is the cold, hard, and sometimes brutal phase of making games.

If the journey ends in a death march of crunch and relentless rationality, the big adventure starts at the opposite end of the spectrum: in the hazy and vague, in the fragile and esoteric, as far from the land of closers as possible.

Making triple-A games is a true marathon, and as almost everyone who has tried to run a real marathon knows, it's all about pacing. Run too fast in the beginning, and at around 30 km, your legs will stiffen, your stomach will cramp, your back will protest, your knees will collapse, and you will run into a mental wall that you can't overcome. You just cannot finish the race, because your aching body protests too aggressively. On the other hand, if you run too slow, you will feel good for a while, but then you realize you are committing yourself to a very, very long race, which might break you before the finishing line due to the endurance and patience it will require. Even the best Kenyan marathoners are extremely particular about their pace (though theirs is twice as fast as the average Joe's). In a four-hour marathon, seconds actually matter, counterintuitively.

Most game studios in the world run too fast. Much too fast. They see early success and feel fantastic at around 20 km, but then they inevitably crash and burn. The gaming industry is jam-packed with stories of insane hours, infamous crunching, pressure, and abusive leaders who push their teams toward physical collapse. Such a studio might manage to release a game, sometimes even two, but when they bring out the champagne to celebrate, two thirds of the staff are burned out, have missed seeing their children grow up, have lost all faith in their leaders, and hate the studio, which quickly spirals into decline.

In Sweden and the rest of Scandinavia, the concept of a work-life balance has been understood and respected for ages. We prefer to work eight-hour days, like efficient Swiss clocks: highly dedicated and with a laser-sharp focus. It doesn't matter if it's in the game industry or not, it's the same everywhere. And as it so happens, this is the perfect pace not only for successfully creating a single game, but for actually giving birth to great studios that last a long time and can steadily build on the experiences gained and create better and better games.

After passing out on an airplane once many years ago when I had worked much too hard, I decided I had to slow down and hit *the right* pace. The dramatic scene in the skies was embarrassing, but what made a bigger impression on me were the words from the doctor onboard who stared into my eyes when I woke up in the chaos I had created: "You are going to work yourself to death if you keep up this tempo."

I don't know how she knew this from just looking at me, but I guess she was a good doctor. I got the message. I was too young to die. As a consequence, I decided that I had to program myself to leave the office at 5 p.m. every day, no matter if the entire studio was on fire.

In the beginning of my new regimen, my young colleagues in the game industry found it very provocative that I was so strict about my pace, and it was seen as anti–gamer culture and antiambitious. But I was playing the long-game, and the five o'clock rule resulted in a reliable day-in-day-out performance in the decade that followed. Balance is a good thing. I believe it has played an important role not just for me, but for all the Swedish game companies.

A large project like *The Division* or *Avatar* is traditionally led by a producer and a creative director, who in turn are surrounded by a team of rock-solid and specialized directors in areas such as audio, art, tech, and narrative. Maybe animation, realization, and cinematics directors too. It all depends on the focus and style of the project. The producer is supported by various associate producers, who oversee different domains. Some producers like to accumulate a tremendous amount of power and are very hands-on; others are great at building a team of loyal officers around them whom they rely on for execution. But at the end of the day, the producer is responsible for time, budget, and execution, while the creative director is responsible for content. Together, they share the quest for quality.

The small group of producers and directors is called the core team, and, in theory, all decisions on the project should trace back to them. I say "in theory" because rather than being an elegant decision-making process, making games is more like a never-ending, winding path of problem solving. The core team needs to rely heavily on the individual experts distributed across the team who are often highly specialized—the best-of-the-best in extremely narrow fields of craft like digital hair, locomotion, matchmaking, optimization, anticheating, data management, dialogue, ambient audio, collision, or pathfinding. A game development team is like a community of exceptionally talented people who have all gone full-nerd into a topic that fascinates them to the extreme. Most of them believe that their respective field is the most important of all and will passionately fight for the right to deliver absolute perfection in it, no matter the reality or feasibility. It's like herding extremely emotional cats, disproportionally attached to an outrageously small detail that only they fully appreciate. But they're right in their attachment. The quality of the final game depends on this obsession.

The director's job is to set goals, broad and narrow, deep and thin, short and long; and the producer's job is to break down the goals and delegate them to the smaller, specialized teams. At the peak of a triple-A project, the team might be more than five hundred people strong.

The level of trust is naturally high, but in order to verify that the production loop is working and that the directors' visions are on their way to being realized (at some distant point in the future), the best method is to develop playable prototypes as soon as possible, which can answer questions such as: *When you say "soft light," is this what you mean? When you say "intention-revealing movement from the AI," is this what you mean?* The only way to know for sure is to build prototypes. They can be tested and evaluated. The results can be discussed, debated, and fought for, which results in plans for improvement. Meanwhile, the producers actively keep an eye on simply cutting features that are too problematic or will take too much time, which to the directors is like removing a guitarist from a band or a main character from a movie. Analyze, improve, adapt. The winding road is long.

Prototypes are not tested arbitrarily or subjectively; the important ones are tested in a laboratory. An audience is hooked up to various devices that will measure their reactions. Pulses are taken, eye movements are tracked, and levels of sweat are measured. Together with interviews and hard data from the games, the directors build an amazing understanding of how their visions are perceived by an audience. The ability to interpret and adapt to all this data, the measurable touchpoints of the gamer's experience, is key to arriving at what gamers colloquially refer to as the "fun factor."

Then, from what was once nebulous and amorphous, fixed points begin to appear like tent poles. Some things get carved into stone and never move again. They will be on the disc; they will be what the gamers experience on release day. Slowly, the various specialists deliver onto this literal backbone, which gradually gets richer and richer. The game grows into life from a black void, like a planet assembled from space dust. It's a beautiful thing to see. Maybe it's a process that does require a closer as midwife?

When *Far Cry 3* was finally wrapped up and delivered, the team had learned to love Cristian the Closer, to respect his craftsmanship, and to appreciate him for the heavy burden he carried. We learned that being a closer was a tough job, one that required a lonely individual to endure a hailstorm of frustration from the team. To our surprise, Cristian had been hiding a creative sensibility behind his hardened surface. His decisions as a closer were respectful, tasteful, elegant, and bold. He was a piano tuner allowing himself to play the Steinway when no one was listening. He turned out to be a virtuoso.

"I'll be back," he said over the farewell beer before departing for another mission in another studio, somewhere.

"Yes, please *do* come back," I said. And in what was beginning to become a habit, I added, "I promise to make it the best decision of your career."

35

GIANT FLIES

Brooks Brown from Lightstorm arrived at the Los Angeles Airport and headed for the lounge immediately after checking in. He had finally zoomed in on a game developer he felt might be the right one to recommend to James Cameron and Jon Landau for the *Avatar* game, and it wasn't Massive.

During our pitches and exploratory meetings, I'd come to know Brooks as a sweet and warm person, although he came wrapped in many layers of attitude and deep skepticism. Behind the anger was a man longing for true creativity, maybe for friendship, but most of all to be involved in a project that would one day become known as one of the finest pieces of entertainment on the planet. His intentions were great, and he had met everyone in the industry he hoped could be the best match for his sky-high expectations. *Never make shit*, he'd been told by Lightstorm when he landed the job. Brooks couldn't agree more. As far as he was concerned, it was almost a moral obligation to avoid making shit.

Most of the developers Brooks met had average and predictable ideas and instantly dropped out of competition. Some just showed screenshots of games they'd already produced, with added blue characters Photoshopped in. *They are all crap*, he thought.

One of the courting game studios blew their chances by telling

Kathy Franklin that they were great at making games specifically for women, "because all women need is something to do between diapers and standing in the grocery line." They lost the gig on the spot. Lightstorm's list of potential partners became shorter by the day.

In the lounge at LAX, Brooks saw someone he did not want to run into on this particular day: Ubisoft's head of Licensing, who'd been trying to woo Lightstorm for years. In typical Brooks fashion, he thought, *Oh no, not that bald motherfucker*, because the timing of the chance encounter was horrible. He didn't want to explain to someone he had no intention to work with why he was flying to Europe. He called his travel partner who was somewhere in the airport and said they both needed to hide. It felt wrong somehow to engage in small talk when they were about to terminate the discussions with Ubisoft in a couple of days.

Half an hour later, Brooks sat down in his designated seat on the plane and prepared for the long flight when suddenly someone tapped him gently on the shoulder.

"Well, HELLO, Brooks!" the Ubisoft executive said happily.

"Oh, uh. Hello," Brooks replied, a lot less excited, realizing that he was seated right in front of the man he'd successfully avoided in the lounge.

"What are you doing in Europe?" came the inevitable follow-up question.

For a second, Brooks thought about being honest and just spilling the beans, but he realized that it was too soon to burn any bridges and he needed an excuse.

"I am. Eh...I'm going to a conference," he said unconvincingly, and began to feel oddly guilty.

"FANTASTIC!" the Ubi executive said. "In that case, why don't you go visit Massive? I can arrange everything for you!"

Brooks felt cornered and out of ideas. His usual bravado failed him, and the words that blurted out of his mouth were not the ones he'd planned to say.

"Sure. Why not?"

What? his inner voice whispered.

Fuck it; let's just do it, Brooks whispered back to himself. He needed to keep up a rapport with Ubisoft, just in case.

In actuality, accepting an invitation made no sense. Hopefully, Lightstorm was about to finalize a deal with someone else, and he had no reason to visit Massive. But in a combination of guilt for avoiding the man, and kind of liking the Swedes, and thinking it would never happen anyway, he decided to stick with the idea. *Sure, I'll go see Massive. Sure. Why not?*

Fate sometimes likes to get involved in our lives, whether we invite it in or not.

The next day, somewhere in Central Europe, Brooks met up with a business partner, Mike Doyle from Fox, who looked like a rugby player from New Zealand but was actually a Canadian lawyer with true philosophical depth. In the cab, Brooks told him they'd probably be going to Sweden before flying home again. Mike sighed and texted his girlfriend. This trip was going to be longer than expected. But at the same time, Mike thought things were about to get more interesting too. He had discovered the qualities of Massive many years before, when he was at Relic, the same Vancouver-based studio that used to be a home to Josh Mosqueira, the creative director who had created the foundation of *Far Cry 3*. Mike had admired the Swedes ever since.

But before making a guilt-driven and pointless detour to the north, Brooks and Mike planned to sign their selected studio and fully celebrate the moment. It was potentially the biggest deal they had done in their lives. They jumped out of the cab, greeted the receptionist, and entered the large, merchandise-filled conference room. But instead of meeting a jubilant team ready to make the finest *Avatar* game anyone could conceive, they found themselves facing broken and desperate people looking over their shoulders, as if in paranoia. Something was wrong. The meeting quickly took a horrible turn for the worse when the studio head offered the visitors some of his cocaine, and suddenly Lightstorm had no choice but to abandon the path they had intended to pursue.

Meanwhile, the enterprising Ubisoft exec had delivered, and everything was lined up and organized in Sweden. "The team will love to see you!" he wrote in an email, outlining the agenda for the visit.

After declining the coke, Brooks and Mike rescheduled their return flights, took the train across Europe and arrived in the Danish capital of Copenhagen, across the strait from Massive's office in Malmö, Sweden. As they embarked from the Central Station, they were surrounded by a bizarre parade of men and women dancing on a string of trucks equipped with powerful sound systems blasting Euro disco that hurt their ears. It looked like a Pride festival, and the entire town seemed to be involved. Was this Denmark?

"What the hell is this?" Brooks asked a passerby.

"It's the Eurovision Song Contest!" the man shouted back, apparently proud that the Danish would host such an event. "The whole town is on fire!"

After a night of constant oompah-oompah from the streets, Brooks and Mike arrived at Massive. The visit had become much more interesting now that their first choice of developer had gone to hell, and they were serious about investigating to see if the trip to Europe could be salvaged some way. Mike spent time with the operational side of the studio, while Brooks spent time with the developers. He locked himself in a room with Soundboy for a while so they could discuss game design at length in peace.

"I want to know what game design means to you," Brooks said on the way in, in a generous question that would force Massive's creative director to show his hand.

But auditing us was fine. We never intended to hide anything. We had our ideas. We believed in them, and through the work we'd been doing on Snowdrop, we felt confident that we could deliver the game everyone dreamt of. I knew Soundboy would succinctly convey the message on behalf of the studio.

During the following hours Brooks spent a lot of time in the smokers' corner, where he sneakily asked unsuspecting Massive employees questions about the studio. He wanted to know what it was really like in production. He wanted to know if Soundboy, Petter, and I were respected. He was looking for a certain kind of energy and a certain kind of culture. Later, he told me that this was his favorite method to get unbiased intel: Hang out with the smokers.

The meeting with Soundboy went extremely well, and the mood was visibly turning positive. But there was one thing still missing from the puzzle, and soon enough, Brooks asked to see Snowdrop in action. We took him to a room where we planned to give him a demo. Everyone was really nervous, and Brooks guessed it was because we knew that this part of the meeting would not hold up, that this was when we would be exposed as liars. But the reality was that we were nervous only because the guy who was supposed to run the presentation had called in sick and we'd been forced to throw in someone who had no time to prepare. We were professionals, we liked to be very well prepared, and last-minute improvising made us uneasy.

After explaining what the engine could do, we could see Brooks's eyes light up. Apparently, this was very exciting to him.

"So, it's systemic?" he asked.

"Of course," the tech dude replied. "Otherwise, we'd have to script everything."

We didn't know it at the time, but this was exactly what Brooks had been looking for. He hated scripted, linear games, and he dreamed about an open-world *Avatar* game, an open-ended game that relied on systems rather than predetermined scripts.

"Okay," Brooks continued. "In that case, let me ask you to do a few things right now."

I had time to think that this might end badly, but there was nothing to do about it. Fate had committed us to this moment.

We were looking at a scene of a street in New York from *The Division*. There was an abandoned police car, some trash, and some simple life-forms like flies and rats.

"Can you put the garbage inside the police car?" Brooks asked.

"Sure," we said, and in the editor, the demoist moved a pile of garbage to the car interior. This was instantly updated in the playable prototype.

"Now make the flies bigger."

The tech guy changed a digit in the editor, and suddenly the flies were the size of small dogs, making the whole thing look like a B movie.

As we watched, the giant flies were attracted to the garbage and started hovering around the police car, but they could not get in, because the glass was still intact.

"Shoot the car windows," Brooks said, and so we did.

The windows broke open and the holes were large enough for the flies to enter.

They flew into the car and enjoyed their snack on the pile of trash. It had all happened without any scripts. Everything had happened because we'd built complicated underlying systems for behavior, movement, collision, destruction, and endless ways for all those things to connect and "understand" one another.

"Wow," Brooks said. "I get it. It's a truly systemic engine."

He turned to me and continued, "Did you know that was going to happen?"

"No," I said truthfully. "But I'm thoroughly relieved that it did."

"Hmm," he said, and looked at me. "How long are you going to pretend you're the outsiders?" he asked, in an intellectual leap that I didn't fully follow.

"I didn't realize that we were pretending to be anything," I said.

"Well. Your team is remarkable. You guys are fucking awesome. You're going to be great," he said, and it sounded as if he'd made up his mind.

"Can you show me the Oregon prototype now, the one you talked about?"

Sure, we said, and then we blew his mind completely. After that, I had no doubts; Hollywood was coming to Malmö.

36

TOM CLANCY'S THE DIVISION

Around June 2015, less than a year before we were scheduled to ship *The Division*, I sat in my office at Massive watching the man standing by my whiteboard. The clock was ticking, literally and symbolically. The guest continued:

"So, you understand the project is like a *big ship*. A big, big ship, with some *small holes* in it. Small, small holes," he said, and started drawing a clumsy image of a boat with a fat green pen.

"BIG ship. SMALL holes! If we don't fix the tiny little problems, the big, big ship will sink, do you see?"

It was very hard to accept, but there I was in my own office, being lectured like a child on how to make games. The room, which usually felt like my second home, had been host to at least a million meetings around the small, round white table from the '70s that stood at one end. But not once in any of those meetings had I been treated like an idiot who knew nothing about developing games. Being handled like a child annoyed me to no end. The really depressing thing, though, I observed, was that apparently someone had given this self-proclaimed nanny the information that I needed to be dealt with like a clueless kid. *Who?* I wondered as I kept pretending to listen.

When Martin had left Massive almost ten years earlier, I initially refused to take over his room, even though it was generally expected that I'd simply move into what was considered "the boss's office." But to me, moving in the day after he left felt like a clumsy power grab, like a childish and symbolic move by an insecure person, so I had it turned into a meeting room instead. After a while, people started complaining that I was still sitting in my old office while at the same time I was basically occupying Martin's abandoned office as my permanent meeting room. I'd essentially ended up with *two* large offices, not just one, so my attempt at being humble had backfired and made me look like a guy who *really* needed to show off with twice as much space as his predecessor. It ended up being logical that I moved into his old space a few months after he left. And for once, counter to my nomad instincts, I thought maybe it could be a place where I'd finally be staying for a while. Or, if not, at least I'd want to enjoy the room while I had it.

I decided to make myself comfortable. I brought in a large old teak desk that I'd once found on a street sale in Stockholm and had been saving in an attic ever since. I bought a cheap copy of an Eames desk chair that suited the desk perfectly. We built a bookshelf out of oak that covered one of the walls from floor to ceiling, and I filled it with Iain M. Banks books and rare Tardi comics. In the end the place looked like a cool Scandinavian office from the '50s or '60s, a little like something from the TV show *Mad Men*.

Every year, I added memorabilia from the Massive adventures, until it began to look like an exclusive toy store: figurines; awards; a personal postcard from Hideo Kojima, with whom I had shared a few laughs; a dollar bill that fell from the roof at the cinema when we announced *The Division*; a photo of me and the Swedish prime minister; and all of our games in large collector's edition boxes. I'd assembled a bunch of items that were truly unique, and each one carried an emotional meaning to me. Everything was neatly organized and meticulously placed in a balanced rhythm by an apparently obsessive-compulsive person.

This was supposed to be my safe space, my home turf, my shelter, a protected bunker away from the trenches. But there I was, being treated like a slow child by a man I hardly knew.

The game was still coming together very late, and the sluggish progress had made everyone nervous to the point where the faith in Massive's ability crumbled completely. Tension was high; trust was depleted. No matter what we did, everything was challenged, questioned, debated, and scrutinized. Everyone involved knew that design by committe was a horrible idea, but nevertheless, the flood-gates of opinion had opened. We had to fight like maniacs every day to create space for the conversations but still make sure that the integrity and the consistency of the design remained intact. It was as if an artist were painting in a auditorium filled with people where every single person in the audience was shouting out opinions.

I had made quite aggressive changes to the core team, replacing and removing key people in the process. Although I was convinced that the decisions were necessary to deliver the game, I was privately plagued by emotions of guilt and regret. I always felt that it was a management failure when an individual got hurt, no matter what they'd done. I took it as a personal defeat when I couldn't puzzle together the right conditions for our talented developers. Usually I'd spend an endless amount of time trying to figure out how to maximize everything and everyone, and I took great pride in often succeeding, but *The Division* was requiring brute force rather than a gentle touch.

Like a blurry shadow that begins to appear in one's peripheral vision, I began to wonder if maybe we'd fail spectacularly after all. It was a depressing thought, and I couldn't see any meaningful future for the studio if we didn't deliver.

Once the aggressive changes to the core team were made and the dust settled, I had, as intended, put my trusted old buddies, Petter and Soundboy, in charge. Massive ended up with the same lineup we'd had for *World in Conflict* and *Far Cry 3*, with Petter as a producer and Soundboy as the creative director. The change had an immediate good effect on the production floor, but it was impossible to tell if it was going to be enough. Those recently demoted stood on the sidelines, glancing bitterly at the new arrivals and quietly hoping for vindication when things got worse.

"Big boat. Small holes! And once the big, big boat is repaired, we will guide it, like small and happy tugboats, toward the harbor," the man went on. I had no choice but to politely nod and tell him how interesting it all was.

Once Paris's patience had run out entirely, they decided it was time to send this man, a senior closer, to Massive. Except they decided that a single person wouldn't suffice, so as a perfect illustration of the seriousness of the situation, they sent five of them: *five closers?!* No one had ever heard of such a thing! The newly formed assembly was dubbed "the Strike Team," and they were given almost unlimited power to do whatever was needed to ship the game. It was hard not to feel insulted by this excessive babysitting. At the same time, I had so many doubts about the project and my own capacity that I had to accept it.

"The harbor, of course, is release day, you understand," he said with infinite patience. He really was drawing out this metaphor.

The man lecturing me about boats and holes in his heavy northern English accent was the Strike Team leader, Richard. In almost all senses of the word he seemed to be my opposite, and we got off to a horrible start. While I was intentionally optimistic, he was unintentionally pessimistic. For me to function, I needed to believe that things would soon be fantastic. I needed a dream to fight for, a Worthy Cause, but Richard took his inspiration from the reverse: He needed to be in the middle of a harsh, horrible, and hopeless war. While I liked to listen to people, he enjoyed lecturing. I liked to trust people and give them very broad mandates, whereas Richard preferred to organize the tasks for everyone in detailed briefs. He would meticulously follow up with highly precise burn-down charts. If I was a hippie, he was a Marine.

Any way one looked at it, we were quite the opposite. It seemed we provoked each other to become even more stereotypical in the most annoying ways. I became the naive, die-hard believer, and he became the energy-draining cynic. I universally encouraged friendliness and trust, while he attacked like a spitfire as soon as anyone made an unwelcome blip on his radar. I liked wine; he liked beer. I had southern European blood from my Italian mother, he had dark northern British blood. It was almost comical how different we were. A casting director couldn't have made it more obvious.

While we were figuring all this out, the project and the world swept by in a crazed storm. The team was working extremely hard, and the dark rings under Petter's and Soundboy's eyes grew blacker by the minute as their hair was doing the opposite, growing white. My old friend Cristian Pana had returned to the studio as a member of the Strike Team, and he was solidly in charge of the online group. It was fantastic to have him back, and in the middle of everything else, he and I started planning his stay for good this time after the project shipped. Assuming it did. Somewhere in the avalanche of everything, I'd hired another old favorite, Julian Gerighty from the editorial team in Paris, the guy who'd once so gently told us that Ubisoft was killing *World in Conflict 2*. He was right behind Soundboy, working as an associate creative director, and with him, too, I had secretly started planning for a future beyond the release date, if such a thing even existed.

"The clock is ticking," Boss Christine told Richard and me, as if we didn't already know.

I got called down to Paris to meet Serge. I was expecting another scolding and braced myself, but, as always, the man was full of surprises. He greeted me with a big smile as I entered the room.

"RRRRROOAAAR! Bonjour, mon ami!" he said.

"Hello. Hi there," I said cautiously, not knowing what to expect.

But before I could find out what was going on, Serge shifted his attention to something else.

"Wait. Your bag is missing? No?"

And in fact, it was. I had arrived on a late-afternoon flight and would need to stay another night at Ubisoft's favorite hotel, the good old Mama Shelter. The small bag I'd checked had gone missing during the trip.

"My bag?" I replied, confused. "Yes, yes it got lost; you're right. It's not a big deal. It'll show up."

"But, mon ami, what will you do for underwear and toothbrushing?" he asked, looking very concerned. Before I could answer that he shouldn't worry, and honestly it wasn't really something for Ubisoft's global creative director and guru genius to waste time on, he leaped out of his chair and grabbed his coat.

"Alors! We will go shopping together."

Serge was the master of setting the stage in unexpected ways and in throwing curveballs, so I probably shouldn't have been so surprised. Suddenly, there we were, discussing the future of our game engine Snowdrop and buying boxer shorts in Paris while *The Division* project was fully ablaze back home.

"I love Snowdrop. I want you to make it possible for other teams to use it. Do you like this color on your underwear? Maybe the first Ubi game for the Nintendo Switch could be a Snowdrop game, oui? Or maybe this color is too bright for you? What does your girlfriend think?" Serge said in one go, equally focused on all the issues at hand.

When they say that Ubisoft is a family company, they're not joking.

Richard came to work every morning and immersed himself in angry pessimism, exactly the kind of attitude from which I'd fought hard to protect Massive. It was not surprising that everyone around was predicting a titanic clash and a brutal battle for power between us. "Shit, this is going to be *so* bad," I heard people say behind our backs, staying clear of the looming tempest.

"FUCK OFF!" Richard shouted at me in my office. He seemed to actually be gearing up to hit me.

A fistfight? Really?

"I asked you for ONE BLOODY THING and you can't even do that?" he continued. "You're fucking USELESS!"

We were arguing about how to manage Eric, the brand director. I was convinced that we needed to keep the marketing team fully in the loop, but the inevitable side effect was that they added a heavy burden to the extremely pressured development team. In order to build the hype for the game successfully, Eric needed an endless amount of attention, screenshots, exclusive content for partners, trailers, builds for events, tools, and much, much more. No doubt, it was making Richard's job a lot harder.

It occurred to me that I might in fact be mixing emotions from different timelines. Once, I had been in Eric's position, trying to make *World in Conflict* look amazing to the world, while the development team under Petter perceived my constant requests for marketability and cool assets as disruptive rather than helpful. Perhaps the discussion with Richard was getting so heated because I was defending not only Eric, but my old self too? Maybe this was making the fight familiar and personal in a way that neither Richard nor I had intended.

"We have to support them," I said, trying but failing to stay calm. "They're a big part of making it possible for us to succeed."

He looked at me with tremendous frustration, and his eyes narrowed into evil cracks, shooting fire. His face painfully twisted into a nightmarish grimace.

"Do you want me to throw this laptop through your glass walls?" he said in a low, growling voice.

He didn't wait for an answer.

"HOW DO YOU WANT ME TO MAKE MY FUCKING POINT?" he shouted loud enough to make my coffee jump out of the cup I was holding in my slightly trembling hands.

"Richard..." I said, immediately regretting my patronizing tone.

This would infuriate him even further, I knew. "*Richard*. We HAVE TO keep the marketing in mind. There is no point in fixing the game if we simultaneously burn all the bridges to the marketing team and starve them of ammunition."

"Fuck you. FUCK YOU. FUUUUCK YOU!" he shouted back. "All I asked for was for you to bloody get them out of my hair so I can do MY JOB. I WILL NOT DO THEIRS! And your solution is just to say BE NICE?!"

"Uh, I didn't say that," I said hopelessly.

"YOU FUCKING LUNATIC. You have no idea what my reality is like. You are living in la-la land, where everyone is friends, happily dancing around in circles singing 'Kumbaya' together. THAT. IS. NOT. HOW. GAMES. ARE. MADE. I asked you for one *single thing* to make my life easier, and all you do is sit here and dream. FUCK YOU!" he said, and stormed out, slamming the door shut.

Clearly, we were bringing out the worst in each other. My job seemed to have evolved into people shouting at me.

I tried to reach out to Richard after a few hours and resolve things, but he refused to answer. I guessed he was shooting emails to Paris, telling them what a useless person I was.

In fact, he did, because soon enough, I got a phone call from HQ.

"Bonjour, David. You've got to fix that," I was told.

Very accurately phrased, I thought. *The Division* needed us to get along; that was unavoidable, and both Richard and I knew it. As much as we seemed to represent the other person's mortal enemy, the truth was that we weren't. We were in it together, and both our careers were at stake.

As opposed to me, Richard thought like a soldier, and that made him a fierce believer in hierarchy. He was simply not comfortable disobeying my request to collaborate with Eric. Two days after our big fight, he suddenly ended the silent treatment, showed up in my office, and calmly said, "Okay, I'll work with marketing," then added, "For the record, it's adding considerable risk." I thanked him with genuine gratitude, and I sensed the beginning of a functional working relationship.

And how could I not be grateful? The man was spending a year living in a lifeless hotel room, far away from the family in Newcastle that he seemed to love dearly. What were we asking of him and the others on the Strike Team? What kind of life was this for them? I decided I needed to show Richard more respect.

Early in 2016, right before the first *Division* public beta, the Ubisoft marketing teams began their work in earnest, and it was welcome magic. We felt like panicked hobbits running across gloomy hills suddenly being swept up by a friendly dragon. We were carried on top of gigantic, powerful wings, and suddenly *Tom Clancy's The Division* was visible everywhere. Wherever I went I saw advertisements for our project. In Sweden, in the US, in Paris. On billboards, in the subway, on buses, in magazines, on my favorite websites, on TV. It was surreal. People started calling from everywhere, offering jobs, threatening to kill me because the game didn't look like what someone was expecting it to, or just to offer congratulations. I had to delete my Facebook account because the noise was unbearable. And *The Division* hadn't even shipped yet!

We were in a frenzy. It was difficult to keep up with everything, but the mojo on the floor was visibly improving, and we were indeed like a big, big boat with small holes repaired, on our way to a safe harbor. Game features and content were being either finalized or cut every day, and I reluctantly had to admit that Richard's ironfisted process was a viable strategy.

Richard and I had discovered ways to forge a fantastic friendship that allowed us to overcome all our differences, no matter how profound they seemed initially. For one, we had a surprisingly similar view on loyalty. We were both fiercely loyal to the project and to the team above all. We were both ready to personally crash and burn to avoid letting the project down, and no matter how I felt about it, he was in the studio to fight for *us*. He was someone I was going to be loyal to. We shared this emotional, personal, slightly irrational, and melodramatic perspective on loyalty, as if it were a question of either eternal brotherhood or bitter betrayal. It didn't matter that I got my worldview from *The Lord of the Rings* while he got his from reading military biographies. Loyalty was crucial to both of us.

The second thing that made it possible for us to get along was even more basic: We were both smart. By relying on rational intelligence, we were ultimately able to see most things the same way, sometimes just minutes after we'd been driving each other crazy. Using raw and clinical observation skills, we realized we could see the best path forward and fight for it together.

"The clock is ticking," Christine called to tell us again, and by then, Richard and I had become a strange symbiotic duo and shouted back in unison, "WE KNOW! We are on top of it!" and immediately went back to our respective tasks. Richard had turned the entire development team into an efficient war machine, and it was like a billion well-oiled parts in a coordinated dance. Singing "Kumbaya."

On March 8, 2016, the game went live. We were in the Live Room on the top floor in the Massive building. The place looked like a makeshift poor man's version of the NASA control room in Houston. Screens everywhere, data from everything, a matrix of incomprehensible charts, and flowing digits, all managed by tired unshaven engineers with steady voices. They were following the game launch through the digital lens of infrastructure and statistics. First Australia came online, then Asia, then the live world map became an explosion of light when the servers opened in Europe, and then, finally, a few hours later, we watched as the Americas joined the party. Everywhere on the globe, on the planet we live on, people were playing *The Division*. The lines on the diagrams shot up as more and more people joined. Millions.

It's a beautiful thing to see a game being born. The game was going ballistic! Way, way beyond our expectations, and we had to purchase more servers and install them on the fly. Things were going exceptionally well, but all we could focus on was keeping up with demand and player requests. There was no time to enjoy the long-awaited success.

Richard had become a pale, chain-smoking version of himself. He looked as if it was time for him to retire or go to rehab. Petter and Soundboy were at home sleeping after too many months of ignoring their health and families. It was hard for me to see anything except the struggle, but from everywhere great numbers started pouring in: The biggest public beta test and the best-selling launch in the history of Ubisoft! Sweden's largest cultural export! Top three on Twitch! Billions of hours played! One of the most successful launches of a new franchise ever in video game history!

It should have been our finest moment, but we were emotionally ragged, worn, and homesick. Richard collapsed from exhaustion in an airport somewhere, while I fell into a strange sort of postpartum depression, thinking more about what I had lost than what we had gained with the birth of *The Division*. The developers at Massive who celebrated the success of the project began to automatically attach the same closing statement to all their war stories: "I'll never do that again."

Petter actively avoided me, and I didn't see Soundboy for a long time. They were apparently not eager to embark on something new, and I wondered if they'd been broken. We became a shattered family. Shattered, perhaps, but with newly formed deep, lifelong bonds. Friendships had been forged in the way they can be forged only during the harshest times. We'd been there for one another when most of the world felt like an enemy.

It should have been a majestic, massive moment of celebration, but the best I could muster was relief. Relief that it was all over, that the pressure would ease. Relief that we had achieved something that very few game industry professionals ever would. Relief that the immense success was in fact already real, tangible history that no one could rewrite or question. The release was on my CV (curriculum vitae), in Massive's history books, carved into the soul of each one of us as an experience we hated and loved in equal parts.

Finally, we had arrived at the top, after twenty years of constant hard work and steady improvement, we were the kings of the video game world. We were number one.

I guess some people really enjoy climbing Mount Everest, and I guess others are more like me: I'll do it if I get a chance, of course I will. But on my way up, I'll begin to wonder about the cost, the sacrifices, the casualties, and the deeper meaning of it. Getting to the peak certainly proves something, but *what* exactly?

As I stood on top of the highest mountain of the game industry in March 2016 and observed the 360-degree horizon around me, I breathed the fresh air for a second, hoping that it would be different or special in some way. But it wasn't.

It was like any other moment in my life, and I realized that being at the top is not the moment that counts, the real change is who you've become when you finally return to the world.

37

MALIBU

Apparently, a scriptwriter for a movie doesn't begin by writing the script itself. Before that, and after pitching some high-level ideas to those in charge, they write something called a "treatment," which is a short version of the story from beginning to end. The treatment doesn't need to describe all the beats, scenes, camera angles, structure, and dialogue. I didn't know that. But what I did know was that almost no one had seen the treatment for *The Division* movie, and I was about to. There it was, in my hands, ready to be read. The printout wasn't too thick, but every page contained an avalanche of text, as if it were written fast, in a single, uninterrupted stream of consciousness.

As I do sometimes when I'm really looking forward to something, I dragged it out, allowing myself to enjoy the wait. The moment before the "Thing" is sometimes as sweet as the experience itself. So I didn't read the treatment as soon as the pages flowed out from the printer in glorious Hollywood black and white. Instead, I put the pages in a binder, then stuffed the binder in my worn leather mailman's bag, hung it over my shoulder, and took it all home to read when the moment was right. This was it, I thought: the origin of *The Division* film, written by Oscar-winning writer/ director Stephen Gaghan.

Later that day, once night had fallen and the house was quiet, I poured myself a glass of wine and started reading.

Being a guy who never liked big cities, it's not strange it took me such a long time to appreciate Los Angeles. As much as I enjoyed traveling there for work and to meet interesting people, I never got a chance to know the city. Sometimes, I'd go directly from the airport to a conference room somewhere and then directly back to the airport for another cross-Atlantic flight. For the longest time, aside from trade shows downtown in the Convention Center, my only memories of LA consisted of long meetings hosted in generic offices. I must have visited the City of Angels more than sixty times, but it still didn't feel familiar.

One time, we allowed ourselves the luxury of a few extra free days to get over the jet lag. Petter rented a car and we finally started exploring the city. We created a wish list of places we wanted to see. Petter chose a distant milk-shake bar on a pier, a run-down café that was frequented by the local police and firemen (where we had morning coffee), and a gigantic store that sold boots. To the itinerary, I added an archery shop that sold Fred Bear bows and a place that perhaps would feature secondhand bowling shirts, which I was into at the time. And then I wanted to drive north, to Malibu, to watch surfers and see if there were any Case Study Houses to marvel at. Somewhere in between all these high-value targets, we'd also need to buy underwear and T-shirts because our luggage had been lost. True to his introvert personality, Soundboy didn't particularly want to see anything, but he was happy enough to join us, making clever and sarcastic comments on everything from our pale Swedish skin to the dysfunctional logic of LA highways.

As it turned out, Petter had a photographic memory for city layouts, and he was perfectly capable of finding everything even when local traffic was being unhelpful. When we got lost, Petter just closed his eyes for a second, looked as if he were reciting an ancient prayer, and then he exclaimed with great certainty that he knew where we were. And he did. Soundboy and I relaxed and felt like we were kids on a school trip looking forward to that milk shake we'd been promised.

In Malibu, we had lunch in a restaurant with a view of the sea where giant birds flew outside the window and nonchalantly caught fish in elegant swooping stunts, barely touching the surface of the water. Our best guess was that they were pelicans, but really, being gamers with limited exposure to nature, we had no idea. In the distance, we saw surfers in black wet suits, paddling out into the water, trying to catch a wave back in.

After lunch, we drove up to the Malibu Hills, hoping to admire some elegant architecture, but we soon found that if you go far enough, the roads are cordoned by gates and bars so that the rich can live in private, I suppose. We turned around and were rewarded with a spectacular view of the California mountains and the sprawling, endless city in the vast valley. It was such a beautiful and rare experience. We were just enjoying ourselves as friends in the humming Dodge. And for once, no one was knocking on our shoulders, urgently needing something or pushing us to work harder. It was a peaceful, blissful, and painfully short moment under a cloudless sky, accompanied by the muted sound of the Pacific from far below the ridge. This was the moment when I finally fell in love with LA.

Many years later, that Malibu postcard moment came back to me in full Technicolor at Massive's twenty-year anniversary party. Hundreds of colleagues were celebrating in a comparatively underwhelming ballroom in a newly constructed hotel. The space was dominated by a giant LED screen at one end of the room. With regular intervals, the screen would jump to life with videos sent by friends, partners, and colleagues from all over the world, congratulating us on our anniversary, and wishing us good luck in the future. One of those friendly little videos came from an LA beach, just like the ones we'd once admired from the Malibu Hills. The sun was about to set, and it looked like a windy evening. All of a sudden, there was Stephen Gaghan, who'd recorded himself with his iPhone. The short clip was shaky and a bit grainy due to the fading light, but still, it somehow looked extremely Hollywood and impressive. For a person like me, who adores the film *Syriana* (written and directed by Gaghan), it was a surreal moment. Later that evening, we received another personal message with well-wishes, from another Oscar-winning superstar, Jon Landau of Lightstorm, producer of *Titanic* and *Avatar*.

Imagine, it all got to this. This is who we've become, I thought.

Through the crowd, I saw Martin Walfisz, my old boss and friend, who had been invited to the party as the founder of the studio, celebrating with a couple of beers. He looked incredibly pleased as he walked over to me.

"MAN! What did you *do* to my studio?" he said with his huge patented smile.

"You like it?" I said.

"Dude! I LOVE IT!" he shouted as beer splashed from his glass. "Honestly, man. This makes me wonder if in fact you're *better than me*, ha-ha! You're a cunning guy, David. So cleverly fooling everyone with that low-key persona. And I think you're secretly holding on to a few more things, yeah? The Frenchies will never know what hit them!"

"Oh, you flatter me," I replied with a big grin on my face, faking embarrassment.

"Well, I certainly hope they pay you well enough!" he said with another laugh, and ran off to catch up with some Massive veterans he'd once hired, twenty years earlier.

Always such a good guy, I thought. And inside, I realized that I'd been waiting a long time to get his blessing and validation.

"HOLLYWOOD, HERE WE COME!" I heard Martin bellow proudly to his old pals, as if he were still a Massive employee.

The first time I heard anyone mention anything about making a movie based on our game *The Division* was in Paris, where the rumor mill never sleeps. Ubisoft had created a small company called Ubisoft Motion Pictures (UMP), with the straightforward idea to turn the game properties into Hollywood films. The man in charge, JJ, was a guy who used to work with French director Luc Besson, and he was exploring different ways to approach the equation. Movies based on games had an unimpressive history, and someone needed to recalibrate the recipe. Originally, UMP was based in Paris and had only three employees, but they soon realized that they'd have to move to LA to get things going. I was jealous of this, of course, with my never-realized California dreams, but I really liked the guys and there was no reason to begrudge their adventure.

I had met JJ and his colleagues a few times when they were preparing the *Assassin's Creed* movie, which eventually came out in 2017 as UMP's first full-length film. They were looking at basing a narrative thread in their script on some of the coma sequences that Massive had worked on for *Assassin's Creed: Revelations*, which I thought was a brilliant idea. I could imagine that our brutalistic part of the game, based on poetry and light, would offer quite spectacular visual opportunities for the movie-to-be. JJ seemed to think so, too, and he was fascinated by the David Lynch–style quality of it. But suddenly he switched his focus to something else.

"Once we're done with this, *The Division* needs to be the next one that we focus on! I don't think you guys even realize how fantastic your setting is, and how many amazing stories it allows us to tell."

Why, thank you, Mister One-Of-the-Few-Who-Believe-in-Us! This was before the launch of *The Division*, at a time when we'd worn down the patience of our dwindling number of remaining fans in the Paris head office. For a long time, Massive was internally considered a bunch of trickster salespeople who'd looted the Ubisoft gold mines, only to run away and spend a fortune on a game that never shipped. But JJ was unfazed by all this, and already saw *The Division*'s strengths, and, to his credit, time would prove him right.

I have a special folder in my brain where I keep track of those who stand by me when things are difficult and risky. It's not that I'm bitter toward the many who show up only when things are going well, but I need to know whom I can trust when times are bad. Producing games is a cyclical process. The job I do very often amounts to putting things back on track when they're spiraling downward. I don't think there is any way to avoid the bad times, and it's pointless to fear them. But yes, it's good to know who believes in you when you look like a loser. Make a note.

JJ was as optimistic as I was about most things. *The game will come out one day. And it will be fantastic! And we will make a* Division *movie! And it will be amazing!* It was all very contagious. And somehow, this story became another one of those fragile dreams that would force the harsh reality to adapt: *The Division* will become a great film! Since then, this has been the conviction of many people, both inside and outside of Ubisoft, and slowly but surely, things have been progressing toward the red carpet.

Actor Jake Gyllenhaal signed on to play one of the leading characters, and shortly thereafter, actress Jessica Chastain signed on too. UMP would hire actors, a director, and a writer. They'd finance the scriptwriting and jell the team around a set of core creative ideas. Once everything was in place, UMP would pitch the entire package to the big studios and see who was ready to turn it into a full-fledged movie.

And now, Stephen Gaghan had committed to both writing and directing the project! It was impossibly exciting, and the realization filled me with awe. The people involved in this project were, in my mind, some of the best and most interesting Hollywood could offer. I rewatched Gaghan's masterpiece *Syriana* and tried to imagine how the peculiar tone and rhythm would translate into a *Division* film. It was spectacular in my head.

To be honest, I had my concerns about Gaghan. Not because

of his writing or directing, which I admired deeply, but because he had produced so comparatively little in his career as a director. He didn't seem like a guy who had many movies in him.

I see modern entertainment projects more as a challenge of execution than a creative challenge. There are so many ideas, so much talent, so much passion and energy, but in fact, there can be too much of those things. And simultaneously, there's a lack of smart money and an even bigger lack of great project managers who can take a magical idea and pull it through the vortex of production. Ideas are cheap. Execution is key. Creativity comes in short flashes of brilliance. Production is an endurance test. This is one of the reasons why I admire Jon Landau and James Cameron so much.

Already in his early fifties, Gaghan had started late in his career, and it seemed to me that he had remarkably few releases under his belt. Most of what he'd created was fantastic, but it made me wonder about his ability to ultimately finish the projects he'd take on. I asked UMP what they thought, and they told me not to worry. The treatment was brilliant, they said. *Well, can I read it then?* I said. And under much secrecy, the precious document was sent to me.

I took a sip of my wine and started reading Gaghan's treatment. I fell in love right away.

The piece was so well-written it was absurd! The words, the language, the twists, and the immediateness of it hit me like a cold November wind. I wanted to marry the typewriter upon which it had been written.

In the game we had created, New York's winter streets were filled with rotting corpses and people trying to survive or, worse, those who saw an opportunity to use the situation to their advantage. In good action movie tradition, this set the background for looters, cultists, revisionists, and all sorts of madness. The player was the sheriff, with the right to decide what it all meant.

It could be anyone. It could happen anywhere. What would *you* do if you were in the middle of it?

I liked the actual writing better than I liked the story, which was a bit too gung ho for my personal taste. Still, it was incredibly easy to see the words I was reading dressed up in Gaghan's direction, visual confidence, and dramatic pace. It was wonderful.

But as it turned out, the world will never see this film.

Gaghan ran out of time, and he had to move on to something else, possibly another unfinished something. I put the treatment printout to rest in my office safe, where I locked it up and never shared it with anyone, even though I've really wanted to, many times.

Sixteen months later, a young writer with wild-grown red hair and an open smile stepped through the doors of Massive to discuss the new screenplay he was going to write for *The Division*. His name was Rafe Judkins, but with my limited interest in Hollywood celebrities, I had no idea who he was. Everyone said he was great, but it didn't matter what I knew or what people said, I planned on judging him on his craftsmanship, not his CV.

"Have you read Gaghan's stuff?" I asked, somewhat clumsily. I made it sound as if I were referring to a previous, more attractive, girlfriend.

"No, I intentionally didn't," he replied, still smiling. "Even though I heard it's supposed to be good. I just don't want to be biased by anything other than what is really in the game. It's such a lovely brand you have created."

"Yeah, well," I said, "in the manner that a story about a virus wiping out society and throwing the world into violent chaos can be described as 'lovely,' I guess I agree."

He laughed at this in an honest way, which seemed to perfectly reflect his personality. He was curious, attentive, and intelligent. He certainly seemed to be at peace with himself, although I soon realized that his life had been far from simple and that he had made many difficult choices in his life. *Another survivor*, I thought. A brother.

Many months later, and for the second time in my life, I got to read a secret script for *The Division* movie with a glass of wine as company, only this time it was Judkin's version from start to finish, and it was truly marvelous.

At E3 2019, Ubisoft proudly announced the partnership with Netflix, where the curtain for the movie will rise one day. I hope there will be a red carpet somewhere, where hundreds of game developers awkwardly dressed in tailcoats will march past the paparazzi, bathing in the lights of fame.

38

SOLAR PANELS

Jon Landau, the most successful movie producer of all time, took the time to meet me, Petter, and Soundboy in the inconspicuous reception downstairs in the gigantic Manhattan Beach Studios (MBS) lot in Los Angeles. This was where some of the finest entertainment products in the world were produced. I noted with interest and gratitude that Landau chose to personally let us in. Throughout the years, I had met so many executives who were buffered by layers of assistants and service personnel who would execute such menial tasks on their behalf, but apparently Landau was just not a person with that kind of ego. It made me relax a little.

To everyone's excitement, Brooks Brown had translated his initial excitement from his visit to Massive many months earlier into this: our final shot at impressing Lightstorm. This was the moment that would decide if we finally had succeeded in winning the trust of James Cameron, Jon Landau, and their team. Once and for all, we were about to discover if years of careful preparation and efforts were going to pay off.

Before we entered the elevator, Jon Landau stopped to point at an aerial photo of the MBS facilities. It was truly impressive. We had not realized how large the place was, because it was impossible to see it all from the ground. But now we were able to discern that it was a huge complex, consisting of several large studios joined like a Hollywood castle, built to protect and celebrate the ambition of the future projects Cameron had in mind. We naively thought this was called a "film set," but Landau corrected us and taught us that the buildings were actually referred to as "sound studios," which made no immediate sense to me, but I trusted the source and asked no further.

Something else on the photo had caught my eye: The entire roof, spanning hundreds of square meters, was covered in shining metallic solar panels.

"Hey, that's pretty cool!" I said. "Solar panels! Did you guys add them, or were they already here when you moved in? How much electricity do they produce?"

Jon Landau paused and looked at me for a moment.

He was about the same height as me, perhaps a bit heavier and with a few more gray hairs that he kept in short curls around his ears like a halo. He had deep-set eyes that he could hide in the shadows of his sockets, seemingly at will. The big, colorful Hawaiian short-sleeved shirt rhymed with his equally big and genuine smile. Occasionally, his bright and intensely active gaze would dart out in a curious manner that made you realize he didn't miss anything that was going on, neither spoken out loud nor between the lines.

"Aren't you going to ask me about celebrities?" he said, with a voice that sounded disappointed. "Aren't you going to ask me about how much this place costs? Or how big it is? Or where Jim's office is?"

I felt as if I had just failed a test of some sort. *Jim?* That's what they called James Cameron around here? I had no idea. And truthfully, I had not even thought about bumping into anyone famous in the coming hours apart from the legendary producer himself. My eyes remained locked on the photo; my ability to respond had faded entirely.

Landau suddenly exploded in laughter. "I'm just kidding! I love your question! You know, usually people look at this photo and all they see is fame and money—but you . . . YOU asked about the only relevant thing, which is the solar panels! That's the first thing that springs to your mind? I LOVE IT!"

He went on to describe how they had made the investment in solar energy as soon as they moved into the studio, because Lightstorm was a company that took its own words seriously, and one of the key messages in the *Avatar* universe was about respecting the environment.

"You have to live as you learn!" Landau exclaimed proudly as we exited the elevator. It was evident that my reading of the aerial photo pleased him greatly. My question had positioned us on his ethical world map with undeniable clarity, and apparently this mattered a whole lot to Lightstorm. Now, I thought, the hard part remained: to convince them that we would do their precious *Avatar* brand justice if we were to translate it into a video game. Before the day was over, we needed to make sure that we'd arrived at a place where a deep collaboration made sense.

No matter how anyone looked at it, it was a long journey. Between different worlds, different lives, different needs. From the old, perpetually melancholic Kingdom of Sweden, across the Atlantic, to the sexy, dry hotness of California, ever prone to forest fires and earthquakes, filled with celebrities and Ferraris. But for a brief moment, everything we had become as individuals condensed into the formation of a singular experience, stuck into a few square meters in the MBS elevator taking us upward, to one of the strongest beating hearts of the movie industry: Lightstorm, James Cameron's personal company, currently working on the near-mythical sequels to the original *Avatar* movie.

And indeed, we were not there as fanboys; we were there to work. Professionals were about to meet professionals. Creatives and producers from the gaming end of the entertainment industry spectrum were gearing up to meet their distant colleagues in the movie business, who, it seemed to us, were living on another planet entirely. Theirs was a place that we had seen many times through the telescopes of our inner observatories, but never properly visited. Now, finally, we were inside, astonishingly as equals! Over coffee we began inspecting each other like old soldiers, normally battling on our respective fronts. Soon, the air was filled with unspoken appreciation and genuine understanding of the others' efforts. "Oel ngati kameie" (I see you), as they say in the *Avatar* universe. But in real life, between artists, such things are not often said out loud. Instead, the language is dry, short, technical, and precise. There is no flattery, just an exploration of craftsmanship, a conversation intended to evaluate mastery, not to validate the ego.

It wasn't surprising that Lightstorm displayed a profound knowledge of the complexities involved in creating world-class entertainment. They coupled their lifelong experience and exceptionally well-developed expertise with a down-to-earth acceptance that there were still things they could learn. To me, curiosity is the ultimate proof of a mature craftsman; understanding that change is good, knowing that discovering you are wrong means growth. The best craftsmen always see the world as an infinite source of potential knowledge, and this was how Jon Landau finally approached me and the team from Massive: with profound curiosity. We were flattered.

As well as we felt things were progressing, the meeting was still a job interview of sorts. It did not escape me that Lightstorm elegantly evaded giving us any clues about the future. We were there to sell; we were supposed to impress and please, but on the other hand we weren't very good at playing games or acting, so we kept going with our only real weapon: honesty.

Soundboy and Petter bluntly dismissed some of the ideas Lightstorm had, without stopping twice to consider if it made them come across as arrogant. They were focused on the game, not on being polite.

I, too, recklessly threw my cards on the table, saying that we simply couldn't do certain things, explaining that we were not in the business of making promises we couldn't keep. As a sales pitch, it was pretty raw.

Landau kept bringing all conversations back to the topic of *quality*. He was simply obsessed with it. It seemed to me that quality was almost an ethical obligation for him, much more so than I had ever encountered before. His preoccupation with it reminded me of some of the people I had met in art school many years earlier. Initially I had lovingly thought that such people had gone overboard, that they were a little bit nuts—but I always ended up admiring them deeply for their utter unwillingness to compromise.

In the end, there was only one question hanging over the assembly: *How did Cameron and Landau actually feel about the potential partnership with Massive?* Had we finally, as Yves Guillemot once asked me to do, succeeded in winning their trust?

The room fell silent. Everything that could be said had been said, and every question that could be addressed had gotten the attention it needed. Slowly, all heads turned toward Jon Landau, who was acting as the chairman of the meeting. His eyes moved quickly back and forth as he processed the conversations of the day. Suddenly, he flew out of his chair and pointed at me.

"David! You. And Petter. And Soundboy. Follow me!"

We, too, got out of our chairs, not sure what to expect.

Landau was already out of the room, pacing quickly down the corridor like a man who had just made an important decision.

We followed him, down the elevator and out a back door that took us into a labyrinth of corridors, then through the building, which without warning opened up to an absolutely enormous soundstage that felt like a cathedral. There were a few people working there, and they turned their heads in surprise toward us. We were the first outsiders they had seen in a long, long time. Landau mumbled something about horses and motion-capture issues, but before we could ask him more, he darted into a narrow staircase on the side of the gigantic room, which finally took us to a conference room that was plastered with concept art, from floor to roof, from wall to wall. It was like looking at the sun through a prism.

"*This*...," he said, followed by a perfectly timed dramatic pause. "*This* is the future of *Avatar*. What you are seeing here is all of the upcoming movies. I want you to take this in. You know how the original *Avatar* ends, right? Well, here's what's going to happen next."

From there, in the words of Jon Landau, the secret stories of Pandora unraveled in front of our wide-eyed joy like a string of glimmering jewels. And I felt a magic door open. Again.

Jon Landau had opened up another enchanted portal: a majestic, private viewing of supreme creativity at work, a universe of sublime vision and color, a string of powerful narrative ideas that were far beyond my imagination, *and direct access to the people who were working on it.*

He walked us through the entire saga, using the concept art as illustrations. Landau turned out to be an amazing storyteller as he let the entire saga unfold, from start to finish. Once he was done, I realized I had no idea how much time had passed, I'd been so mesmerized by Landau's passionate and gripping retelling of the multilayered stories they had crafted. I felt gratitude and, more than ever, a strong desire to become a part of the creative endeavor.

Landau looked at me and with a big smile, which confirmed that we were about to be invited to become magicians of Pandora too.

"I thought you should know what you're getting yourselves into," he said. "We'll be working together for more than a decade!"

It had taken me four years to be invited through that door.

Four years of building a key relationship based on genuine trust, of carefully selected prototyping, of internal politics. Four years of finding the right way forward into the future of Pandora and interactive entertainment.

Or maybe it took me twenty years, depending on how you looked at it.

39

IN THE GLADE

I once spent a few dreamlike days in the city of Porto, pacing the sun-drenched streets with someone I love.

Situated on the Atlantic coast of Portugal, Porto is an old city founded in 1123, and it has inevitably seen quite a few highs and lows throughout the years. Today, it's rich and poor simultaneously, and it looks as if someone built a city upon a city upon yet another even older city. It's as if the place exists in a bubble where life progresses without ever abandoning anything. In Porto, no memory is ever lost, and nothing can really die. Like a strange puzzle, the laminations of time are added on top of one another and merged into one until they become an enchanted varnish.

Normally in a city, there are dead ends and clearly defined boundaries between the accessible and the hidden places that some-one has claimed, private or corporate. But in Porto, you can just keep walking down every street and dead end, only to find that, surprisingly, there will be yet another corner to turn, another narrow alley to follow. This pattern repeats itself in an endless spiral of exploration. What looks like a wall will turn out to contain a small, almost invisible portal, and when you walk through it, you happily find yourself in a magnificent park with ancient cork trees that look perfectly sentient and wise. Turn toward a dark alleyway, and you might find that in the shadows from the old city wall there's a café that makes the best espresso you've ever had. Keep moving, drifting, and you'll travel through layers and coats of history in a never-ending fractal.

Porto rewards the curious, the slightly aimless, and the non-judgmental. It rewards those who optimistically suspect that the city will share a small gem with them if they only trust it to. It's the kind of place I love. And you know what? I think that life might just be the same: a series of paths we can choose to follow, some of them older than others, and some of them new and unknown. Some of those lanes are dark, frightening, and lead to bad places. But keep looking, and you will find others that honor your inquis-itiveness with magical discoveries and beautiful memories that last a lifetime. The only way to find out is to have an open mind and begin exploring.

In a similar way, I once started my journey in the game industry by taking a job I didn't really want, only so I could make a little bit of money and survive as an artist. It was a small, crooked alley called Out There. In the beginning it looked like I was going nowhere, as if I were heading down a dead end, but like Porto, it turned out to lead me someplace new, someplace entirely different.

During my journey, even when I thought I was stuck or had walked into a bad neighborhood, life always seemed to throw another surprise at me. *Hey you! The wall you just smashed into has a small doorway over here, and on the other side there might be a reward for you. Keep moving, keep discovering.* And so it went, on and on, through avenues and highways, boulevards and roads, in an amazing and endless network of mysteriously con-nected points that took me from a dark basement in Stockholm to the coolest offices in Hollywood. It was as if I had an invisible map that always made sure I didn't get lost. At times I thought I was lucky. At other times I thought, *No, it's not luck; it's the paths I've chosen.*

When I became a manager, I had no training, no tools, no hunger for power or money, and no desire to lead. I thought of management as a heavy responsibility, and I approached the challenge entirely from the craftsman's perspective: The single role a manager has is to set people up for success.

In the face of impossible challenges, the only answers I had were to focus on quality and to use my imagination. They became and remained my trusted guides throughout, even though I could see that I sometimes imagined too much, too soon, and came across as a dreamer to some, perhaps a person to dismiss. *Stellar or seller?* I wish I could say I always knew exactly what I was doing, but that would be a lie. Often, guessing was the only path forward, and in those moments, I found comfort in consciously choosing the most ambitious guess I could think of.

Slowly but surely, I was able to prove that the ability to dream is necessary to achieve greatness, and I focused on protecting and supporting everyone else who had the ability to think far beyond. I saw it as my duty to create conditions that allowed others to thrive. Over the years, my job translated from creating pixels to creating a studio with a culture that promoted and nurtured those same values: quality and imagination. After I personally stepped out of the trenches, letting my hands rest, I focused on nothing else. On that quest, I forged important alliances, and I formed a team of developers that was good enough to compete with the best.

Many times, I became defiant and felt bitterness toward those who tried to put a hole in the small balloon I was trying to turn into a majestic vehicle that would take us to fantastic places. I thought of their negative energy as an unwelcome and destructive attack on the things I believed in so strongly. The creative spirit is a sensitive one, and it needs to breathe the high, clear air of big dreams. Skeptics have the advantage of often being right, but to what end? What does it mean to be right when you expect failure? What does it bring to the world?

Quality was the answer to everything, and for Massive, it paid off.

Once we released *The Division*, reality shifted quickly. Suddenly, we were geniuses, a studio that could propel Ubisoft into the future, into the online space, and into the big, big league of games that sell more than twenty million copies. After the launch, it took me some time to process and enjoy the success. It had been so hard to get to that level, and getting there had taken a very, very long time. More than pleased and excited, I felt vindicated.

Apart from the celebrations and congratulations coming in from everywhere, the joy and satisfaction on Yves's and Serge's faces was particularly special, and it was obvious that they were exceptionally pleased that their big gamble on Massive had paid off. Buying the studio and asking us to modernize the Clancy brand had turned out to be a stroke of genius, and I had to admit that they could sometimes dream of bigger and bolder things than I could. This was their victory too.

At BlizzCon I met J. Allen Brack, who would later succeed Mike Morhaime as CEO of Blizzard. Over a cup of coffee, we chatted about *World of WarCraft*, which was still offering a fantastically playful and imaginative alternative online life after ten years. No other game had achieved anything like it. As game developers tend to do when they feel safe and among friends, we discussed our challenges and fears going forward. We had no reason to act confident in front of our own employees or to put on a show for our publishers; we could speak our minds, unfiltered.

I threw out some thoughts about *World of WarCraft*, where I would take the franchise if it was my responsibility, and somewhere in those loose ideas I weaved in properly bringing the genre to consoles. J. Allen Brack looked at me for a little while.

"Yeah, but you know what, we could never do what you guys have done with *The Division*," he said. "We have tried. It's just too hard. I have no idea how you managed to succeed with that."

I was astonished. And as I thought back to my visit to their offices, years earlier, it struck me that nowadays we, too, had a mission control room, servers running our game all across the world, and that we, too, were watching the global news to be ready for anything.

Ubisoft reacted quickly to the launch of *The Division*, and the roller-coaster ride went into hyperspeed. Two months after the release of *Division*, four years of determined investment in mutual trust resulted in the signing of the *Avatar* deal. Brooks and Mike and I celebrated in our respective parts of the world and exchanged an imaginary toast to Jon Landau through the ether. Petter and Soundboy departed *The Division* team and began chiseling out the founding blocks of the future release of the *Avatar* game.

My boss, Christine, bought an entire city block in Malmö, where the future Massive office will host more than seven hundred talented game developers. It's a beautiful old redbrick building, and our moving there is a perfect illustration of the old Malmö transitioning to the new. Out of nowhere, we were asked to open a sibling studio in Stockholm, which we did, and as I write this, the team in the north is over seventy people strong, working on very fascinating stuff for the future. With the growth of Massive and Stockholm in parallel, my kids noted over dinner one evening that I might soon be the boss of in excess of a thousand people.

As every successful entertainer knows, success demands a sequel, and once we were out of the complicated shipping waters of the first *Division*, we embarked on a new journey, *The Division 2*, with my old friends Cristian Pana and Julian Gerighty at the helm, both now full-time Massive employees with their lives solidly set in the Scandinavian Kingdoms.

Even though there had originally been a lot of debate about our choice to build our own engine, Snowdrop, the results in *The Division* proved that we'd been right to make the complex investment in new tech. After seeing it live and in action, many other Ubisoft studios asked to switch their projects to Snowdrop too. Some of them are still unannounced, but some have already shipped, like *Mario + Rabbids*, *South Park*, and *Starlink*. And of course, the engine supports all projects in Malmö and Stockholm. Snowdrop is no longer a sensitive spring flower, it's a rock-solid proven, powerful, and incredible feat of engineering.

Behind the scenes, more things are going on, some of them obvious and predictable, while others are not ready for the light of day just yet. There is much to do. Too much. And so little time to do it all. With sadness I must admit that we can never embrace all the opportunities we're faced with; we have to choose wisely. I have to choose wisely.

When we ride this wave of success, where do we stop to breathe? In a pattern of constant escalation, with larger projects, bigger audiences, more pressure, an increasing number of opinionated stakeholders, greater responsibility, and growing teams all playing out in the brightest spotlight—where does the creative spirit find nourishment? For a surfer on top of a wave that just gets higher and higher, is there even time to reflect and enjoy the moment itself? Can that surfer afford the luxury to consider what waves to surf tomorrow, or is he entirely blinded by a nearsighted mix of excitement and adrenaline, consumed by the potent cocktail of joy and fear?

In many ways, Massive is a result of a year of thinking that lasted a decade. When we were waiting for the antitrust bureaus to approve the Vivendi/Activision deal, we laid the foundation for almost everything that followed. Our success was born out of our sense of duty toward the craft itself; our journey was never a result of anyone telling us what to do.

As a child, I escaped to my drawings to find peace in those dream worlds. They gave me a quiet place to escape to, a safe place, where rules were logical and events could be controlled. Stories and adventures emerged from my head through the hand that held the pen. Epic journeys appeared like magic. Sometimes I let go and allowed them to live on their own, and I traveled along with them as a passenger. Later, I realized that games offer almost exactly the same experience to millions of gamers all across the world. In a sense, what once drew me to art is what draws gamers to games.

I often think about that disastrous career moment in Paris when I had lost control over *The Division* and was scolded by upper management. Destroyed, and on the way back home, I fell asleep on an airplane and had a nightmare about being lost in a forest. But as terrifying as the nightmare was, it ended with an unexpected sense of acceptance; I could feel peace, even though I clearly didn't know my way out. Somehow, the forest had turned into home. The menacing labyrinth had become a wondrous adventure, one that I could enjoy, though I didn't know where it would take me next. It was when I stopped running that I started to live.

I want to remain curious. I want to explore the exciting woods around me and see new forms of magic and excitement. It seems to me that there are many great adventures to be had, many new worlds waiting to be dreamed into being.

To see everything clearly, I have stopped to breathe in a glade where I can easily spot what matters most. In that place where I don't ask for any more from life, I stay with my fellow dreamers and wait for a magic door to open once more.

APPENDIX

Rules for an (Allegedly) Classic
Italian Pool Game

In dimly lit bars in Lazio, Tuscany, and Piemonte, from Rome to Siena to Torino, it is said that the Italians play a game of pool that has never been shared with the outside world. The rules are simple and fair. Every match guarantees a constant increase of the stakes, and it is the player with the best focus at the end of the match who will take home the win.

* * *

The objective of the game is to pocket all the balls in numerical order, starting from lowest and gradually proceeding to the highest.

1. Place all the balls, except the cue ball (the white ball), in the triangular rack.
2. Toss a coin to decide who starts.
3. The loser of the coin toss uses the cue ball to break the other balls apart.
4. From here on, the goal is to pocket all the balls in numerical order, starting from the lowest and gradually proceeding to the highest.
5. For each ball that is pocketed, the player who is shooting will receive points equivalent to the number on the ball (e.g., Ball #1 is worth one point; Ball #7 is worth seven points; Ball #14 is worth fourteen points).
6. All points are accumulated progressively, ensuring that the last couple of balls can change the outcome of the entire match.

7. Throughout the match, both players must always hit all the balls in numerical order, without touching any other ball before hitting the relevant target.

8. After hitting the relevant ball, the cue ball (and all others) may proceed to collide and touch other balls on the table.

9. Hitting and pocketing the right ball means that the same player continues to play, aiming for the next ball in numerical order.

10. Hitting but not pocketing the right ball means that the turn goes to the next player, who will start the turn from wherever the cue ball is located after the previous shot.

11. Failing to hit the right ball means that the turn goes to the next player, who will be given the freedom to start the turn from anywhere on the table, essentially being able to line up a perfect shot on the next target (a.k.a. ball-in-hand).

12. The winner of the match is the player with the highest number of total points after all balls have been pocketed.

13. Due to the sometimes-cascading score accumulation at the end of a match, the game is more enjoyable in best-of-five rounds, where each match counts as one point, and the first player to reach three victories is declared the winner.

14. Buona fortuna!

ACKNOWLEDGMENTS

I want to thank all the hundreds of game developers I have had the pleasure to work with throughout my career. In this book, the vast majority of the talented people involved in developing games like *WiC*, *Penrose*, *Far Cry*, *The Division*, and *Avatar* remain unnamed, but trust me: Without them, none of this would have ever happened! It is a true pleasure to work with pedantic and obsessive craftspeople, and as a coworker once phrased it, I feel like I am walking among astronauts every day. The most prominent astronauts of this story are, of course, Petter and Soundboy.

Speaking of fantastic colleagues, I wish there had been more space dedicated to Creative Director Julian Gerighty and Senior Producer Cristian Pana, who have been absolutely instrumental in taking Massive to where it is today, but most of those adventures took place after the events covered in this book.

More than anyone, two special people have been directly involved in the creation of *The Dream Architects*, and without their amazing dedication, skill, and patient support, I would not have made it. First of all, my agent, William LoTurco, believed in the story and my writing when, to be honest, he had no real reason to. He invested an enormous amount of time and attention to detail in the early stages of the project, remembering to flatter my ego often enough to keep the ghosts of self-doubt at bay. Second, my editor at Grand Central, Wes Miller, identified and strengthened themes in the book that I had touched upon only vaguely. Like a good therapist, he saw obvious and intricate patterns that I had no idea were there. In my own (very humble!) eyes, the editing phase made me appear a lot smarter than I actually am. Both William and Wes are diligent, honest, hardworking dreamers and stubborn Knights of Quality. They should be in the game industry!

I admire the bravery of Ubisoft for allowing me to write this book without expecting me to add any corporate gloss. It is rare for corporations to trust the truth to be the best PR, but if you are truly great, it actually is. I hope I have been able to convey my view of Ubisoft as an amazing home for dreamers and creatives, both developers and gamers. This is Yves's creation, the work of a persistent visionary.

A few individuals stand out as absolutely vital to both my story and the creation of this book: *Jonas*, my best buddy from art school who helped me stay true to my early dreams many years ago when we shared an office in the Old Town of Stockholm. I often think about him when I need to calibrate my ethical and artistic compass, because he sets such a good example. *Kim*, who introduced me to the real magic of creating games and who was my wingman for many years. His never-ending optimism and work ethic both remain benchmarks. *Martin*, who hired me without hesitation when most people had dismissed me as a nobody and then taught me everything I needed to make it in the big league. I am forever indebted (and hey, thanks for getting the heck out of Massive so I could steal your job!). We still meet every so often to exchange war stories, and it is always a tremendous pleasure. *Jason* and *Pierre* were there and helped Massive in the early days after the acquisition. When it all was about to go to hell, they gently steered everything in a positive direction and set the foundation of the powerful Ubi-Massive alliance we have enjoyed ever since. The last decade of growth for Massive and me personally would not have been possible without *Serge*, the ultimate creative warrior, the lion guru. *Jon Landau*, my smiling producer friend in Hollywood, recognized the Massive team for what it is, a kindred spirit to Lightstorm. His uncompromising yet masterful management of exceptionally complex problems is a true inspiration.

Louise, my love, thank you for being an angel and of course also for encouraging me to write this book (and for reading ever-changing versions so many times you must have come to hate it).

Behind all entertainers, there are parents, siblings, loved ones, children, and relatives who have to suffer the never-ending emotional roller-coaster ride as the self-obsessed artist hurls himself toward failures and successes. Sorry about that.

Nevertheless, I would like to thank everyone in my extended family, with all the many members attached to it since childhood. In different ways, you all contributed, and in the end, no professional achievement is more important than each of you.

Finally, I wish to declare my sincere support and love to all the stargazers of the world, especially my two children, Isa and Harry. To those who dream about enchanted stories to tell, of art to paint, arias to sing, books to write, languages to discover, and fantastic worlds to create: Please, do it! Allow yourself to make the world more beautiful. And once your creation is a real thing, no longer a fantasy, please leave a magical portal behind so that the rest of us might one day discover and enjoy the fragile elegance of your poetry.

ABOUT THE AUTHOR

David Polfeldt is the managing director of Massive Entertainment, a world-leading video game studio and part of the Ubisoft family. At Massive, David has worked on industry-defining, triple-A games such as *Assassin's Creed: Revelations*, *Far Cry 3*, and *Tom Clancy's The Division*, which together have generated billions in revenue worldwide. Massive is currently developing a series of *Avatar* video games in collaboration with James Cameron and Lightstorm, which will be released in conjunction with the forthcoming *Avatar* movies.